P9-DFB-768

BARBECUE

BARBECUE

Sizzling recipes for grills and barbecues: over 400 step-by-step recipes for
successful outdoor eating and entertaining

Christine France and Steven Wheeler

BARNES & NOBLE BOOKS

NEW YORK

This edition published by Barnes & Noble, Inc.,
by arrangement with Anness Publishing Limited

2004 Barnes & Noble Books

M 10 9 8 7 6 5 4 3 2 1

ISBN 0-7607-6242-2

Publisher: Joanna Lorenz
Editorial Director: Helen Sudell
Project Editor: Valerie Ferguson
Copy Editor: Linda Doeser
Designers: Bill Mason, Nigel Partridge and Ian Sandom

Illustrations: Madeleine David, Lucinda Ganderton
and Anna Koska
Consultant Editors: Christine France and Steven Wheeler
Photographers: William Adams-Lingwood, Karl Adamson,
Edward Allwright, Steve Baxter, James Duncan, John
Freeman, Michelle Garrett, Amanda Heywood, David
Jordan, Dave King, Don Last, Patrick McLeavey, Michael
Michaels, Thomas Odulate, Debbie Patterson, Juliet
Piddington, Craig Robertson and Simon Smith
Recipes contributed by: Michelle Berriedale Johnson, Angela
Boggiano, Janet Brinkworth,Carla Capalbo, Kit Chan,
Jacqueline Clark, Carole Clements, Roz Denny, Nicola
Diggins, Matthew Drennan, Joanna Farrow, Rafi Fernandez,
Christine France, Silvana Franco, Brian Glover, Rosamund
Grant, Rebekah Hassan, Deh-Ta Hsiung, Christine Ingram,
Judy Jackson, Soheila Kimberley, Lucy Knox, Elisabeth
Lambert Ortiz, Ruby Le Bois, Lesley Mackley, Sue Maggs,
Maggie Mayhew, Jane Milton, Sallie Morris, Annie Nichols,
Maggie Pannell, Katherine Richmond, Keith Richmond, Anne
Sheasby, Liz Trigg, Hilaire Walden, Steven Wheeler, Kate
Whiteman, Elizabeth Wolf-Cohen and Jeni Wright

Previously published as *Barbecues and Salads*

Standard spoon and cup measures are level.
Large eggs are used unless otherwise stated.

CONTENTS

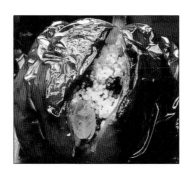

INTRODUCTION

o o o

There is something special about eating outdoors – the appetite is sharpened, the aroma is more tempting, the flavor is enhanced and it is altogether more fun. Whether you are planning an *al fresco* family lunch in the garden, a barbecue for family and friends, a picnic at the coast or a sophisticated summer evening dinner party, you will find the perfect recipe for success here.

The first part of the book focuses on barbecues, offering a huge choice, from family favorites, such as homemade burgers and kebabs, to more exotic dishes inspired by cuisines from around the world. There are recipes for all occasions and every course, including delicious vegetable accompaniments, vegetarian dishes and fabulous grilled desserts. A chapter is dedicated to salsas, dips and marinades to inspire your creativity, and there is also advice on salad accompaniments and outdoor entertaining.

The second part concentrates on salads – from simple side dishes to luxurious special occasion menus and from quick and easy accompaniments to substantial main courses. You can mix and match with the recipes in the first part of the book, pick and choose delicious and healthy side salads to go with an ordinary family meal or plan an entire menu from the appetizer to a refreshing fruit salad dessert. Forget boring sandwiches – most of the salads featured can be transported in cool bags and plastic containers for a wonderful picnic, whether in the country, on the beach or simply in the local park. Make the best of both worlds and take a portable barbecue with you as well.

Both parts of the book include a wealth of practical information about ingredients, cooking and preparation techniques, types of barbecue and fuel, and dressings, marinades and other accompaniments to ensure success every time you cook.

Planning a Barbecue

A well-run barbecue is one of the most enjoyable ways to spend a warm afternoon or evening, and it is not at all difficult to make sure that everything runs smoothly. In the following pages, you will find advice, hints and tips on how to do this.

Cooking on the barbecue is always fun, and you will probably have plenty of volunteers who are willing to help. However, if too many cooks can spoil the broth, think of the havoc they can wreak with hot coals. You can make use of their enthusiasm by asking them to carry bowls of salad, dishes, cutlery and so on between the kitchen and the

backyard. It is also sensible to have a designated adult to watch the barbecue if you need to leave it for any reason – once lit, it should never be left unattended, especially if there are children present.

One reason why barbecues are such a good way to entertain is that much of the work can be done in advance. Marinades, which not only tenderize ingredients but also give them flavor, need time to take effect, so you can often start the preparation the evening before. Meat and fish can be cut up for kebabs, and burgers can be made and stored, covered with plastic wrap in the refrigerator.

Safety First

It is all too easy to get carried away with enthusiasm and invite half the neighbourhood to your barbecue. Be sensible about the numbers that can be safely contained at the venue and for whom you can cook without ending up limp and exhausted with scorched food. Serving large numbers of people increases the risk of not cooking the food sufficiently. While part of the charm of a barbecue is that instead of being hidden in the kitchen, you are at the center of things and can chat to your guests, you won't want to spend the whole time slaving over a hot grill.

Although you don't have to be totally abstemious, remember that cooking on a barbecue is thirsty work and it is very easy to underestimate how much you are drinking. Too high an alcohol intake and hot charcoal could be a lethal combination. Keep an eye on the safety of drinking guests, too. Make sure that you have a good supply of soft drinks for children, drivers and those who prefer them. In the chapter on Outdoor Entertaining, you will find some delicious recipes for both alcoholic and non-alcoholic drinks.

Selecting the Food

Offering a choice of foods is part of the pleasure, but don't be over-ambitious. Depending on how many people you

will be serving, a good selection would include two or three different main ingredients, such as fish, meat and poultry, a vegetarian option and, perhaps, child-friendly food, such as burgers. However, you may be surprised to discover a toddler happily consuming a spicy chicken satay or a plateful of stuffed squid. There is nothing like a barbecue for bringing out everyone's sense of adventure.

The one thing no one has any control over is the weather. Even when the forecast is promising and there have been weeks of clear blue skies, a sudden downpour or gusting wind can spoil the best-laid plans. It is therefore worth making some contingency arrangements. Before inviting your guests, think about the available space indoors if they need sudden shelter.

Most of the recipes in this book are easily adapted for cooking in the kitchen. Kebabs, drumsticks, steaks, chops and chunky fish fillets can all be cooked under a conventional broiler for the same length of time. Parcels can be cooked in a moderate oven, for about the same length of time as given in the recipe. Otherwise, if you have a

barbecue with a lid, grab an umbrella, put a smile on your face and pass the plates through the nearest window into the house.

Salad for all Seasons

When the temperature soars and the evenings are long and light, no one wants to spend time cooking. Happily, this is just the time when baby vegetables are in season, salad leaves flourish and tomatoes, eggplant and zucchini ripen in the warm sunshine.

Nowadays, the range of salad ingredients is almost endless. Even the choice of salad leaves has expanded enormously. Supermarkets and other stores are packed with both familiar and exotic vegetables in a tempting array of colors, shapes and sizes.

While salads are, understandably, at their most popular in the summer, they are also a refreshing and healthy option all year around. All the chapters in the second half of this book include some winter specialities, based on seasonal produce, such as potatoes, fennel or celeriac, or on pasta and rice. However, with modern transportation, almost all vegetables are available at any time of year so that you can have greater variety of ingredients.

Side salads, whether made from raw or cooked ingredients, are versatile accompaniments to almost every main course dish, whether pasta, casseroles or grills. You can serve them as an appetizer, with the main course or, French-style, as a palate cleanser afterward. They can range from a simple selection of salad leaves tossed in a vinaigrette to a colorful compilation of several different ingredients in a spicy or creamy dressing. You are sure to find a recipe with flavors that are the perfect complement to your chosen main course. Most can be prepared or partially prepared in advance, making entertaining easy.

Main Course Salads

It is during the summer months that main course salads reign supreme. They can be based around almost any ingredients, from duck breast fillets to smoked trout, and from mussels to steak. A quick and easy salad can provide an economical and filling midweek family supper, while a more elaborate and luxurious dish makes a wonderful centerpiece for a party

buffet or can play a starring role at an *al fresco* dinner. The chapter on Special Occasion Salads will be an eye-opener for those whose imagination has not stretched much beyond ham, hard-boiled eggs and lettuce. However, if these are your favorite salad

ingredients, you will be pleased to find them presented in new and ingenious ways in the chapter called Main Course Salads.

Perfect Picnics

Salads are an excellent choice for picnics and packed lunches. Make the dressing in a screw-top jar and transport it this way to your picnic site or workplace. Assemble the salad in advance or pack the separate ingredients in rigid plastic containers or plastic bags. Then all you have to do is toss it in the dressing and serve.

Use this book to plan an entire menu for a dinner party or special occasion, or simply dip into it for ideas and suggestions for family meals. Whatever your taste, budget and level of culinary skill, you will find a recipe for every course and every kind of occasion to delight your family and friends.

SIZZLING
BARBECUES

o o o

Just a glance through this mouthwatering selection of recipes, from seared scallops to glazed duck and from sirloin steaks to fruit kebabs, will give you an idea of just how versatile and tasty grilled food can be.

This section of the book begins with some practical guidance about cooking on a barbecue, including safety tips, cooking times and choosing the equipment and fuel. It also offers some handy hints on the magic of marinating.

The remaining chapters cover every aspect of the barbecue menu – from appetizers and snacks to desserts – and include some unusual and delicious vegetable accompaniments, as well as an entire chapter on salsas, dips and marinades and a special section on outdoor entertaining that will inspire you to party throughout the summer.

While steaks, chicken drumsticks, chops and burgers are traditional barbecue fare, the range of suitable ingredients is far more extensive. Firm-textured fish, such as monkfish and tuna, can be cooked directly on the grill and respond beautifully to the smoky flavor imparted by the fire, while shrimp make fabulous and colorful kebabs. More delicate fish can be wrapped in foil parcels to protect their texture from the fierce heat. Foil parcels are an ideal way of cooking vegetables, too, and this section of the book includes a chapter of succulent vegetable recipes, many of which are wonderful, main-course vegetarian dishes.

Whatever your plan, from an impromptu midweek supper on a hot summer evening to a full-scale barbecue party at the weekend, you will find the recipes you want here. Accompany cold canapés with hot snacks straight from the grill, cook an entire meal, or even choose an unusual grilled dessert to follow an *al fresco* meal.

CHOOSING A BARBECUE

• • •

ABOVE: *Hibachi barbecue*

There is a huge choice of ready-made barbecues on the market, and it's important to choose one that suits your needs. First decide how many people you want to cook for and where you are likely to use the barbecue. For instance, do you usually have barbecues just for the family, or are you likely to have barbecue parties for lots of friends? Once you've decided on your basic requirements, you will be able to choose between the different types more easily.

Hibachi Barbecues

These small cast-iron barbecues originated in Japan – the word *hibachi* translates literally as "firebox". They are inexpensive, easy to use and easily transportable. Lightweight versions are now made in steel or aluminum.

Disposable Barbecues

These will last for about an hour and are a convenient idea for picnic-style barbecues or for cooking just a few small pieces of food.

Portable Barbecues

These are usually quite light and fold away to fit into a car trunk so that you can take them on picnics. Some are even small enough to fit into a backpack.

Brazier Barbecues

These open barbecues are suitable for use on a patio or in the backyard. Most have legs or wheels and it's a good idea to check that the height suits you. The grill area of a brazier barbecue varies in size, and the barbecue may be round or rectangular. It's useful to choose one that has a shelf attached to the side. Other extras may include an electric, battery-powered or clockwork spit: choose one on which you can adjust the height of the spit. Many brazier barbecues have a hood, which is useful as a windbreak and gives a place to mount the spit.

LEFT: *Brazier barbecue*
BELOW: *Disposable barbecue*
RIGHT: *Portable barbecue*

ABOVE: Gas barbecue

Kettle-grill Barbecues

These have a large, hinged lid which can be used as a windbreak; when closed, the lid allows you to use the barbecue like an oven. Even large pieces of meat or whole chickens cook successfully, as the heat reflected within the dome helps to brown the meat evenly. The heat is easily controlled by the use of efficient air vents. This type of barbecue can also be used for home-smoking foods.

Gas Barbecues

The main advantage of these is their convenience – the heat is instant and easily controllable. The disadvantage is that they tend to be quite expensive.

Permanent Barbecues

These are a good idea if you often have barbecues at home. They can be built simply and cheaply. Choose a sheltered site that is a little way from the house, but with easy access to the kitchen. Permanent barbecues can be built with ordinary house bricks, but it's best to line the inside with firebricks, which will withstand the heat better. Use a metal shelf for the fuel and a grid at whatever height you choose. Packs are available containing all you need to build a barbecue.

Improvised Barbecues

Barbecue cooking adds to the fun of eating outdoors on picnics and camping trips, but transporting the barbecue for the rest of the day can make the idea more of a chore than a treat. Basic barbecues can be built at almost no cost and can be dismantled after use as quickly as they were put together. A pile of stones topped with chicken wire and fuelled with driftwood or kindling makes a very efficient barbecue. Or take a large metal cookie container with you and punch a few holes in it; fill it with charcoal and place a grid on top. With just a little planning, you can turn your trip into a truly memorable event.

ABOVE: Improvised barbecue

ABOVE: Permanent barbecue

TYPES OF FUEL

• • •

If you have a gas or electric barbecue, you will not need to buy extra fuel, but other barbecues require either charcoal or wood. Choose good-quality fuel from sustainable sources, and always store it in a dry place.

Lumpwood Charcoal

Lumpwood charcoal is usually made from softwood, and comes in lumps of varying size. It is easier to ignite than briquettes, but tends to burn up faster.

Charcoal Briquettes

Briquettes are a cost-effective choice of fuel, since they burn for a long time with the minimum of smell and smoke. They can take a long time to ignite, however.

LIGHTING THE FIRE

Follow these basic instructions for lighting the fire unless you are using self-igniting charcoal, in which case you should follow the manufacturer's instructions.

1 Spread a layer of foil over the base of the barbecue, to reflect the heat and make cleaning easier.

2 Spread a layer of wood, charcoal or briquettes on the fire grate about 2 inches deep. Pile the fuel in a small pyramid in the center.

3 Push one or two firelighters into the pyramid or pour over about 3 tablespoons liquid firelighter and leave for 1 minute. Light with a long match or taper and leave to burn for 15 minutes. Spread the coals evenly and leave for 30–45 minutes, until they are covered with a film of gray ash, before cooking.

ABOVE: Charcoal briquettes

Self-igniting Charcoal

This is simply lumpwood charcoal or briquettes, treated with a flammable substance that catches light very easily. It's important to wait until the ignition agent has burned off before cooking food, or the smell may taint the food.

Coconut-shell Charcoal

This makes a good fuel for small barbecues. It's best used on a fire grate with small holes, as the small pieces tend to fall through the gaps.

Wood

Hardwoods, such as oak and olive, are best for barbecues, as they burn slowly with a pleasant aroma. Softwoods tend to burn too fast and give off sparks and smoke, making them unsuitable for most barbecues. Wood fires need constant attention to achieve an even, steady heat.

BELOW: Lumpwood charcoal

CONTROLLING THE HEAT

There are three basic ways to control the heat of the barbecue during cooking time.

1 Adjust the height of the grill rack. Raise it for slow cooking, or use the bottom level for searing foods. For a medium heat, the rack should be about 4 inches from the fire.

2 Push the burning coals apart for a lower heat; pile them closer together to increase the heat of the fire.

3 Most barbecues have air vents to allow air into the fire. Open the vents to make the fire hotter, or close them in order to lower the temperature.

Woodchips and Herbs

These are designed to be added to the fire to impart a pleasant aroma to the food. They can be soaked to make them last longer. Sprinkle woodchips and herbs straight onto the coals during cooking, or place them on a metal tray under the grill rack. Packs of hickory or oak chips are widely available, or you can simply spread twigs of juniper, rosemary, thyme, sage or fennel over the fire.

BELOW: Coconut shell

SAFETY TIPS

Barbecuing is a perfectly safe method of cooking if it's done sensibly – use these simple guidelines as a basic checklist to safeguard against accidents. If you have never organized a barbecue before, keep your first few attempts as simple as possible, with just one or two types of food. When you have mastered the technique of cooking on a barbecue, you can start to become more ambitious. Soon you will progress from burgers for two to meals for large parties of family and friends.

ABOVE: *Light the fire with a long match or taper, and leave it to burn for about 15 minutes.*

☆ Make sure the barbecue is sited on a firm surface and is stable and level before lighting the fire. Once the barbecue is lit, do not move it.

☆ Keep the barbecue sheltered from the wind, and keep it well away from trees and shrubs.

☆ Always follow the manufacturer's instructions for your barbecue, as there are some barbecues that can use only one type of fuel.

☆ Don't try to hasten the fire – some fuels may take quite a time to build up heat. Never pour flammable liquid onto the barbecue.

☆ Keep children and pets away from the fire, and make sure the cooking is always supervised by adults.

☆ Keep perishable foods cold until you're ready to cook – especially in hot weather. If you take them outdoors, place them in a cool bag until needed.

☆ Make sure meats, such as burgers, sausages and poultry, are thoroughly cooked – there should be no trace of pink in the juices. Pierce a thick part of the flesh as a test: the juices should run clear.

RIGHT: *Poultry can be pre-cooked in the oven or microwave, before being finished off on the barbecue.*

☆ Wash your hands after handling raw meat and before touching other foods. Don't use the same utensils for raw ingredients and cooked food.

☆ You may prefer to precook poultry in the microwave or oven and then transfer it to the barbecue to finish off cooking and to attain the flavor of chargrilled food. Don't allow meat to cool down before transferring it to the barbecue; poultry should never be reheated once it has cooled.

☆ In case the fire should get out of control, have a bucket of sand and a water spray on hand to douse the flames.

☆ Keep a first-aid kit handy. If someone burns themselves, hold the burn under cold running water.

☆ Trim excess fat from meat and don't use too much oil in marinades. Fat can cause dangerous flare-ups if too much is allowed to drip onto the fuel.

☆ Use long-handled barbecue tools, such as forks, tongs and brushes, for turning and basting food; keep some oven gloves at hand, preferably the extra-long type, to protect your hands.

☆ Always keep the raw foods to be cooked away from foods that are ready to eat, to prevent cross-contamination.

BASIC TIMING GUIDE

. . .

It is almost impossible to give precise timing guides for barbecue cooking, since there are so many factors to consider. The heat will depend on the type and size of barbecue, the type of fuel used, the height of the grill above the fire and, of course, the weather. Cooking times will also be affected by the thickness and type of food, the quality of the meat, and whereabouts on the grill it is placed.

Bearing this in mind, the chart below provides only a rough guide to timing. Food should always be tested to make sure it is thoroughly cooked. The times given here are total cooking times, allowing for the food to be turned. Most foods need turning only once, but smaller items, such as kebabs and sausages, should be turned more frequently to be sure of even cooking. Foods wrapped in foil cook more slowly and will need longer on the barbecue.

Type of Food	Weight/ Thickness	Heat	Total Cooking Time	Type of Food	Weight/ Thickness	Heat	Total Cooking Time
BEEF				CHICKEN			
steaks	1 inch	hot	rare: 5 minutes	whole	3½ pounds	spit	1–1¼ hours
			medium: 8 minutes	quarters		medium	30–35 minutes
			well done: 12 minutes	boneless breasts		medium	10–15 minutes
burgers	¾ inch	hot	6–8 minutes	drumsticks		medium	25–30 minutes
kebabs	1 inch	hot	5–8 minutes	kebabs		medium	6–10 minutes
joints	3½ pounds	spit	2–3 hours	poussin, whole	1 pound	spit	25–30 minutes
				poussin, spatchcocked	1 pound	medium	25–30 minutes
LAMB							
leg steaks	¾ inch	medium	10–15 minutes	DUCKLING			
chops	1 inch	medium	10–15 minutes	whole	5 pounds	spit	1–1½ hours
kebabs	1 inch	medium	6–15 minutes	half		medium	35–45 minutes
butterfly leg	3 inch	low	rare: 40–45 minutes	breasts, boneless		medium	15–20 minutes
			well done: 1 hour				
rolled shoulder	3½ pounds	spit	1¼–1½ hours	FISH			
				large, whole	5–10 pounds	low/ medium	allow 10 minutes per 1 inch thickness
PORK				small, whole	1¼–2 pounds	hot/ medium	12–20 minutes
chops	1 inch	medium	15–18 minutes				
kebabs	1 inch	medium	12–15 minutes	sardines		hot/ medium	4–6 minutes
spare ribs		medium	30–40 minutes				
sausages	thick	medium	8–10 minutes	steaks or fillets	1 inch	medium	6–10 minutes
joints	3½ pounds	spit	2–3 hours	kebabs	1 inch	medium	5–8 minutes
				large shrimp, in shell	medium	6–8 minutes	
				large shrimp, shelled		medium	4–6 minutes
				scallops/mussels, in shell		medium	until open
				scallops/mussels, shelled, skewered		medium	5–8 minutes
				half lobster		low/ medium	15–20 minutes

MARINATING

Marinades are used to add flavor and to moisten or tenderize foods, particularly meat. Marinades can be either savory or sweet and are as varied as you want to make them: spicy, fruity, fragrant or exotic. Particular classic combinations always work well with certain foods. Usually, it is best to choose oily marinades for dry foods, such as lean meat or white fish, and wine- or vinegar-based marinades for rich foods with a higher fat content. Most marinades don't contain salt, which can draw out the juices from meat. It's better to add salt just before or after cooking.

1 Place the food for marinating in a wide, non-metallic dish or bowl, preferably a dish that is large enough to allow the food to lie in a single layer.

2 Mix together the ingredients for the marinade according to the recipe. The marinade can usually be prepared in advance and stored in a jar with a screw-top lid until needed.

Cook's Tip
The amount of marinade you will need depends on the amount of food. As a rough guide, about ¼ pint/⅔ cup is enough for about 1¼ pounds of food.

3 Pour the marinade over the food and turn the food to coat it evenly.

4 Cover the dish or bowl with plastic wrap and chill in the refrigerator for anything from about 30 minutes up to several hours or even overnight, depending on the recipe. Turn the food over occasionally and spoon the marinade over it to make sure that it is well coated.

5 Remove the food with a slotted spoon, or lift it out with tongs, and drain off and reserve the marinade. If necessary, allow the food to come to room temperature before cooking.

6 Use the marinade for basting or brushing the food during cooking.

BELOW: Marinating foods before cooking adds to the flavor and makes sure the food is kept tender and moist.

BASIC BARBECUE MARINADE
This can be used for meat or fish.

1 garlic clove, crushed
3 tablespoons sunflower or olive oil
3 tablespoons dry sherry
1 tablespoon Worcestershire sauce
1 tablespoon dark soy sauce
freshly ground black pepper

RED WINE MARINADE
This is good with red meats and game.

¼ pint/⅔ cup dry red wine
1 tablespoon olive oil
1 tablespoon red wine vinegar
2 garlic cloves, crushed
2 dried bay leaves, crumbled
freshly ground black pepper

To keep your guests happy while they wait for the main event,

begin your barbecue with exciting appetizers that are quick to

cook and fun to eat. Here is a collection of flavorsome dishes

guaranteed to disappear from the grill rack as soon as they're

cool enough to snatch away.

APPETIZERS AND
SNACKS

ROASTED GARLIC TOASTS

. . .

Cooking garlic in its skin on the barbecue produces a soft, aromatic purée with a sweet, nutty flavor. Spread on crisp toast to make a delicious appetizer.

INGREDIENTS

2 whole garlic heads
extra virgin olive oil
fresh rosemary sprigs
ciabatta loaf or thick baguette
chopped fresh rosemary
salt and freshly ground
black pepper

SERVES 4

1 Slice the tops from the heads of garlic, using a sharp kitchen knife.

2 Brush the garlic heads with extra virgin olive oil and add a few sprigs of fresh rosemary, before wrapping in kitchen foil. Cook the foil parcels on a medium-hot barbecue for about 25–30 minutes, turning occasionally, until the garlic is soft.

3 Slice the bread and brush each slice generously with olive oil. Toast the slices on the barbecue until crisp and golden, turning once.

4 Squeeze the garlic cloves from their skins onto the toast. Sprinkle with the chopped fresh rosemary and olive oil, and add salt and black pepper to taste.

ROASTED BELL PEPPER ANTIPASTO

Jars of Italian mixed peppers in olive oil are a common sight in supermarkets, yet none can compete with this freshly made version, perfect as an appetizer.

INGREDIENTS

3 red bell peppers
2 yellow or orange bell peppers
2 green bell peppers
2 ounces/½ cup sun-dried
tomatoes in oil, drained
1 garlic clove
2 tablespoons balsamic vinegar
5 tablespoons olive oil
few drops of chili sauce
4 canned artichoke hearts, drained
and sliced
salt and freshly ground
black pepper
fresh basil leaves, to garnish

SERVES 6

1 Cook the whole bell peppers on a medium-hot barbecue, turning frequently, for about 10–15 minutes, until they begin to char. Cover the peppers with a clean dish towel and leave to cool for 5 minutes.

2 Use a sharp kitchen knife to slice the sun-dried tomatoes into thin strips. Thinly slice the garlic clove.

3 Beat together the balsamic vinegar, olive oil and chili sauce in a small bowl, then season with a little salt and freshly ground black pepper.

4 Stalk and slice the peppers. Mix with the sliced artichokes, sun-dried tomatoes and garlic. Pour over the dressing and sprinkle with basil leaves.

Cook's Tip

If you prefer your peppers to have a softer texture and sweeter flavor, peel them once they have cooled down after grilling, using a small sharp knife. They will then be very easy to slice.

HERB-STUFFED MINI VEGETABLES
• • •

*These little hors d'oeuvres are ideal for parties, since they can be prepared in advance,
and simply assembled and cooked at the last minute.*

INGREDIENTS

30 mini vegetables: zucchini,
pattypan squashes and
large white mushrooms
2 tablespoons olive oil
fresh basil or parsley, to garnish

FOR THE STUFFING

2 tablespoons olive oil
1 onion, finely chopped
1 garlic clove, finely chopped
4 ounces/1½ cups finely chopped
white mushrooms
1 zucchini, finely chopped
1 red bell pepper, finely chopped
2½ ounces/⅓ cup orzo pasta
6 tablespoons/⅓ cup bottled
strained tomatoes
½ teaspoon dried thyme
4 fluid ounces/½ cup chicken stock
1–2 teaspoons chopped
fresh basil
2 ounces/½ cup coarsely grated
mozzarella or fontina cheese
salt and freshly ground
black pepper

MAKES 30

2 Stir in the pasta, tomatoes, thyme
and chicken stock and bring to the boil,
stirring. Reduce the heat and simmer
for 10–12 minutes, until reduced and
thickened. Remove from the heat and
cool slightly. Stir in the basil and the
grated cheese.

3 Drop the zucchini and squashes into
a pan of boiling water and cook for
3 minutes. Drain and refresh under
cold running water. Trim the bottoms
so they are flat, trim a small slice off
the tops and scoop out the centers with
a spoon or melon baller. Remove the
stems from the mushrooms. Brush all
the vegetables with olive oil.

4 Using a teaspoon, fill the vegetables
with the stuffing and arrange on a rack.
Cook on a medium-hot barbecue for
10–15 minutes, until the filling is hot
and bubbling. Garnish with the fresh
basil or parsley. The vegetables can be
served either warm or cool.

1 For the stuffing, heat the oil over a
medium heat in a pan. Add the onion
and cook for 2 minutes, until tender. Stir
in the garlic, mushrooms, zucchini and
red bell pepper. Season and cook for
2 minutes, until the vegetables soften.

POLPETTES WITH MOZZARELLA AND TOMATO

These Italian-style meatballs are made with beef and topped with creamy melted mozzarella and savory anchovies.

INGREDIENTS

½ slice white bread,
crust removed
3 tablespoons milk
1½ pounds/6 cups ground beef
1 egg, beaten
2 ounces/⅔ cup dry bread crumbs
olive oil for brushing
2 beefsteak tomatoes, sliced
1 tablespoon chopped
fresh oregano
1 mozzarella cheese, cut into
6 slices
6 drained, canned anchovy fillets,
cut in half lengthwise
salt and freshly ground
black pepper

SERVES 6

1 Put the bread and milk into a small pan and heat very gently, until the bread absorbs all the milk. Mash it to a pulp and set aside to cool.

2 Put the minced beef into a bowl with the bread mixture and the egg and season with plenty of salt and freshly ground black pepper. Mix well, then shape the mixture into six patties, using your hands. Sprinkle the bread crumbs onto a plate and dredge the patties, coating them thoroughly.

3 Brush the polpettes with olive oil and cook them on a hot barbecue for 2–3 minutes on one side, until brown. Turn them over.

4 Without removing the polpettes from the barbecue, lay a slice of tomato on top of each polpette, sprinkle with chopped oregano and season with salt and pepper. Place a mozzarella slice on top and arrange two strips of anchovy in a cross over the cheese.

5 Cook for 4–5 minutes more until the polpettes are cooked through and the mozzarella has melted.

23

STUFFED KIBBEH

. . .

Kibbeh is a tasty Middle Eastern speciality of ground lamb and bulgur wheat, which can be eaten with no further cooking or shaped into patties and cooked on the barbecue.

INGREDIENTS

1 pound lean lamb
3 tablespoons olive oil
avocado slices and fresh cilantro
sprigs, to serve

FOR THE KIBBEH
8 ounces/1⅓ cups bulghur wheat
1 fresh red chile, seeded and
roughly chopped
1 onion, coarsely chopped
salt and freshly ground
black pepper

FOR THE STUFFING
1 onion, finely chopped
2 ounces/⅔ cup pine nuts
2 tablespoons olive oil
1½ teaspoons ground allspice
4 tablespoons chopped
fresh cilantro

SERVES 4–6

1 Cut the lamb into coarse chunks, using a heavy kitchen knife. Process the chunks in a blender or food processor until finely ground. Divide the ground meat into two equal portions and set aside until needed.

2 To make the kibbeh, soak the bulghur wheat for 15 minutes in cold water. Drain well, then process in the blender or food processor with the chopped chile and onion, half the meat and plenty of salt and pepper.

3 To make the stuffing, cook the onion and pine nuts in the olive oil for 5 minutes. Add the allspice and remaining ground meat and cook gently, breaking up the meat with a wooden spoon, until browned. Stir in the cilantro and a little seasoning.

4 Turn the kibbeh mixture out onto a clean work surface and use your hands to shape the mixture into a cake. Divide the cake into 12 wedges.

5 Flatten one wedge in the palm of your hand and spoon a little stuffing into the center. Bring the edges of the kibbeh over the stuffing to enclose it. Make into a firm, egg-shaped mold between the palms of your hands, checking that the filling is completely encased. Repeat with the other kibbeh.

6 To barbecue the kibbeh, lightly brush with olive oil and cook on a medium barbecue for 10–15 minutes, turning carefully, until evenly browned and cooked through. To fry the kibbeh, heat oil to a depth of 2 inches in a large pan until a few kibbeh crumbs sizzle on the surface. Lower half the kibbeh into the oil and fry for about 5 minutes, until golden. Drain on paper towels and keep hot while frying the remainder. Serve hot with avocado slices and fresh cilantro sprigs.

HERB POLENTA

∘ ∘ ∘

Golden polenta with fresh summer herbs makes a delicious appetizer or light snack, served with barbecue-cooked tomatoes.

INGREDIENTS

1¼ pints/3 cups stock
or water
1 teaspoon salt
6 ounces/1 cup polenta
1 ounce/2 tablespoons butter
5 tablespoons mixed chopped
fresh parsley, chives and basil,
plus extra to garnish
olive oil for brushing
4 large plum or beefsteak
tomatoes, halved
salt and freshly ground
black pepper

SERVES 4

1 Prepare the polenta in advance: place the stock or water in a pan, with the salt, and bring to the boil. Reduce the heat and stir in the polenta.

2 Stir constantly over a moderate heat for 5 minutes, until the polenta begins to thicken and come away from the sides of the pan.

Cook's Tip

Try using fresh basil or fresh chives alone, for a distinctive flavor.

3 Remove from the heat and stir in the butter, chopped herbs and pepper.

4 Lightly grease a wide dish and tip the polenta into it, spreading it evenly. Leave until cool and set.

5 Turn out the polenta and cut into squares or stamp out round pieces with a large cookie cutter. Brush with olive oil. Lightly brush the tomatoes with olive oil and sprinkle with salt and pepper to taste. Cook the tomatoes and polenta on a medium-hot barbecue for about 5 minutes, turning once. Serve garnished with fresh herbs.

BRIE PARCELS WITH ALMONDS

° ° °

*Creamy French Brie makes a sophisticated appetizer or light meal, wrapped in
grape leaves and served hot with chunks of bread.*

2 Cut the Brie into four chunks and
place each chunk on a grape leaf.

3 Mix together the chives, ground
almonds, peppercorns and olive oil, and
place a spoonful on top of each piece of
cheese. Sprinkle with sliced almonds.

4 Fold the grape leaves over tightly
to enclose the cheese completely. Brush
the parcels with olive oil and cook on
a hot barbecue for about 3–4 minutes,
until the cheese is hot and melting.
Serve immediately.

INGREDIENTS

4 large grape leaves, preserved
in brine
7 ounce piece Brie cheese
2 tablespoons chopped fresh chives
2 tablespoons ground almonds
1 teaspoon crushed
black peppercorns
1 tablespoon olive oil
sliced almonds

SERVES 4

1 Rinse the grape leaves thoroughly
under cold running water and dry them
well. Spread the leaves out on a clean
work surface or chopping board.

TOFU STEAKS

Vegetarians and meat-eaters alike will enjoy these grilled tofu steaks. The combination of ingredients in the marinade gives the steaks a distinctly Japanese flavor.

INGREDIENTS

1 packet fresh tofu (4 x 3 1/4 x 1 1/4 inches), 11 ounces drained weight
2 scallions, thinly sliced, to garnish
mixed salad leaves, to garnish

FOR THE MARINADE
3 tablespoons sake
2 tablespoons soy sauce
1 teaspoon sesame oil
1 garlic clove, crushed
1 tablespoon grated fresh root ginger
1 scallion, chopped

SERVES 4

1 Wrap the tofu in a clean dish towel and place it on a chopping board. Put a large plate on top and leave the tofu for 30 minutes to remove any excess water.

2 Slice the tofu horizontally into three pieces, then cut the slices into quarters. Set aside. Combine all the ingredients for the marinade in a large bowl. Add the tofu to the bowl in a single layer and set aside to marinate for about 30 minutes. Drain the tofu steaks and reserve the marinade to use for basting while cooking.

3 Cook the steaks on the barbecue for 3 minutes on each side, basting regularly with the marinade, or fry them for 3 minutes in a large pan.

4 Arrange three tofu steaks on each plate. Any remaining marinade can be heated in a pan and then poured over the steaks. Sprinkle with the scallions and garnish with mixed salad leaves. Serve immediately.

Cook's Tip
Firm tofu is easily obtainable from supermarkets and health-food stores, and is an ideal alternative to meat.

GRILLED ASPARAGUS WITH SALT-CURED HAM

Barbecue-cooked asparagus has a wonderfully intense flavor that stands up well to the wrapping of crisp, salty ham. Serve this traditional tapas dish with drinks before a meal.

INGREDIENTS

6 slices of serrano ham
12 asparagus spears
1 tablespoon olive oil
sea salt and coarsely ground
black pepper

SERVES 4

1 Halve each slice of ham lengthwise and wrap one half around each of the asparagus spears.

2 Brush the ham and asparagus lightly with olive oil and sprinkle with salt and pepper. Cook on a medium barbecue for about 4 minutes, turning frequently, until the asparagus is tender but still firm. Serve immediately.

Cook's Tip

If you can't find serrano ham, try using Italian prosciutto or Portuguese presunto.

POTATO SKINS WITH CAJUN DIP

* * *

As an alternative to deep-frying, cooking potato skins on the barbecue crisps them up in no time
and gives them a wonderful chargrilled flavor. This spicy dip makes the perfect partner.

INGREDIENTS

4 large baking potatoes
olive oil for brushing
8 fluid ounces/1 cup
plain yogurt
2 garlic cloves, crushed
2 teaspoons tomato paste
1 small fresh green chile, chopped
1/2 teaspoon celery salt
salt and freshly ground
black pepper

SERVES 4

1 Bake or microwave the potatoes until tender. Cut them in half and scoop out the flesh, leaving a thin layer of potato on the skins. The scooped-out potato can be reserved in the refrigerator or freezer for another meal.

2 Cut each potato shell in half again and lightly brush the skins with olive oil. Cook on a medium-hot barbecue for 4–5 minutes, or until crisp.

3 Mix together the remaining ingredients in a bowl to make the dip. Serve the potato skins with the Cajun dip on the side.

Cook's Tip
If you don't have any fresh chiles, add 1 teaspoon green chili paste or one or two drops of hot pepper sauce to the dip instead.

31

SPICY CHICKEN WINGS

° ° °

*These deliciously sticky bites will appeal to adults and children alike, although
younger eaters might prefer a little less chilli.*

INGREDIENTS

8 plump chicken wings
2 large garlic cloves, cut
into slivers
1 tablespoon olive oil
1 tablespoon paprika
1 teaspoon chili powder
1 teaspoon dried oregano
salt and freshly ground
black pepper
lime wedges, to serve

SERVES 4

1 Using a small, sharp kitchen knife,
make one or two cuts in the skin of
each chicken wing and slide a sliver of
garlic under the skin. Brush the wings
generously with the olive oil.

2 In a large bowl, stir together the
paprika, chili powder and oregano
and season with plenty of salt and
pepper. Add the chicken wings and
toss together until very lightly coated
in the mixture.

3 Cook the chicken wings on a
medium barbecue for 15 minutes,
until they are cooked through, with
a blackened, crispy skin. Serve with
fresh lime wedges to squeeze over.

CHICKEN WINGS TERIYAKI STYLE

This Japanese glaze is very simple to prepare and adds a unique flavor to the meat. The glaze can be used with any cut of chicken or with fish.

INGREDIENTS

1 garlic clove, crushed
3 tablespoons soy sauce
2 tablespoons dry sherry
2 teaspoons clear honey
2 teaspoons grated fresh root ginger
1 teaspoon sesame oil
12 chicken wings
1 tablespoon sesame seeds, toasted

SERVES 4

1 Place the garlic, soy sauce, sherry, honey, grated ginger and sesame oil in a large bowl and beat with a fork to mix the ingredients together evenly.

2 Add the chicken wings and toss thoroughly, to coat in the marinade. Cover the bowl with plastic wrap and chill in the refrigerator for about 30 minutes, or longer.

3 Cook the chicken wings on a fairly hot barbecue for about 20–25 minutes, turning occasionally and basting with the remaining marinade.

4 Sprinkle the chicken wings with sesame seeds. Serve the wings on their own as an appetizer or side dish, or with a crisp green salad.

SKEWERED LAMB WITH RED ONION SALSA
° ° °

A simple salsa makes a refreshing accompaniment to this summery dish – make sure you use a mild-flavored red onion that is fresh and crisp, and a tomato that is ripe and full of flavor.

INGREDIENTS
8 ounces lean lamb, cubed
½ teaspoon ground cumin
1 teaspoon ground paprika
1 tablespoon olive oil
salt and freshly ground black pepper

FOR THE SALSA
1 red onion, very thinly sliced
1 large tomato, seeded and chopped
1 tablespoon red wine vinegar
3–4 fresh basil or mint leaves, roughly torn
small mint leaves, to garnish

SERVES 4

1 Place the lamb in a large bowl with the cumin, paprika and olive oil and season with plenty of salt and freshly ground black pepper. Toss well. Cover the bowl with plastic wrap and leave in a cool place for several hours, or in the refrigerator overnight, so that the lamb absorbs the flavors.

2 Spear the lamb cubes on four small skewers. If using wooden skewers, soak them first in cold water for at least 30 minutes to prevent them from burning when placed on the barbecue.

3 To make the salsa, put the sliced onion, tomato, red wine vinegar and torn fresh basil or mint leaves in a small bowl and stir together until thoroughly blended. Season to taste with salt and garnish with mint.

4 Cook the skewered lamb on a hot barbecue for about 5–10 minutes, turning the skewers frequently, until the lamb is well browned on the outside, but still slightly pink in the center. Serve hot, with the salsa.

SPICY MEATBALLS

These meatballs are delicious served piping hot with chili sauce. Keep the sauce on the side so that everyone can add as much heat as they like.

2 Add the ground beef, shallots, garlic, bread crumbs, beaten egg and parsley, with plenty of salt and pepper. Mix well, then use your hands to shape the mixture into 18 small balls.

3 Brush the meatballs with olive oil and cook on a medium barbecue, or fry them in a large pan, for 10–15 minutes, turning regularly until evenly browned and cooked through.

INGREDIENTS

4 ounces fresh spicy sausages
4 ounces/1 cup ground beef
2 shallots, finely chopped
2 garlic cloves, finely chopped
3 ounces/1½ cups fresh
white bread crumbs
1 egg, beaten
2 tablespoons chopped
fresh parsley, plus extra
to garnish
1 tablespoon olive oil
salt and freshly ground
black pepper
Tabasco sauce, to serve

SERVES 6

1 Use your hands to remove the skins from the spicy sausages, placing the sausage meat in a mixing bowl and breaking it up with a fork.

4 Transfer the meatballs to a warm dish and sprinkle with chopped fresh parsley. Serve with Tabasco sauce.

FIVE-SPICE RIB-STICKERS
. . .

Choose the meatiest spareribs you can find, to make these a real success, and
remember to keep a supply of paper napkins within easy reach.

2 Mix together all the remaining
ingredients, except the scallions, and
pour over the ribs. Toss to coat evenly.
Cover the bowl and leave to marinate
in the refrigerator overnight.

3 Cook the ribs on a medium-hot
barbecue, turning frequently, for about
30–40 minutes. Brush occasionally
with the remaining marinade.

INGREDIENTS

2¹/₄ pouncs Chinese-style
pork spareribs
2 teaspoons Chinese five-
spice powder
2 garlic cloves, crushed
1 tablespoon grated fresh
root ginger
¹/₂ teaspoon chili sauce
4 tablespoons dark soy sauce
3 tablespoons dark molasses sugar
1 tablespoon sunflower oil
4 scallions

SERVES 4

1 If the spareribs are still attached
to each other, cut between them to
separate them (or you could ask your
butcher to do this when you buy them).
Place the spareribs in a large bowl.

4 While the ribs are cooking, finely
slice the scallions. Sprinkle them over
the ribs and serve immediately.

SALMON WITH SPICY PESTO

° ° °

This is a great way to bone salmon steaks to give a solid piece of fish. The pesto uses
sunflower seeds and chilli as its flavoring, rather than the classic basil and pine nuts.

INGREDIENTS

4 salmon steaks, about
8 ounces each
2 tablesoons sunflower oil
finely grated rind and juice
of 1 lime
salt and freshly ground
black pepper

FOR THE PESTO
6 mild fresh red chiles
2 garlic cloves
2 tablespoons sunflower or
pumpkin seeds
juice and finely grated rind
of 1 lime
5 tablespoons olive oil

SERVES 4

1 Insert a very sharp knife close to the top of the bone. Working closely to the bone, cut your way to the end of the steak to release one side. Repeat with the other side. Pull out any extra visible bones with a pair of tweezers.

2 Sprinkle salt on the work surface and take hold of the end of the salmon piece, skin-side down. Insert the knife between the skin and the flesh and, working away from you, remove the skin, keeping the knife as close to it as possible. Repeat for each piece of fish.

3 Curl each piece of fish into a round shape, with the thinner end wrapped around the fatter end. Secure the shape tightly with a length of string.

4 Rub the sunflower oil into the boneless fish rounds. Put the salmon into a large bowl or dish and add the lime juice and rind and the salt and pepper. Leave the salmon to marinate in the refrigerator for up to 2 hours.

5 For the pesto, seed the chiles and place with the garlic cloves, sunflower or pumpkin seeds, lime juice, rind and seasoning in a food processor. Process until well mixed. With the motor running, gradually pour in the olive oil until the sauce has thickened and emulsified. Drain the salmon from its marinade. Cook the fish steaks on a medium barbecue for 5 minutes each side and serve with the spicy pesto.

GRILLED JUMBO SHRIMP WITH ROMESCO SAUCE

• • •

This sauce comes from the Catalan region of Spain and is served with fish and seafood.
Its main ingredients are pimiento, tomatoes, garlic and almonds.

INGREDIENTS

24 raw jumbo shrimp
2–3 tablespoons olive oil
flat leaf parsley, to garnish
lemon wedges, to serve

FOR THE SAUCE

2 well-flavored tomatoes
4 tablespoons olive oil
1 onion, chopped
4 garlic cloves, chopped
1 canned pimiento, chopped
1/2 teaspoon dried chili flakes
5 tablespoons fish stock
2 tablespoons white wine
10 blanched almonds
1 tablespoon red
wine vinegar
salt

SERVES 4

1 To make the sauce, immerse the tomatoes in boiling water for about 30 seconds, then refresh them under cold running water. Peel off the skins and coarsely chop the flesh.

2 Heat 2 tablespoons of the oil. Add the onion and three of the garlic cloves and cook until soft. Add the pimiento, tomatoes, chili, fish stock and wine. Cover and simmer for 30 minutes.

3 Toast the almonds under the broiler until golden. Transfer to a blender or food processor and grind coarsely. Add the remaining oil, the vinegar and the last garlic clove and process until evenly combined. Add the tomato and pimiento sauce and process until smooth. Season with salt.

4 Remove the heads from the shrimp, leaving them otherwise unpeeled and, with a sharp knife, slit each one down the back and remove the dark vein. Rinse and pat dry on paper towels. Toss the shrimp in olive oil, then spread them out on the barbecue and cook over a medium heat for about 2–3 minutes on each side, until pink. Serve immediately, garnished with parsley and accompanied by lemon wedges and the romesco sauce.

GRILLED MUSSELS WITH PARSLEY AND PARMESAN

° ° °

*Mussels release an irresistible aroma as they cook on the barbecue. Don't be surprised
if they are devoured the moment they are ready.*

INGREDIENTS

1 pound fresh mussels
3 tablespoons water
1 tablespoon melted butter
1 tablespoon olive oil
3 tablespoons freshly grated
Parmesan cheese
2 tablespoons chopped fresh parsley
2 garlic cloves, finely chopped
½ teaspoon coarsely ground
black pepper

SERVES 4

2 Place the mussels with the water
in a large pan. Cover with the lid and
steam for 5 minutes, or until all of the
mussels have opened.

4 In a large bowl, mix together
the melted butter, olive oil, grated
Parmesan cheese, chopped parsley,
garlic and ground black pepper.

1 Scrub the mussels, scraping off any
barnacles and pulling out the beards.
Tap any open mussels sharply with a
knife and discard any that fail to close.

3 Drain the mussels, discarding any
that remain closed. Snap the top shell
off each, leaving the mussel still
attached to the bottom shell.

5 Using a teaspoon, place a small
amount of the cheese mixture on top
of each mussel.

6 Cook the mussels in a pan on a
medium barbecue for 2–3 minutes or
until the mussels are sizzling hot. Serve
immediately, with French bread.

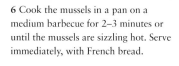

QUICK SHELLFISH PIZZA

Make four mini pizzas or one large one with the same quantities of ingredients.
If you are short of time, use a pizza-base mix instead of making the dough.

INGREDIENTS

FOR THE PIZZA BASE
1 teaspoon active dry yeast
1 pound/4 cups strong white
bread flour
1 tablespoon sugar
1 teaspoon sea salt
1/2 pint/1 1/4 cups lukewarm water
2 tablespoons extra virgin
olive oil

FOR THE FISH TOPPING
1 tablespoon olive oil
1 onion, finely chopped
1 3/4 pounds canned or fresh plum
tomatoes, chopped
salt and ground black pepper
1 tablespoon chopped
fresh thyme
4 ounces cherry tomatoes, halved
12 fresh anchovy fillets, or 1 can
anchovy fillets, drained
8 fresh, peeled shrimp
fresh thyme sprigs, to garnish

SERVES 4

1 Stir the active dry yeast into the flour
in a large bowl. Add the sugar and sea
salt and mix together well.

2 Add the water and olive oil to the
bowl, and stir to make a firm dough.

3 Knead the dough for 10 minutes.
Cover and leave in a warm place until
it has doubled in size.

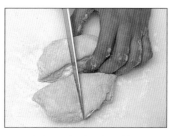

4 Punch down the dough and knead
for 5 minutes, then cut the dough
into four. Form each of the four pieces
of dough into 5-inch round shapes.

5 Cook the onions until soft. Add the
canned tomatoes, seasoning and thyme
and simmer for 15 minutes. Brush the
pizza bases with olive oil and cook on a
medium-hot barbecue, oiled-side down,
for 6–8 minutes, until firm and golden
underneath. Oil the uncooked side and
turn the pizzas over.

6 Cut the cherry tomatoes in half.
Assemble each of the pizzas with a
spoonful of the sauce, a couple of
anchovy fillets and shrimp and the
cherry tomatoes. Return the pizzas
to the barbecue and cook for a further
8–10 minutes until golden and crispy.
Sprinkle a few fresh sprigs of thyme on
top of the pizzas to serve.

Variation

Add your favorite shellfish,
such as fresh or canned mussels,
to the topping.

CIABATTA WITH MOZZARELLA AND ONIONS

*Ciabatta bread is readily available and is even more delicious when made with spinach,
sun-dried tomatoes or olives: you can find these variations in most supermarkets.*

INGREDIENTS
1 ciabatta loaf
4 tablespoons red pesto
2 small onions
olive oil, for brushing
8 ounces mozzarella cheese, sliced
8 black olives, halved and pitted

MAKES 4

1 Cut the bread in half horizontally
and toast the cut sides lightly on the
barbecue. Spread with the red pesto.

2 Peel the onions and then slice them
horizontally. Brush with oil and cook
on a hot barbecue for 4–5 minutes,
until the edges are caramelized.

3 Arrange the cheese on the bread. Add
the onion slices and sprinkle some
olives over. Cut in half. Return to the
barbecue to melt the cheese.

CROSTINI WITH TOMATO AND ANCHOVY

Crostini are little rounds of bread cut from a baguette and crisply toasted, then covered with a topping, such as this savory mixture of tomato and anchovy.

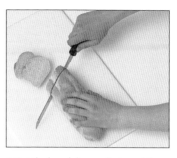

2 Cut the bread diagonally into eight slices about ½-inch thick and brush with the remaining oil. Toast on the barbecue until golden, turning once.

3 Spoon a little tomato mixture onto each slice of bread. Place an anchovy fillet on each one and dot with the halved olives. Serve the crostini garnished with a sprig of fresh basil.

INGREDIENTS

4 tablespoons olive oil
2 garlic cloves
4 tomatoes, peeled and chopped
1 tablespoon chopped fresh basil
1 tablespoon tomato paste
1 small baguette (large enough
to give 8 slices)
8 canned anchovy fillets
12 black olives, halved and pitted
salt and freshly ground
black pepper
fresh basil, to garnish

MAKES 8

1 Heat half the olive oil in a frying pan and cook the whole garlic cloves with the chopped tomatoes for about 4 minutes. Stir in the chopped basil, tomato paste and season with plenty of salt and freshly ground black pepper.

Variation

CROSTINI WITH ONION AND OLIVE
Cook 2 large onions, sliced, in 2 tablespoons olive oil until golden. Stir in 8 chopped anchovy fillets, 12 halved, pitted black olives, some seasoning and 1 teaspoon dried thyme. Spread the bread with 1 tablespoon black olive paste and cover with the onion mixture.

Succulent grilled cuts of meat are often the starting point when
planning a barbecue, and chargrilling gives meat a unique flavor.
The recipes in this chapter draw on cuisines from all over the
world to offer an exciting range of dishes that are easy to
prepare and deliciously succulent.

MEAT
DISHES

MIXED GRILL SKEWERS WITH HORSERADISH SAUCE

o o o

This hearty selection of meats, cooked on a skewer and drizzled with horseradish sauce, makes a popular main course. Keep all the pieces of meat about the same thickness so they cook evenly.

INGREDIENTS

4 small lamb noisettes
4 lamb's kidneys
4 fatty bacon strips
8 cherry tomatoes
8 chipolata sausages
12–16 bay leaves
salt and freshly ground
    black pepper

FOR THE HORSERADISH SAUCE
2 tablespoons horseradish relish
3 tablespoons melted butter

SERVES 4

1 Trim any excess fat from the lamb noisettes with a sharp knife. Halve the kidneys and remove the cores, using kitchen scissors.

2 Cut each bacon strip in half and wrap around the tomatoes or kidneys.

3 Thread the lamb noisettes, bacon-wrapped kidneys and cherry tomatoes, chipolatas and bay leaves onto four long metal skewers. Set aside while you prepare the sauce.

4 Mix the horseradish relish with the melted butter in a small bowl and stir until thoroughly mixed.

5 Brush a little of the horseradish sauce over the meat and sprinkle with salt and freshly ground black pepper.

6 Cook the skewers on a medium barbecue for 12 minutes, turning occasionally, until the meat is golden brown and thoroughly cooked. Serve hot, drizzled with the remaining sauce.

SAUSAGES WITH PRUNES AND BACON

• • •

Sausages are a perennial barbecue favorite and this is a delicious way to ring the changes.
Serve with French bread or warmed ciabatta.

2 Spread the cut surface with the mustard and then place three prunes in each sausage, pressing them in firmly.

3 Stretch the bacon strips out thinly, using a round-bladed knife.

4 Wrap one bacon strip tightly around each of the sausages, to hold them in shape. Cook on a hot barbecue for 15–18 minutes, turning occasionally, until evenly browned and thoroughly cooked. Serve immediately, with lots of fresh rustic bread and the additional mustard.

INGREDIENTS

8 large, meaty sausages, such as
Toulouse or other good-quality
pork sausages
2 tablespoons Dijon mustard,
plus extra to serve
24 ready-to-eat prunes
8 smoked fatty
bacon strips

SERVES 4

1 Use a sharp knife to cut a long slit down the length of each sausage, about three-quarters of the way through.

SHISH KEBAB

• • •

Many different kinds of kebab are eaten throughout the Middle East, and they are almost always cooked over an open wood or charcoal fire.

INGREDIENTS

1 pound boned leg of
lamb, cubed
1 large green bell pepper, seeded
and cut into squares
1 large yellow bell pepper, seeded
and cut into squares
8 pearl onions, halved
8 ounces white mushrooms
4 tomatoes, halved
1 tablespoon melted butter

FOR THE MARINADE
3 tablespoons olive oil
juice of 1 lemon
2 garlic cloves, crushed
1 large onion, grated
1 tablespoon fresh oregano
salt and freshly ground
black pepper

SERVES 4

1 First make the marinade: blend together the olive oil, lemon juice, crushed garlic, onion, fresh oregano and seasoning. Place the cubed meat in a shallow dish and pour over the marinade. Cover with plastic wrap and leave to marinate for several hours, or overnight, in the refrigerator.

2 Thread the lamb onto metal skewers, alternating with pieces of pepper, onions and mushrooms. Thread the tomatoes onto separate skewers.

3 Cook the kebabs and tomatoes on a hot barbecue for 10 minutes, turning occasionally and basting with butter. Serve with bulghur wheat.

BACON KOFTA KEBABS AND SALAD

* * *

Kofta kebabs can be made with any type of minced meat, but bacon is very successful, if you have a food processor.

INGREDIENTS

*9 ounces lean bacon strips,
coarsely chopped
1 small onion, coarsely chopped
1 celery stick, coarsely chopped
5 tablespoons fresh whole-wheat
breadcrumbs
3 tablespoons chopped fresh thyme
2 tablespoons Worcestershire sauce
1 egg, beaten
salt and freshly ground
black pepper
olive oil, for brushing*

FOR THE SALAD

*4 ounces/3/4 cup bulghur wheat
4 tablespoons toasted
sunflower seeds
1 tablespoon olive oil
salt and freshly ground
black pepper
handful of celery leaves, chopped*

SERVES 4

1 Place the bacon, onion, celery and bread crumbs in a food processor and process until chopped. Add the thyme, Worcestershire sauce and seasoning. Bind to a firm mixture with the egg.

2 Divide the mixture into eight equal portions and use your hands to shape them around eight bamboo skewers.

3 For the salad, place the bulghur wheat in a bowl and pour over boiling water to cover. Leave to stand for 30 minutes, until the grains are tender.

4 Drain well, then stir in the sunflower seeds, olive oil, salt and pepper. Stir in the celery leaves.

5 Cook the skewers on a medium-hot barbecue for 8–10 minutes, turning occasionally, until golden brown. Serve with the salad.

PEPPERED STEAKS IN BEER AND GARLIC

The robust flavors of this dish will satisfy the heartiest appetites.
Serve the steaks with baked potatoes and a crisp mixed salad.

2 Remove the steaks from the dish and reserve the marinade. Sprinkle the peppercorns over the steaks and press them into the surface.

3 Cook the steaks on a hot barbecue, basting them occasionally with the reserved marinade during cooking. (Take care when basting, as the alcohol will tend to flare up: spoon or brush on just a small amount at a time.)

INGREDIENTS

4 beef sirloin or round steaks,
about 6 ounces each
2 garlic cloves, crushed
4 fluid ounces/½ cup stout
2 tablespoons dark
brown sugar
2 tablespoons Worcestershire sauce
1 tablespoon corn oil
1 tablespoon crushed
black peppercorns

SERVES 4

1 Place the steaks in a dish and add the garlic, stout, sugar, Worcestershire sauce and oil. Turn to coat evenly, then leave to marinate in the refrigerator for 2–3 hours or overnight.

4 Turn the steaks once during cooking, and cook them for 3–6 minutes on each side, depending on whether you like them rare, medium or well done.

SIRLOIN STEAKS WITH BLOODY MARY SAUCE

This cocktail of ingredients is just as delicious as the drink that inspired it, and since the alcohol evaporates during cooking, you need not worry about a hangover.

INGREDIENTS

4 sirloin steaks, about
8 ounces each
2 tablespoons dark soy sauce
4 tablespoons balsamic vinegar
2 tablespoons extra virgin
olive oil

FOR THE BLOODY MARY SAUCE
2 1/4 pounds very ripe tomatoes,
peeled and chopped
tomato paste, if required
2 ounces/1/2 cup chopped onions
2 scallions
1 teaspoon chopped
fresh cilantro
1 teaspoon ground cumin
1 teaspoon salt
1 tablespoon fresh lime juice
4 fluid ounces/1/2 cup beef
consommé
4 tablespoons vodka
1 tablespoon Worcestershire sauce

SERVES 4

1 Lay the steaks in a shallow dish. Mix together the soy sauce, vinegar and olive oil, pour over the steaks and leave to marinate in the refrigerator for at least 2 hours, turning once or twice.

2 Place all the sauce ingredients in a food processor and blend to a fairly smooth texture. If the tomatoes are not quite ripe, add a little tomato paste. Put in a pan, bring to the boil and simmer for about 5 minutes.

3 Remove the steaks from the dish and discard the marinade. Cook the steaks on a medium-hot barbecue for about 3–6 minutes each side, depending on how rare you like them, turning once during cooking. Serve the steaks with the Bloody Mary sauce.

BEEF RIB WITH ONION SAUCE

· · ·

Rib of beef is a classic large roasting joint, but just one rib, barbecue-cooked on the bone, then carved into succulent slices, makes a perfect dish for two. Serve with a mellow red onion sauce.

INGREDIENTS

1 beef rib on the bone, about
2¼ pounds and about 1½ inches
thick, well trimmed of fat
1 teaspoon "steak pepper" or
lightly crushed black peppercorns
1 tablespoon coarse sea
salt, crushed
2–3 tablespoons olive oil

FOR THE RED ONION SAUCE
1½ ounces butter
1 large red onion or
8–10 shallots, sliced
8 fluid ounces/1 cup fruity red wine
8 fluid ounces/1 cup beef or
chicken stock
1–2 tablespoons red currant jelly
or seedless raspberry preserve
¼ teaspoon dried thyme
salt and freshly ground
black pepper

SERVES 2–4

1 Wipe the beef with damp paper towels. Mix the "steak pepper" or crushed peppercorns with the crushed salt and press onto both sides of the meat. Leave the meat to stand, loosely covered, for 30 minutes.

2 To make the sauce, melt the butter over a medium heat. Add the onion or shallots and cook for 3 minutes, until softened. Add the wine, stock, jelly or preserve and thyme and bring to the boil. Reduce the heat and simmer for 30–35 minutes until the liquid has evaporated and the sauce has thickened. Season and keep warm.

3 Brush the meat with olive oil and cook on a hot barbecue, or in a pan over a high heat, for 5–8 minutes each side, depending on how rare you like it. Transfer the beef to a board, cover loosely and leave to stand for about 10 minutes. Using a knife, loosen the meat from the rib bone, then carve into slices. Serve with the red onion sauce.

STILTON BURGERS

° ° °

A variation on the traditional burger, this tasty recipe contains a delicious surprise:
a creamy filling of lightly melted Stilton cheese.

INGREDIENTS

1 pound/4 cups ground beef
1 onion, chopped
1 celery stick, chopped
1 teaspoon dried mixed herbs
1 teaspoon prepared mustard
2 ounces Stilton cheese
4 burger buns
salt and freshly ground
black pepper

SERVES 4

1 Mix the ground beef with the chopped onion, celery, mixed herbs and mustard. Season well with salt and pepper, and bring together with your hands to form a firm mixture.

2 Divide the mixture into eight equal portions. Shape four portions into rounds and flatten each one slightly. Crumble a little of the cheese in the center of each round.

3 Shape and flatten the remaining four portions and place on top. Use your hands to mold the rounds together, encasing the crumbled cheese, and shaping them into four burgers.

4 Cook on a medium barbecue for about 10 minutes, or until cooked through, turning once. Split the burger buns and place a burger inside each. Serve with salad and mustard relish.

SPICED BEEF SATAY

Tender strips of steak threaded on skewers and spiced with the characteristic flavors
of Indonesia are popular with everyone.

INGREDIENTS

1 pound round steak, cut in
½ inch strips
1 teaspoon coriander seeds,
dry-fried and ground
½ teaspoon cumin seeds,
dry-fried and ground
1 teaspoon tamarind pulp
1 small onion
2 garlic cloves
1 tablespoon brown sugar
1 tablespoon dark soy sauce
salt

TO SERVE
cucumber chunks
lemon or lime wedges
Sambal Kecap

MAKES 18 SKEWERS

1 Mix the meat and spices in a large non-metallic bowl. Soak the tamarind pulp in 5 tablespoons water.

2 Strain the tamarind and reserve the juice. Put the onion, garlic, tamarind juice, sugar and soy sauce in a food processor and blend well.

3 Pour the marinade over the meat and spices in the bowl and toss together well. Leave for at least 1 hour.

4 Meanwhile, soak some bamboo skewers in water to prevent them from burning while cooking. Thread 5 or 6 pieces of meat onto each skewer and sprinkle with salt. Cook on a medium-hot barbecue, turning the skewers frequently and basting with the marinade, until the meat is tender.

5 Serve with cucumber chunks and wedges of lemon or lime for squeezing over the meat. Sambal Kecap makes a traditional accompaniment.

SAMBAL KECAP
Mix 1 fresh red chile,
seeded and finely chopped,
2 crushed garlic cloves and
4 tablespoons dark soy sauce with
4 teaspoons lemon juice and
2 tablespoons hot water in a bowl.
Leave to stand for 30 minutes
before serving.

VEGETABLE-STUFFED BEEF ROLLS

These Japanese-style beef rolls are very popular for al fresco *meals. You could roll up many other vegetables in the sliced beef. Pork is also very good cooked this way.*

INGREDIENTS

2 ounces carrot
2 ounces green bell pepper, seeded
bunch of scallions
14 ounces beef pot roast,
thinly sliced
all-purpose flour, for dusting
1 tablespoon olive oil
fresh parsley sprigs, to garnish

FOR THE SAUCE
2 tablespoons sugar
3 tablespoons soy sauce
3 tablespoons mirin

SERVES 4

1 Use a sharp knife to shred the carrot and green bell pepper into 1½–2-inch lengths. Wash and peel the outer skins from the scallions, then halve them lengthwise. Shred the scallions diagonally into 1½–2-inch lengths.

2 The beef slices should be no more than ¹⁄₁₂ of an inch thick, and about 6 inches square. Lay a slice of beef on a chopping board and top with strips of the carrot, green bell pepper and scallion. Roll up quite tightly and dust lightly with flour. Repeat with the remaining beef and vegetables.

3 Secure the beef rolls with toothpicks, soaked in water to prevent them from burning, and cook on a medium barbecue or in a pan over a medium heat, for 10–15 minutes, turning frequently, until golden brown and thoroughly cooked.

4 Blend the ingredients for the sauce in a small pan and cook to dissolve the sugar and form a glaze. Halve the cooked rolls, cutting at a slant, and stand them on a plate with the sloping cut ends facing upward. Dress with the sauce and garnish with fresh parsley.

LAMB STEAKS MARINATED IN MINT AND SHERRY

∘ ∘ ∘

The marinade in this recipe is extremely quick to prepare, and is the key
to its success: the sherry imparts a wonderful tang to the meat.

INGREDIENTS

6 large lamb steaks or
12 smaller chops

FOR THE MARINADE
2 tablespoons chopped fresh
mint leaves
1 tablespoon black peppercorns
1 medium onion, chopped
4 fluid ounces/¹/₂ cup sherry
4 tablespoons extra virgin olive oil
2 garlic cloves

SERVES 6

1 Process the fresh mint leaves and peppercorns in a food processor until finely chopped. Add the onion and process again until smooth. Add the rest of the marinade ingredients and process until completely mixed. The marinade should be a thick consistency.

2 Add the marinade to the lamb and cover with plastic wrap. Marinate in the refrigerator overnight.

3 Cook the steaks on a medium barbecue for 10–15 minutes, basting occasionally with the marinade.

SKEWERED LAMB WITH HERB YOGURT

These Turkish kebabs are traditionally made with lamb, but lean beef or pork work equally well.
You can alternate pieces of pepper, lemon or onions with the meat for extra flavor and color.

INGREDIENTS
2 pounds lean boneless lamb
1 large onion, grated
3 bay leaves
5 sprigs of thyme or rosemary
grated rind and juice of 1 lemon
pinch of superfine sugar
3 fluid ounces/⅓ cup olive oil
salt and freshly ground
black pepper
sprigs of fresh rosemary,
to garnish
lemon wedges, to serve

FOR THE HERB YOGURT
¼ pint/⅔ cup thick plain yogurt
1 tablespoon chopped fresh mint
1 tablespoon chopped
fresh cilantro
2 teaspoons grated onion

SERVES 4

1 To make the herb yogurt, mix together the plain yogurt, chopped fresh mint, chopped fresh cilantro and grated onion. Transfer the yogurt to a serving bowl.

2 To make the kebabs, cut the lamb into 1-inch cubes and put in a bowl. Mix together the onion, herbs, lemon rind and juice, sugar and oil, then season to taste.

3 Pour the marinade over the meat and stir to ensure it is covered. Cover with plastic wrap and leave to marinate in the refrigerator for several hours or overnight.

4 Drain the meat and thread onto metal skewers. Cook on a hot barbecue for about 10 minutes. Garnish with rosemary and lemon wedges and serve with the herb yogurt.

LAMB BURGERS WITH RED-CURRANT CHUTNEY

∘ ∘ ∘

These rather special burgers take a little extra time to prepare but are well worth it.
The red-currant chutney is the perfect complement to the minty lamb taste.

INGREDIENTS

1¼ pounds/5 cups ground
lean lamb
1 small onion, finely chopped
2 tablespoons finely chopped
fresh mint
2 tablespoons finely chopped
fresh parsley
4 ounces mozzarella cheese
2 tablespoons oil, for basting
salt and freshly ground
black pepper

FOR THE RED-CURRANT CHUTNEY
4 ounces/1½ cups red currants
2 teaspoons clear honey
1 teaspoon balsamic vinegar
2 tablespoons finely chopped mint

SERVES 4

1 In a large bowl, mix together the ground lamb, chopped onion, mint and parsley until evenly combined. Season well with plenty of salt and freshly ground black pepper.

Cook's Tip

If time is short, or if fresh red currants are not available, serve the burgers with ready-made red-currant sauce.

2 Roughly divide the meat mixture into eight equal pieces and use your hands to press each of the pieces into flat round shapes.

3 Cut the mozzarella cheese into four chunks. Place one chunk of cheese on half the lamb rounds. Top each with another round of meat mixture.

4 Press each of the two rounds of meat together firmly, making four flattish burger shapes. Use your fingers to blend the edges neatly and seal in the cheese completely.

5 Place all the ingredients for the chutney in a bowl and mash them together with a fork. Season well with salt and freshly ground black pepper.

6 Brush the lamb burgers with olive oil and cook them over a moderately hot barbecue for about 15 minutes, turning once, until golden brown. Serve with the red-currant chutney.

BARBECUE-COOKED LAMB WITH POTATO SLICES

A traditional mixture of fresh herbs adds a summery flavor to this simple lamb dish.
A leg of lamb is easier to cook evenly on the barbecue if it's boned out, or "butterflied" first.

INGREDIENTS

1 leg of lamb, about 4¹/₂ pounds
1 garlic clove, thinly sliced
handful of fresh flat leaf parsley
handful of fresh sage
handful of fresh rosemary
handful of fresh thyme
6 tablespoons dry sherry
4 tablespoons walnut oil
1¹/₄ pounds medium-size potatoes
salt and freshly ground
black pepper

SERVES 4

2 Use a sharp kitchen knife to scrape away the meat from the bone on both sides, until the bone is completely exposed. Carefully remove the bone and cut away any sinews and excess fat from the meat.

4 Place the meat in a bowl and pour over the sherry and walnut oil. Chop half the remaining herbs and sprinkle over the meat. Cover the bowl with a clean dish towel and leave to marinate in the refrigerator for 30 minutes.

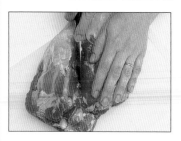

1 Place the lamb on a board, smooth-side downward, so that you can see where the bone lies. Using a sharp heavy knife, make a long cut through the flesh down to the bone.

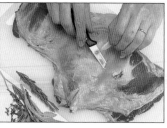

3 Cut through the thickest part of the meat so that you can open it out as flat as possible. Make several cuts in the lamb with a sharp kitchen knife, and push slivers of garlic and sprigs of fresh herbs into the cuts.

5 Remove the lamb from the marinade and season. Cook on a medium-hot barbecue for 30–35 minutes, turning occasionally and basting with the reserved marinade.

Cook's Tip

If you have a spit-roasting attachment, the lamb can be rolled and tied with herbs inside, and spit roasted for 1–1¹/₂ hours. A spit makes it much easier to cook larger pieces of lamb.

6 Scrub the potatoes, then cut them in thick slices. Brush with the marinade and place around the lamb. Cook for about 15 minutes, until golden brown.

LAMB WITH LAVENDER BALSAMIC MARINADE

° ° °

Lavender is an unusual flavor to use with meat, but its heady, summery scent works well with lamb cooked on the barbecue. If you like, rosemary can take its place.

2 Sprinkle the chopped fresh lavender over the lamb in the bowl.

3 Beat together the vinegar, olive oil and lemon juice and pour them over the lamb. Season well with salt and pepper and then turn to coat evenly.

4 Scatter a few lavender sprigs over the grill or on the coals of a medium-hot barbecue. Cook the lamb for about 15–20 minutes, turning once and basting with any remaining marinade, until golden brown on the outside and still slightly pink in the center.

INGREDIENTS

4 racks of lamb, with
3–4 cutlets each
1 shallot, finely chopped
3 tablespoons chopped
fresh lavender
1 tablespoon balsamic vinegar
2 tablespoons olive oil
1 tablespoon lemon juice
salt and freshly ground
black pepper
handful of lavender sprigs

SERVES 4

1 Place the racks of lamb in a large mixing bowl or wide dish and sprinkle over the chopped shallot.

LAMB WITH MINT AND LEMON

∘ ∘ ∘

Use this simple and traditional marinade to make the most of fine quality lamb leg steaks.
Lemon and fresh mint combine extremely well with the flavor of lamb cooked on the barbecue.

INGREDIENTS

4 lamb steaks, about 8 ounces each
fresh mint leaves, to garnish

FOR THE MARINADE
grated rind and juice of ½ lemon
1 garlic clove, crushed
1 scallion, chopped
1 teaspoon finely chopped
fresh mint
2 tablespoons extra virgin olive oil
salt and freshly ground
black pepper

SERVES 4

1 Mix all the marinade ingredients and season to taste. Place the lamb steaks in a shallow dish and add the marinade. Cover with plastic wrap and marinate in the refrigerator for several hours or overnight.

2 Drain the lamb steaks and cook on a medium-hot barbecue for about 10–15 minutes until just cooked, basting with the marinade occasionally and turning once. Garnish the lamb steaks with the fresh mint leaves.

STUFFED EGGPLANT WITH LAMB

• • •

Ground lamb and eggplant go together beautifully. This is an attractive dish,
using different-colored peppers in the lightly spiced stuffing mixture.

INGREDIENTS

2 medium eggplant
2 tablespoons vegetable oil
1 medium onion, sliced
1 teaspoon grated fresh root ginger
1 teaspoon chili powder
1 garlic clove, crushed
1/4 teaspoon ground turmeric
1 teaspoon ground coriander
1 medium tomato, chopped
12 ounces/3 cups ground
lean lamb
1 medium green bell pepper,
coarsely chopped
1 medium orange bell pepper,
coarsely chopped
2 tablespoons chopped
fresh cilantro

FOR THE GARNISH
1/2 onion, sliced
2 cherry tomatoes, quartered
fresh cilantro sprigs

SERVES 4

1 Cut the eggplant in half lengthwise
with a heavy sharp knife. Scoop out
most of the flesh and reserve it for
another dish. Brush the shells with a
little vegetable oil.

2 In a medium pan, heat 1 tablespoon
of oil and cook the sliced onion until
golden brown. Stir in the grated ginger,
chili powder, garlic, turmeric and
ground coriander. Add the chopped
tomato, lower the heat and cook for
about 5 minutes, stirring constantly.

3 Add the ground lamb to the pan and
continue to cook over a medium heat
for about 7–10 minutes. Stir in the
chopped green and orange bell peppers
and the fresh cilantro.

4 Spoon the lamb mixture into the
eggplant shells and brush the edges
of the shells with the remaining oil.
Cook on a medium-hot barbecue for
15–20 minutes, until cooked through.
Garnish with sliced onion, cherry
tomatoes and cilantro and serve.

VEAL CHOPS WITH BASIL BUTTER

o o o

Veal chops from the loin are an expensive cut and are best cooked quickly and simply.
The flavor of basil goes well with veal, but other herbs can be used instead if you like.

INGREDIENTS

1 ounce/2 tablespoons
butter, softened
1 tablespoon Dijon mustard
1 tablespoon chopped fresh basil
olive oil, for brushing
2 veal loin chops, 1-inch thick,
about 8 ounces each
salt and freshly ground black pepper
fresh basil sprigs, to garnish

SERVES 2

1 To make the basil butter, cream the softened butter with the Dijon mustard and chopped fresh basil in a large mixing bowl, then season with plenty of freshly ground black pepper.

2 Brush both sides of each chop with olive oil and season with a little salt.

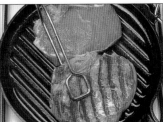

3 Cook the chops on a hot barbecue for 7–10 minutes, basting with oil and turning once, until done to your liking. (Medium-rare meat will still be slightly soft when pressed, medium will be springy and well-done firm.) Top each chop with half the basil butter and serve immediately, garnished with basil.

PORK AND PINEAPPLE SATAY

○ ○ ○

This variation on the classic satay has added pineapple, but keeps the traditional coconut and peanut sauce.

INGREDIENTS

1¼ pounds pork tenderloin
1 small onion, chopped
1 garlic clove, chopped
4 tablespoons soy sauce
finely grated rind of ½ lemon
1 teaspoon ground cumin
1 teaspoon ground coriander
1 teaspoon ground turmeric
1 teaspoon molasses sugar
8-ounce can pineapple chunks,
or 1 small pineapple, peeled
and diced
salt and freshly ground
black pepper

FOR THE SATAY SAUCE
6 fluid ounces/¾ cup coconut milk
6 tablespoons crunchy
peanut butter
1 garlic clove, crushed
2 teaspoons soy sauce
1 teaspoon dark brown sugar

SERVES 4

1 Using a sharp kitchen knife, trim any fat from the pork tenderloin and cut it into 1-inch cubes. Place the meat in a large mixing bowl and set aside.

2 Place the onion, garlic, soy sauce, lemon rind, spices and sugar in a blender or food processor. Add two pieces of pineapple and process until the mixture is almost smooth.

3 Add the paste to the pork, tossing well to coat evenly. Thread the pieces of pork onto bamboo skewers, with the remaining pineapple pieces.

4 To make the sauce, pour the coconut milk into a small pan and stir in the peanut butter. Stir in the remaining sauce ingredients and heat gently over the barbecue, stirring until smooth and hot. Cover and keep warm on the edge of the barbecue.

5 Cook the pork and pineapple skewers on a medium-hot barbecue, turning occasionally, for 10–12 minutes, until golden brown and thoroughly cooked. Serve with the satay sauce.

Cook's Tip

If you cannot buy coconut milk, you can use ¼ pint/⅔ cup coconut cream instead. Thin it to the correct consistency with about 2 tablespoons of water.

LEMON GRASS PORK CHOPS WITH MUSHROOMS

· · ·

Thai flavorings are used to make an aromatic marinade and a spicy sauce. The sauce can be put together in a pan on the barbecue while the chops and mushrooms are cooking.

INGREDIENTS

4 pork chops, about 8 ounces each
4 large portabello mushrooms
3 tablespoons vegetable oil
4 red chiles, seeded and sliced
3 tablespoons Thai fish sauce
6 tablespoons lime juice
4 shallots, chopped
1 teaspoon roasted ground rice
2 tablespoons scallions,
chopped
fresh cilantro leaves and
4 shredded scallions,
to garnish

FOR THE MARINADE
2 garlic cloves, chopped
1 tablespoon sugar
1 tablespoon Thai fish sauce
2 tablespoons soy sauce
1 tablespoon sesame oil
1 tablespoon whisky or
dry sherry
2 lemon grass stalks,
finely chopped
2 scallions, chopped

SERVES 4

2 Place the mushrooms and marinated pork chops on a rack and brush with 1 tablespoon of vegetable oil. Cook the pork chops on a medium-hot barbecue for 10–15 minutes and the mushrooms for about 2 minutes, turning once. Brush both with the marinade while they are cooking.

3 Meanwhile, heat the remaining oil in a small frying pan, then remove from the heat and mix in the remaining ingredients. Put the pork chops and mushrooms on a serving plate and spoon over the sauce. Garnish with the fresh cilantro leaves and shredded scallions.

1 To make the marinade, mix all the ingredients together. Arrange the pork chops in a shallow dish. Pour over the marinade and leave for 1–2 hours.

FARMHOUSE PIZZA

° ° °

*Pizza is not a dish usually associated with barbecue cooking, but in fact the open fire gives the
base a wonderfully crisp texture. Shape the dough to fit the grill rack of your barbecue.*

INGREDIENTS
6 tablespoons olive oil
8 ounces white mushrooms,
sliced
11-ounce packet pizza-dough mix
$\frac{1}{2}$ pint/$1\frac{1}{4}$ cups tomato sauce
11 ounces mozzarella cheese,
thinly sliced
4 ounces extra-thin smoked
ham slices
6 bottled artichoke hearts in oil,
drained and sliced
2-ounce can anchovy fillets,
drained and halved lengthwise
10 pitted black olives, halved
2 tablespoons chopped
fresh oregano
3 tablespoons freshly grated
Parmesan cheese
freshly ground black pepper

SERVES 8

1 Heat 2 tablespoons of oil in a pan,
add the mushrooms and cook until all
the juices have evaporated. Leave to cool.

2 Make up the pizza dough according
to the directions on the packet. Roll it
out on a lightly floured surface to a
12 x 10-inch rectangle. Brush with
oil and place, oiled-side down, on a
medium-hot barbecue. Cook for
6 minutes until firm.

3 Brush the uncooked side of the dough
with oil and turn over. Spread with the
tomato sauce and arrange the sliced
mozzarella on top. Scrunch up the
smoked ham and arrange on top with
the artichoke hearts, anchovies and
cooked mushrooms.

4 Dot with the halved olives, then
sprinkle over the fresh oregano and
Parmesan. Drizzle over the remaining
olive oil and season with black pepper.
Return to the barbecue and cook for
a further 8–10 minutes, or until the
dough is golden brown and crisp.

73

Chicken cooked on a barbecue is unfailingly popular with both

adults and children, and it can be as simple or sophisticated as

you choose. Don't forget other types of poultry, particularly

duck, which stays beautifully juicy and moist when prepared

in this way.

POULTRY AND
GAME

CHICKEN WITH PINEAPPLE

o o o

The pineapple juice in this Indian recipe is used to tenderize the meat, but it also gives the chicken a deliciously tangy sweetness.

INGREDIENTS

8-ounce can pineapple chunks
in juice
1 teaspoon ground cumin
1 teaspoon ground coriander
1 garlic clove, crushed
1 teaspoon chili powder
1 teaspoon salt
2 tablespoons plain yogurt
1 tablespoon chopped
fresh cilantro
few drops orange food
coloring (optional)
10 ounces skinless, boneless
chicken breast and thigh meat
½ red bell pepper
½ yellow or green bell pepper
1 large onion
6 cherry tomatoes
1 tablespoon vegetable oil

SERVES 6

2 In a large bowl, blend together the cumin, ground coriander, garlic, chili powder, salt, yogurt, fresh cilantro and food coloring, if using. Pour in the pineapple juice and mix together.

4 Arrange the chicken pieces, vegetables and reserved pineapple chunks alternately on six skewers.

3 Cut the chicken into cubes, add to the yogurt and spice mixture and leave to marinate for about 1–1½ hours. Cut the peppers and onion into chunks.

5 Brush the kebabs with oil and cook on a medium barbecue for about 10 minutes, turning and basting the chicken pieces regularly with the marinade, until cooked through. Serve with salad or plain boiled rice.

1 Drain the canned pineapple into a bowl. Reserve twelve large chunks of pineapple. Squeeze the juice from the remaining chunks into the bowl, then discard the chunks. You should be left with about 4 fluid ounces/½ cup pineapple juice.

CITRUS KEBABS

Serve these succulent grilled chicken kebabs on a bed of lettuce leaves, garnished with sprigs of fresh mint and orange and lemon slices.

INGREDIENTS

*4 skinless, boneless chicken
breast portions
fresh mint sprigs, to garnish
orange and lemon or lime slices,
to garnish*

FOR THE MARINADE
*finely grated rind and juice of
½ orange
finely grated rind and juice of
½ lemon or lime
2 tablespoons olive oil
2 tablespoons clear honey
2 tablespoons chopped fresh mint
¼ teaspoon ground cumin
salt and freshly ground
black pepper*

SERVES 4

1 Use a heavy knife to cut the chicken into 1-inch cubes.

2 Combine the marinade ingredients in a large bowl, add the chicken and cover with plastic wrap. Leave to marinate for at least 2 hours, or overnight in the refrigerator.

3 Thread the chicken onto metal skewers and cook on a medium barbecue for 10 minutes, basting with the marinade and turning frequently. Garnish with mint and citrus slices.

78

SWEET AND SOUR KEBABS

. . .

*This marinade contains sugar and will burn very easily, so cook the kebabs slowly
and turn them often. Serve these kebabs with harlequin rice.*

INGREDIENTS

2 skinless, boneless chicken
breast portions
8 pearl onions or
2 medium onions
4 rindless fatty bacon strips
3 firm bananas
1 red bell pepper, diced

FOR THE MARINADE
2 tablespoons brown sugar
1 tablespoon Worcestershire sauce
2 tablespoons lemon juice
salt and freshly ground
black pepper

FOR THE HARLEQUIN RICE
2 tablespoons olive oil
1 small red bell pepper, diced
8 ounces/1⅓ cup cooked rice
4 ounces/1 cup cooked peas

SERVES 4

1 Combine the marinade ingredients.
Cut each chicken portion into four
pieces, add to the marinade, cover and
leave for at least 4 hours, or preferably
overnight in the refrigerator.

2 Peel the pearl onions, blanch them in
boiling water for 5 minutes and drain.
If using medium onions, quarter them
after blanching.

3 Cut each strip of bacon in half with a
sharp knife. Peel the bananas and cut
each one into three pieces. Wrap half
a bacon strip around each of the
banana pieces.

4 Thread the bacon and bananas
onto metal skewers with the chicken
pieces, onions and pepper pieces. Brush
generously with the marinade.

5 Cook on a low barbecue for about
15 minutes, turning and basting
frequently with the marinade.

6 Meanwhile, heat the oil in a
frying pan and stir-fry the diced pepper
briefly. Add the rice and peas and stir
until heated through. Serve the
harlequin rice with the kebabs.

BLACKENED CAJUN CHICKEN AND CORN

° ° °

This is a classic American Deep-South method of cooking in a spiced coating, which can be used for poultry, meat or fish. The coating should begin to char and blacken slightly at the edges.

INGREDIENTS

8 chicken joints (drumsticks, thighs or wings)
2 whole corn cobs
2 teaspoons garlic salt
2 teaspoons ground black pepper
1½ teaspoon ground cumin
1½ teaspoon paprika
1 teaspoon cayenne pepper
3 tablespoons melted butter
chopped parsley, to garnish

SERVES 4

1 Trim any excess fat from the chicken, but leave the skin in place. Slash the thickest parts with a knife, to allow the flavors to penetrate the meat as thoroughly as possible.

2 Pull the husks and silks off the corn cobs, then rinse them under cold running water and pat them dry with paper towels. Cut the cobs into thick slices, using a heavy kitchen knife.

3 Mix together all the spices. Brush the chicken and corn with the melted butter and sprinkle the spices over them. Toss well to coat evenly.

4 Cook the chicken pieces on a medium-hot barbecue for about 25 minutes, turning occasionally. Add the corn after 15 minutes, and grill, turning often, until golden brown. Serve garnished with chopped parsley.

CHICKEN WITH HERB AND RICOTTA STUFFING

*These little chicken drumsticks are full of flavor, and the stuffing and bacon help to
keep them moist and tender.*

INGREDIENTS

*4 tablespoons ricotta cheese
1 garlic clove, crushed
3 tablespoons mixed chopped
fresh mixed herbs
2 tablespoons fresh brown
bread crumbs
8 chicken drumsticks
8 smoked fatty bacon strips
1 teaspoon whole-grain mustard
1 tablespoon sunflower oil
salt and freshly ground
black pepper*

SERVES 4

Mix together the ricotta, garlic, herbs
and bread crumbs. Season well with
plenty of salt and pepper.

Carefully loosen the skin from each
drumstick and spoon a little of the herb
stuffing under each, smoothing the skin
back over firmly.

3 Wrap a bacon strip tightly around the
wide end of each drumstick, to hold
the skin in place over the stuffing
during the cooking time.

4 Mix together the mustard and oil and
brush them over the chicken. Cook on
a medium-hot barbecue for about
25 minutes, turning occasionally.

BABY CHICKENS WITH LIME AND CHILI

Cornish hens are small birds that are ideal for one to two portions. The best way to prepare them is "spatchcocked" – flattened out – to ensure more even cooking.

INGREDIENTS

4 Cornish hens, about
1 pound each
3 tablespoons butter
2 tablespoons sun-dried
tomato paste
finely grated rind of 1 lime
2 teaspoons chili sauce
juice of ½ lime
lime wedges, to serve
fresh flat leaf parsley sprigs,
to garnish

SERVES 4

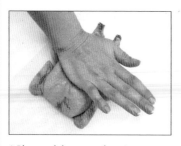

1 Place each hen on a chopping board, breast-side upward, and press down firmly with your hand, to break the breastbone.

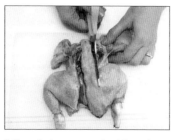

2 Turn the hen over and, with poultry shears or strong kitchen scissors, cut down either side of the backbone. Remove it and discard.

3 Turn the hen breast-side up and flatten it gently. Lift the breast skin carefully and gently ease your fingertips underneath, to loosen it from the flesh.

4 Mix together the butter, sun-dried tomato paste, lime rind and chili sauce in a small bowl. Spread about three-quarters of the mixture under the skin of the hens, smoothing it evenly over the surface of the flesh.

5 To hold the hens flat during cooking, thread two bamboo skewers through each bird, crossing at the center. Each skewer should pass through a drumstick and then out through a wing on the other side.

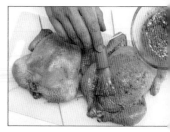

6 Mix the reserved paste with the lime juice and brush it over the skin of the hens. Cook on a medium-hot barbecue, turning occasionally, for 25–30 minutes, or until there is no trace of pink in the juices when the flesh is pierced. Garnish with lime wedges and fresh flat leaf parsley.

CHICKEN COOKED IN SPICES AND COCONUT

This chicken dish can be prepared in advance and then placed in the refrigerator until you are ready to light the barbecue. Serve the chicken with naan bread.

INGREDIENTS

*½ pint/1¼ cups coconut
cream
3 garlic cloves, chopped
2 scallions, chopped
1 fresh green chile, chopped
2-inch piece fresh root
ginger, chopped
1 teaspoon fennel seeds
½ teaspoon black peppercorns
seeds from 4 cardamom pods
2 tablespoons ground
coriander
1 teaspoon ground cumin
1 teaspoon ground star anise
1 teaspoon ground nutmeg
½ teaspoon ground cloves
½ teaspoon ground turmeric
4 large, skinless, boneless chicken
breast portions
onion rings and fresh cilantro
sprigs, to garnish*

SERVES 4

2 Make several diagonal cuts across the chicken. Arrange in a shallow dish. Spoon over half the coconut mixture and toss well to coat the chicken evenly. Cover the dish and leave to marinate for at least 30 minutes, or overnight in the refrigerator.

3 Cook the chicken on a medium barbecue for about 12–15 minutes, turning once, until well browned and thoroughly cooked. Heat the remaining coconut mixture gently until boiling. Serve with the chicken, garnished with onion rings and sprigs of cilantro.

1 Pour the coconut cream into a blender or food processor, then add the chopped garlic, scallions, green chile, fresh root ginger and all of the spices. Blend to form a smooth paste.

GRILLED CASHEW NUT CHICKEN

*This dish comes from the beautiful Indonesian island of Bali, where nuts are widely used as a
base for sauces and marinades. Serve it with a green salad and a hot chili dipping sauce.*

INGREDIENTS

4 chicken legs
radishes, sliced, to garnish
¹/₂ cucumber, sliced, to garnish
Chinese cabbage, to serve

FOR THE MARINADE
2 ounces raw cashew nuts
*2 shallots, or 1 small onion,
finely chopped*
2 garlic cloves, crushed
2 small red chilies, chopped
2-inch piece lemon grass
1 tablespoon tamarind sauce
2 tablespoons dark soy sauce
1 tablespoon Thai fish sauce
2 teaspoons sugar
¹/₂ teaspoon salt
*1 tablespoon rice or white
wine vinegar*

SERVES 4

1 Using a sharp, heavy kitchen knife,
slash the chicken legs several times
through to the bone. Chop off the
knuckle end and discard.

2 To make the marinade, place the
cashew nuts in a food processor or
pestle and mortar and grind until fine.

3 Add the chopped shallots or onion,
garlic, chilies and lemon grass and
process. Add the remaining marinade
ingredients and process again.

4 Spread the marinade over the chicken
and leave for up to 8 hours in the
refrigerator. Cook the chicken on a
medium barbecue for 25 minutes,
basting and turning occasionally.
Garnish with radishes and cucumber
and serve on a bed of Chinese cabbage.

THAI GRILLED CHICKEN

*Thai-style chicken is especially delicious when cooked on the barbecue.
Serve it on a bed of crisp salad with lime wedges to offset its richness.*

INGREDIENTS

*2 pounds chicken drumsticks
or thighs
salt and freshly ground
black pepper
1/2 cucumber, cut into strips,
to garnish
4 scallions, trimmed,
to garnish
2 limes, quartered, to garnish
crisp lettuce leaves, to serve*

FOR THE MARINADE
*1 teaspoon black peppercorns
1/2 teaspoon caraway or
cumin seeds
4 teaspoons sugar
2 teaspoons paprika
3/4-inch piece fresh root ginger,
chopped
3 garlic cloves, crushed
1/2 ounce cilantro, white root or
stem, finely chopped
3 tablespoons vegetable oil*

SERVES 4–6

1 Chop through the narrow end of each drumstick with a heavy knife. Score the chicken pieces deeply to allow the marinade to penetrate and arrange in a shallow bowl.

2 Grind the peppercorns, caraway or cumin seeds and sugar in a pestle and mortar or a food processor. Add the paprika, ginger, garlic, cilantro and oil and grind to a paste.

3 Spread the marinade over the chicken and set aside in the refrigerator to marinate for 6 hours. Cook the chicken on a medium barbecue for 20 minutes, basting with the marinade and turning once. Season, arrange on a bed of lettuce and garnish before serving.

MEDITERRANEAN TURKEY SKEWERS

*These attractive kebabs can be assembled in advance and left to marinate until you are ready
to cook them. Cooking on the barbecue intensifies the Mediterranean flavors of the vegetables.*

INGREDIENTS

2 medium zucchini
1 long thin eggplant
*11 ounces boneless turkey, cut
into 2-inch cubes*
12–16 pearl onions
*1 red or yellow bell pepper, cut
into 2-inch squares*

FOR THE MARINADE
6 tablespoons olive oil
3 tablespoons fresh lemon juice
1 garlic clove, finely chopped
*2 tablespoons chopped fresh basil
salt and freshly ground
black pepper*

SERVES 4

3 Prepare the skewers by alternating
the turkey, onions and pepper pieces.
Lay the prepared skewers on a platter
and sprinkle with the flavored oil.
Leave to marinate for 30 minutes.

4 Cook on a medium barbecue or
under a grill for about 10 minutes,
or until the turkey is cooked and the
vegetables are tender, turning the
skewers occasionally.

1 To make the marinade, mix the olive
oil with the lemon juice, garlic and
chopped fresh basil. Season well with
plenty of salt and black pepper.

2 Slice the zucchini and eggplant
lengthwise into strips ¼-inch thick.
Cut them crosswise about two-thirds
down their length. Discard the shorter
lengths. Wrap half the turkey pieces
with the zucchini slices and the other
half with the eggplant slices.

QUAIL WITH A FIVE-SPICE MARINADE

Blending and grinding your own five-spice powder for this Vietnamese dish will give the freshest-tasting results. If you are short of time, buy a ready-mixed blend from the supermarket.

INGREDIENTS

6 quails, cleaned
2 scallions, coarsely chopped,
to garnish
mandarin orange or satsuma
orange, to garnish
banana leaves, to serve

FOR THE MARINADE
2 pieces star anise
2 teaspoons ground cinnamon
2 teaspoons fennel seeds
2 teaspoons Sichuan pepper
a pinch ground cloves
1 small onion, finely chopped
1 garlic clove, crushed
4 tablespoons clear honey
2 tablespoons dark soy sauce

SERVES 4–6

1 Remove the backbones from the quails by cutting down either side with a pair of strong kitchen scissors.

2 Flatten the birds with the palm of your hand and secure each bird using two bamboo skewers.

3 To make the marinade, place the five spices in a mortar or spice mill and grind to a fine powder. Add the onion, garlic, clear honey and soy sauce, and combine until thoroughly mixed.

4 Arrange the quails on a flat dish and pour over the marinade. Cover with plastic wrap and leave in the refrigerator for 8 hours or overnight for the flavors to mingle.

5 Cook the quails on a medium barbecue for 15–20 minutes until golden brown, basting occasionally with the marinade and turning once.

6 To garnish, remove the outer rind from the mandarin or satsuma orange, using a vegetable peeler. Shred the rind finely and combine with the chopped scallions. Arrange the quails on a bed of banana leaves and garnish with the orange rind and scallions.

Cook's Tip

If you prefer, or if quails are not available, you could use other poultry, such as Cornish hens, as a substitute.

PHEASANTS WITH SAGE AND LEMON

Pheasant is quick to cook and makes a really special summer meal.
This recipe can also be used for guinea fowl.

INGREDIENTS

2 pheasants, about 1 pound each
1 lemon
4 tablespoons chopped fresh sage
3 shallots
1 teaspoon Dijon mustard
1 tablespoon brandy or dry sherry
5 fluid ounces/²⁄₃ cup crème fraîche
salt and freshly ground
black pepper
lemon wedges and sage sprigs,
to garnish

SERVES 4

2 Finely grate the rind from half the lemon and slice the rest thinly. Mix together the lemon rind and half the chopped sage in a small bowl.

5 Meanwhile, cook the shallots on the barbecue for about 10–12 minutes, turning occasionally, until the skin is blackened and the inside very soft. Peel off the skins, chop the flesh roughly and mash it with the Dijon mustard and brandy or sherry.

1 Place the pheasants, breast-side upward, on a chopping board and cut them in half lengthwise, using poultry shears or a sharp kitchen knife.

3 Loosen the skin on the breasts and legs of the pheasants and push a little of the sage mixture under each. Tuck the lemon slices under the skin, smoothing the skin back firmly.

6 Stir in the crème fraîche and add the reserved chopped sage. Season with plenty of salt and freshly ground black pepper. Serve the dressing with the pheasants, garnished with lemon wedges and sprigs of fresh sage.

4 Place the half-pheasants on a medium-hot barbecue and cook for about 25–30 minutes, turning once.

Cook's Tip
Try to choose pheasants with undamaged skins, so that the flavorings stay in place during cooking.

SPICED DUCK WITH PEARS

. . .

This delicious casserole can be cooked on the barbecue or stove. The browned pears are added toward the end of cooking, along with a pine nut and garlic paste to flavor and thicken.

INGREDIENTS

*6 duck portions, either breast
or leg pieces
1 tablespoon olive oil
1 large onion, thinly sliced
1 cinnamon stick, halved
2 sprigs of fresh thyme
16 fluid ounces/2 cups duck or
chicken stock*

TO FINISH

*3 firm ripe pears, peeled and cored
2 tablespoons olive oil
2 garlic cloves, sliced
1 ounce/⅓ cup pine nuts
½ teaspoon saffron threads
1 ounce/2 tablespoons raisins
salt and freshly ground
black pepper
thyme sprigs or parsley, to garnish*

SERVES 6

1 Fry the duck portions in olive oil for 5 minutes, until golden, or brush the portions with oil and cook them on a hot barbecue for 8–10 minutes, until golden. Transfer the duck to a large flameproof dish. If frying, drain off all but 1 tablespoon of fat left in the pan.

2 Cook the onion in the frying pan for 5 minutes until golden. Add the cinnamon stick, thyme and stock and bring to the boil. Pour over the duck in the dish and cook slowly on a low barbecue for about 1¼ hours.

3 Halve the pears, brush with oil and cook on the barbecue until brown, or fry them in the oil on the stovetop. Pound the garlic, pine nuts and saffron with a pestle and mortar, to a paste.

4 Add the paste, raisins and pears to the flameproof dish. Cook for 15 minutes until the pears are tender.

5 Season to taste and garnish with the fresh herbs. Serve with mashed potato and a green vegetable, if you like.

Cook's Tip

A good stock is essential for this dish. Buy a large duck (plus two extra duck breasts if you want portions to be generous) and cut it up yourself, using the giblets and carcass for stock. If you buy duck portions, use a well-flavored chicken stock.

DUCK WITH RED PEPPER JELLY GLAZE

*Sweet potatoes have pinkish skins and flesh varying from creamy white to deep orange.
Choose a long cylindrical tuber to make neat round slices for this Cajun dish.*

INGREDIENTS

2 duck breasts
1 sweet potato, about 14 ounces
2 tablespoons red bell pepper jelly
1 tablespoon sherry vinegar
2 ounces/4 tablespoons butter, melted
coarse sea salt and freshly ground
black pepper

SERVES 2

1 Slash the skin of the duck diagonally at 1-inch intervals and rub plenty of salt and pepper over the skin and into the cuts.

2 Scrub the sweet potato and cut into ½-inch slices, discarding the ends.

3 Cook the duck breasts on a medium barbecue, skin-side down, for about 5 minutes. Turn them over and cook for 8–10 minutes more, according to how pink you like your duck.

4 Meanwhile, warm the red bell pepper jelly and sherry vinegar together in a bowl set over a pan of hot water, stirring to mix them as the jelly melts. Brush the skin of the duck with this jelly glaze and return to the barbecue, skin-side down, for 2–3 minutes more to caramelize it.

5 Brush the sweet potato slices with melted butter and sprinkle with coarse sea salt. Cook on a hot barbecue for 8–10 minutes until soft, brushing with more butter and sprinkling with salt and pepper when you turn them. Serve the duck sliced with the sweet potatoes and accompany with a green salad.

DUCK WITH RED PLUMS

* * *

The rich fruity sauce for this dish combines brandy and red plums with heavy cream and cilantro. The sauce can be made in a pan on the barbecue while the duck is cooking.

INGREDIENTS

4 duck breasts, 6 ounces each
2 teaspoons crushed
cinnamon stick
2 ounces/¼ cup butter
1 tablespoon plum brandy
8 fluid ounces/1 cup chicken stock
8 fl ounces/1 cup heavy cream
6 fresh red plums, pitted
and sliced
6 sprigs fresh cilantro leaves,
plus extra to garnish
salt and freshly ground
black pepper

SERVES 4

1 Skin the duck breasts, score them and sprinkle with salt. Press the crushed cinnamon onto both sides of the duck breasts. Brush with butter and cook on a medium barbecue for 15–20 minutes, turning once, until the duck is tender.

2 To make the sauce, melt half the remaining butter in a pan. Add the plum brandy and set it alight. When the flames have died down, add the stock and cream and simmer gently until reduced and thick. Season to taste with salt and pepper.

3 In a pan, melt the other half of the butter and cook the plums and cilantro just enough to cook the fruit through. Slice the duck breasts and pour some sauce around each one, then garnish with the plum slices and the chopped fresh cilantro.

JUNIPER-SPICED VENISON CHOPS

Depending on the type of venison available, the chops will vary in size,
so you will need either one or two per person.

INGREDIENTS

4–8 venison chops
8 fluid ounces/1 cup red wine
2 medium red onions
6 juniper berries, crushed
1 cinnamon stick, crumbled
1 dried bay leaf, crumbled
thinly pared strip of orange rind
olive oil, for brushing
salt and freshly ground
black pepper

SERVES 4

2 Add the juniper berries, cinnamon, bay leaf and orange rind. Toss well to coat evenly and then cover the bowl and leave to marinate for at least an hour, or overnight in the refrigerator.

1 Place the venison chops in a large mixing bowl and pour over the red wine. Using a sharp knife, cut the red onions in half crosswise and add them to the bowl.

3 Drain the venison and onions and reserve the marinade. Brush the venison and onions generously with the olive oil and sprinkle with plenty of salt and freshly ground black pepper.

4 Cook the venison and onions on a medium-hot barbecue for about 8–10 minutes on each side, basting regularly with the marinade. The venison should still be slightly pink inside even when fully cooked.

Cook's Tip

Tender farmed venison
is now widely available
from supermarkets, but
if venison is difficult to find,
beef steaks could be
used instead.

Oily fish, such as tuna, are perfectly suited to grilling and won't

dry out. Use plump shrimp or firm-textured fish, such as

monkfish, for kebabs, but marinate them first to keep them

moist. More delicate fish can be cooked wrapped in foil,

either on the rack or directly on the coals.

FISH AND
SHELLFISH

SPICED SHRIMP WITH VEGETABLES

* * *

This is a light and nutritious Indian dish, excellent served either on a bed of lettuce leaves,
or with plain boiled rice or chappatis.

INGREDIENTS

20 cooked jumbo shrimp, peeled
1 zucchini, sliced
1 medium onion, cut into
8 chunks
8 cherry tomatoes
8 baby corn cobs
mixed salad leaves, to serve

FOR THE MARINADE
2 tablespoons chopped
fresh cilantro
1 teaspoon salt
2 fresh green chiles, seeded
3 tablespoons lemon juice
2 tablespoons vegetable oil

SERVES 4

1 To make the marinade, process the cilantro, salt, chiles, lemon juice and oil together in a food processor.

2 Empty the contents from the processor and transfer to a bowl.

3 Add the peeled jumbo shrimp to the mixture in the bowl and stir to make sure that all the shrimp are thoroughly coated. Cover the bowl with plastic wrap and set aside in a cool place, to marinate for 30 minutes.

4 Arrange the vegetables and shrimp alternately on four long skewers. Cook on a medium barbecue for 5 minutes, turning frequently, until cooked and browned. Serve immediately, on a bed of mixed salad leaves.

JUMBO SHRIMP SKEWERS WITH WALNUT PESTO

This is an unusual appetizer or main course, which can be prepared in advance and kept in the refrigerator until you're ready to cook it.

INGREDIENTS

12–16 large, raw, unpeeled
jumbo shrimp
2 ounces/¹/2 cup walnut pieces
4 tablespoons chopped fresh
flat leaf parsley
4 tablespoons chopped fresh basil
2 garlic cloves, chopped
3 tablespoons freshly grated
Parmesan cheese
2 tablespoons extra virgin olive oil
2 tablespoons walnut oil
salt and freshly ground
black pepper

SERVES 4

3 Add half the pesto to the shrimp, toss them well, then cover and chill in the refrigerator for a minimum of 1 hour, or leave them overnight.

4 Thread the shrimp onto skewers and cook them on a hot barbecue for 3–4 minutes, turning once. Serve with the remaining pesto and a green salad.

Peel the shrimp, removing the head but leaving the tail. Devein and then put the shrimp in a large mixing bowl.

To make the pesto, place the walnuts, parsley, basil, garlic, cheese and oils in a food processor and process until finely chopped. Season to taste.

MACKEREL KEBABS WITH SWEET PEPPER SALAD

° ° °

Mackerel is an excellent fish for barbecue-cooking because its natural oils keep it moist and tasty.
This recipe combines mackerel with peppers and tomatoes in a flavorsome summer salad.

INGREDIENTS

4 medium mackerel, about
8 ounces each, filleted
2 small red onions, cut in wedges
2 tablespoons chopped
fresh marjoram
4 tablespoons dry white wine
3 tablespoons olive oil
juice of 1 lime

FOR THE SALAD
1 red bell pepper
1 yellow bell pepper
1 small red onion
2 large plum tomatoes
1 tablespoon chopped
fresh marjoram
2 teaspoons balsamic vinegar
salt and freshly ground
black pepper

SERVES 4

2 Combine the marjoram, wine, oil and lime juice and spoon over the mackerel. Cover and chill in the refrigerator for at least 30 minutes, turning once.

3 To make the salad, quarter and seed both peppers and halve the onion. Place the peppers and onion, skin-side down, with the whole tomatoes, on a hot barbecue and leave until the skins are blackened and charred.

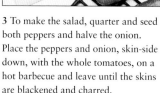

4 Remove the vegetables from the barbecue and leave until they are cool enough to handle. Use a sharp knife to peel off and discard the skins.

5 Chop the vegetables coarsely and put them in a bowl. Stir in the marjoram and balsamic vinegar and season to taste. Toss thoroughly.

6 Remove the kebabs from the refrigerator and cook on a hot barbecue for about 10–12 minutes, turning occasionally and basting with the marinade. Serve with the sweet pepper salad.

1 Thread each mackerel fillet onto a skewer, with an onion wedge on each end. Arrange the skewers in a dish.

Cook's Tip
Other oily fish can be used for this dish: try fillets or cubes of herring, rainbow trout or salmon, instead.

SWORDFISH KEBABS

. . .

Swordfish has a firm meaty texture that makes it ideal for cooking on a barbecue.
Marinate the fish first to keep it moist.

INGREDIENTS

2 pounds swordfish steaks
3 tablespoons olive oil
juice of ½ lemon
1 garlic clove, crushed
1 teaspoon paprika
3 tomatoes, quartered
2 onions, cut into wedges
salt and freshly ground
black pepper
salad and pitta bread, to serve

SERVES 4–6

1 Use a large kitchen knife to cut the swordfish steaks into large cubes. Arrange the cubes in a single layer in a large shallow dish.

2 Blend together the olive oil, lemon juice, garlic, paprika and seasoning in a bowl, and pour over the fish. Cover the dish loosely with plastic wrap and leave to marinate in a cool place for up to 2 hours.

3 Thread the fish cubes onto metal skewers, alternating them with the pieces of tomato and onion wedges.

4 Cook the kebabs on a hot barbecue for about 5–10 minutes, basting frequently with the remaining marinade and turning occasionally. Serve with salad and pitta bread.

HERBED CHARGRILLED SHARK STEAKS

Shark is very low in fat, with dense, well-flavored flesh. Other close-textured fish such as tuna, bonito and marlin work equally well in this recipe, which is ideal for a barbecue.

INGREDIENTS

3 tablespoons olive oil
2 fresh bay leaves, chopped
1 tablespoon chopped fresh basil
1 tablespoon chopped fresh oregano
2 tablespoons chopped fresh parsley
1 teaspoon finely chopped
fresh rosemary
1 teaspoon fresh thyme leaves
2 garlic cloves, crushed
4 pieces drained sun-dried
tomatoes in oil, chopped
4 shark steaks, about
7 ounces each
juice of 1 lemon
1 tablespoon drained small capers
in vinegar (optional)
salt and ground black pepper
grilled tomatoes, to serve

SERVES 4

1 Mix together the oil, herbs, garlic and sun-dried tomatoes in a bowl, then pour the mixture into a shallow dish that is large enough to hold the shark steaks in a single layer.

2 Season the shark steaks with salt and pepper and brush the lemon juice over both sides. Lay the fish in the dish, turning the steaks to coat them all over. Cover with plastic wrap and leave in the refrigerator to marinate for 1–2 hours to allow the flavors to develop.

3 Drain the shark steaks, reserving the marinade, and pat dry with paper towels. Cook on a hot barbecue or ridged griddle pan for about 5 minutes on each side, until cooked through.

4 Meanwhile, pour the marinade into a small pan and bring to the boil either on the barbecue or on the stovetop. Stir in the capers, if using. Spoon the sauce over the grilled shark steaks and serve immediately with grilled tomatoes.

MOROCCAN SPICED MACKEREL

*Mackerel is extremely good for you, but some people find its healthy oiliness too much to take.
The Moroccan spices in this recipe counteract the richness of the fish.*

INGREDIENTS

¼ pint/⅔ cup sunflower oil
1 tablespoon paprika
1–2 teaspoons harissa or
chili powder
2 teaspoons ground cumin
2 teaspoons ground coriander
2 garlic cloves, crushed
juice of 2 lemons
2 tablespoons chopped fresh
mint leaves
2 tablespoons chopped
fresh cilantro
4 mackerel, cleaned
salt and ground black pepper
fresh mint sprigs, to garnish
couscous or rice, and lemon
wedges, to serve

SERVES 4

1 Whisk the sunflower oil with the spices, crushed garlic and lemon juice in a bowl. Season with salt and ground black pepper, then stir in the mint and fresh cilantro.

2 With a sharp knife, make five or six evenly-spaced diagonal slashes on either side of each fish.

Cook's Tip

If you have one, arrange the mackerel on a large hinged rack before placing on the barbecue to make turning easier. It will also produce an attractive striped effect on the skin.

3 Place the mackerel in a single layer in a shallow dish and pour the marinade evenly over them. Cover with plastic wrap and leave to marinate in the refrigerator for a minimum of 3 hours.

4 Drain the mackerel, reserving the marinade. Grill the fish on a medium-hot barbecue or under a preheated broiler, basting them several times with the marinade, for 5–7 minutes on each side, until just cooked. Serve hot or cold, with couscous or rice, lemon wedges and garnished with mint.

Variations

Trout, bonito, trevally and bluefish are also good cooked this way.

CALAMARI WITH TWO-TOMATO STUFFING

Calamari, or baby squid, are quick to cook, but you must turn and baste them often and take care not to overcook them.

INGREDIENTS

1¼ pounds baby squid, cleaned
1 garlic clove, crushed
3 plum tomatoes, peeled
and chopped
8 sun-dried tomatoes in oil,
drained and chopped
4 tablespoons chopped fresh basil,
plus extra, to serve
4 tablespoons fresh white
bread crumbs
3 tablespoons olive oil
1 tablespoon red wine vinegar
salt and freshly ground
black pepper
lemon juice, to serve

SERVES 4

1 Remove the tentacles from the squid and coarsely chop them; leave the main part of the squid whole.

2 Mix together the crushed garlic, plum tomatoes, sun-dried tomatoes, chopped fresh basil, bread crumbs and chopped squid tentacles. Stir in 1 tablespoon of the olive oil and the red wine vinegar. Season well with plenty of salt and black pepper. Soak some wooden toothpicks in water for 10 minutes before use, to prevent them from burning on the barbecue.

3 Using a teaspoon, fill the squid with the stuffing mixture. Secure the open ends with the toothpicks to hold the stuffing mixture in place.

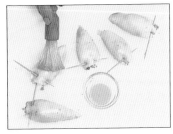

4 Brush the squid with the remaining olive oil and cook on a medium-hot barbecue for 4–5 minutes, turning often. Sprinkle with lemon juice and extra chopped fresh basil to serve.

SCALLOPS WITH LIME BUTTER

° ° °

Fresh scallops are quick to cook and ideal for barbecues. This recipe combines them simply with lime and fennel.

INGREDIENTS

1 fennel bulb
2 limes
12 large prepared scallops
1 egg yolk
6 tablespoons melted butter
olive oil for brushing
salt and freshly ground
black pepper

SERVES 4

3 Place the egg yolk and remaining lime rind and juice in a small bowl and whisk until pale and smooth.

5 Brush the fennel wedges with olive o and cook them on a hot barbecue for 3–4 minutes, turning once.

1 Trim any feathery leaves from the fennel and reserve them. Slice the bulb lengthwise into thin wedges.

4 Gradually whisk in the melted butter and continue whisking until thick and smooth. Finely chop the reserved fennel leaves and stir them in, with salt and pepper to taste.

6 Add the scallops and cook for 3–4 minutes more, turning once. Serve immediately with the lime and fennel butter and the lime wedges.

2 Cut one lime into wedges. Finely grate the rind and squeeze the juice of the other lime and toss half the juice and rind on to the scallops. Season well with salt and pepper.

Cook's Tip

If the scallops are small, you may wish to thread them onto flat skewers to make turning them easier.

SARDINES WITH WARM HERB SALSA

. . .

Plain grilling is the very best way to cook fresh sardines. If they are served with this luscious herb salsa, the only other essential item is fresh bread with a thick crust, to mop up the tasty juices.

INGREDIENTS

12–16 fresh sardines
oil for brushing
juice of 1 lemon

FOR THE SALSA
1 tablespoon butter
4 scallions, chopped
1 garlic clove, finely chopped
rind of 1 lemon, shredded
2 tablespoons finely chopped
fresh parsley
2 tablespoons chopped
fresh chives
2 tablespoons finely chopped
fresh basil
2 tablespoons green olive paste
2 teaspoons balsamic vinegar
salt and freshly ground
black pepper

SERVES 4

1 To clean the sardines, slit the fish along the belly with kitchen scissors and pull out the innards. Wipe the fish with paper towels and then arrange on a hinged rack.

2 To make the salsa, melt the butter in a small pan and gently sauté the scallions and garlic for about 2 minutes, shaking the pan occasionally, until softened but not browned.

3 Add the lemon rind and remaining salsa ingredients to the onions and garlic in the pan and keep warm on the edge of the barbecue, stirring occasionally. Do not allow to boil.

4 Brush the sardines lightly with oil and sprinkle with lemon juice, salt and pepper. Cook on a medium barbecue for about 2 minutes on each side. Serve with the warm salsa and rustic bread.

STUFFED SARDINES

• • •

This Middle Eastern-inspired dish doesn't take much preparation and is a meal in itself.
Just serve with a crisp green salad tossed in a fresh lemon vinaigrette to make it complete.

INGREDIENTS

1/4 ounce/1/4 cup fresh parsley
3–4 garlic cloves, crushed
8–12 fresh or frozen
sardines, cleaned
2 tablespoons lemon juice
2 ounces/1/2 cup all-purpose flour
1/2 teaspoon ground cumin
olive oil, for brushing
salt and freshly ground
black pepper
naan bread and green salad,
to serve

SERVES 4

1 Finely chop the parsley and mix
in a small bowl with the garlic. Pat the
parsley and garlic mixture all over the
outsides and insides of the prepared
sardines. Sprinkle the sardines with
lemon juice, then place them in a dish,
cover and set aside in a cool place for
up to 2 hours, to absorb the flavors.

2 Place the flour on a large plate and
season with the cumin, salt and pepper.
Roll the sardines in the flour.

3 Brush the sardines with olive oil and
cook on a medium-hot barbecue for
about 3 minutes each side. Serve with
naan bread and a green salad.

MONKFISH WITH PEPPERED CITRUS MARINADE

*Monkfish is a firm, meaty fish that cooks well on the barbecue and keeps its shape.
Serve with a green salad.*

INGREDIENTS

2 monkfish tails, about
12 ounces each
1 lime
1 lemon
2 oranges
handful of fresh thyme sprigs
2 tablespoons olive oil
1 tablespoon mixed peppercorns,
coarsely crushed
salt and freshly ground
black pepper

SERVES 4

2 Turn the fish and repeat on the other side, to remove the second fillet. Repeat on the second tail. (If you prefer, you can ask the person at your fish counter to do this for you.) Lay the four fillets out flat on a chopping board.

5 Squeeze the juice from the citrus fruits and mix it with the olive oil and more salt and pepper. Spoon over the fish. Cover with plastic wrap and leave to marinate in the refrigerator for about 1 hour, turning the fish occasionally.

1 Using a sharp kitchen knife, remove any skin from the monkfish tails. Cut carefully down one side of the backbone, sliding the knife between the bone and flesh, to remove the fillet on one side.

3 Cut two slices from each of the citrus fruits and arrange them over two of the fillets. Add a few sprigs of fresh thyme and sprinkle with plenty of salt and freshly ground black pepper. Finely grate the rind from the remaining fruit and sprinkle it over the fish.

6 Drain the monkfish, reserving the marinade, and sprinkle evenly with the crushed peppercorns. Cook the fish on a medium-hot barbecue for about 15–20 minutes, turning occasionally and basting with the marinade, until the fish is evenly cooked.

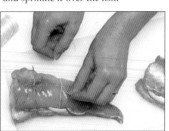

4 Lay the other two fillets on top and tie them firmly at intervals.

SMOKED MACKEREL WITH BLUEBERRIES

*Fresh blueberries burst with flavor when cooked, and their sharpness complements
the rich flesh of mackerel very well.*

INGREDIENTS

2 tablespoons all-purpose flour
4 hot-smoked mackerel fillets
2 ounces/4 tablespoons butter
juice of ½ lemon
salt and freshly ground
black pepper

FOR THE BLUEBERRY SAUCE
1 pound/4 cups blueberries
2 tablespoons superfine sugar
½ ounce/1 tablespoons
sweet butter

SERVES 4

1 Season the flour with salt and freshly ground black pepper. Coat each fish fillet in the flour, covering it well.

2 Brush the fillets with butter and cook on a medium barbecue for a few minutes until heated through with a crisp coating.

3 To make the sauce, place the blueberries, sugar, butter and salt and pepper in a small roasting pan and cook on the barbecue, stirring occasionally, for about 10 minutes. Serve immediately, drizzling the lemon juice over the mackerel and with the blueberries on the side.

MACKEREL WITH TOMATOES, PESTO AND ONION

Rich oily fish like mackerel needs a sharp, fresh-tasting sauce to go with it, and this aromatic pesto is excellent drizzled over the top.

INGREDIENTS

4 mackerel, cleaned and gutted
2 tablespoons olive oil
4 ounces onion, coarsely chopped
1 pound tomatoes,
coarsely chopped
salt and freshly ground
black pepper

FOR THE PESTO
2 ounces/1/2 cup pine nuts
2 tablespoons fresh basil leaves
2 garlic cloves, crushed
2 tablespoons freshly grated
Parmesan cheese
1/4 pint/2/3 cup extra virgin
olive oil

SERVES 4

1 To make the pesto, place the pine nuts, fresh basil leaves and garlic in a food processor and blend to a coarse paste. Add the Parmesan and, with the motor running, gradually add the oil.

2 Season the mackerel well with plenty of salt and freshly ground black pepper and cook on a medium-hot barbecue for about 12–15 minutes, turning the fish once.

3 Meanwhile, heat the olive oil in a large, heavy pan. Add the chopped onions and sauté, stirring occasionally, until soft and golden brown.

4 Stir the chopped tomatoes into the contents of the pan and cook for about 5 minutes. Serve the fish on top of the tomato mixture and top with a generous spoonful of the pesto.

CHARGRILLED TUNA WITH FIERY PEPPER PURÉE

*Tuna is an oily fish that barbecues well and is meaty enough to combine successfully with strong
flavors – even hot chiles, as in this red pepper purée, which is excellent served with rustic bread.*

INGREDIENTS

*4 tuna steaks, about 6 ounces each
finely grated rind and juice of 1 lime
2 tablespoons olive oil
salt and freshly ground black pepper
lime wedges, to serve*

FOR THE PEPPER PURÉE
*2 red bell peppers, halved
3 tablespoons olive oil, plus
extra for brushing
1 small onion
2 garlic cloves, crushed
2 red chiles
1 slice white bread without
crusts, diced
salt*

SERVES 4

2 To make the pepper purée, brush the
pepper halves with a little olive oil and
cook them, skin-side down, on a hot
barbecue, until the skin is charred and
blackened. Place the onion in its skin
on the barbecue and cook until
browned, turning it occasionally.

3 Leave the peppers and onion until
cool enough to handle, then remove the
skins, using a sharp kitchen knife.

4 Place the cooked peppers and onion
with the garlic, chiles, bread and olive
oil in a food processor. Process until
smooth. Add salt to taste.

5 Drain the tuna steaks from the
marinade and cook them on a hot
barbecue for 8–10 minutes, turning
once, until golden brown. Serve with
the pepper purée and lime wedges, with
rustic bread if you like.

1 Trim any skin from the tuna and
place the steaks in a single layer in a
dish. Sprinkle over the lime rind and
juice, olive oil, salt and pepper. Cover
with plastic wrap and chill in the
refrigerator until required.

Cook's Tip

The bell pepper purée can be made
in advance, cooking the peppers
and onion under a hot broiler;
chill until required.

TROUT WITH BACON

∘ ∘ ∘

*The smoky, savory flavor of crispy grilled bacon perfectly complements
the delicate flesh of the trout in this simple dish.*

INGREDIENTS

4 trout, cleaned and gutted
1 tablespoon all-purpose flour
4 strips smoked bacon
2 tablespoons olive oil
juice of ½ lemon
*salt and freshly ground
black pepper*

SERVES 4

1 Place the trout on a chopping board
and pat them dry with paper towels.
Season the flour with the salt and
freshly ground black pepper. Stretch
the bacon strips out thinly using the
back of a heavy kitchen knife.

2 Roll the fish in the seasoned flour
mixture and wrap them tightly in the
bacon. Brush with olive oil and cook
on a medium-hot barbecue for
10–15 minutes, turning once. Serve at
once, drizzled with the lemon juice.

RED MULLET WITH BASIL AND CITRUS

° ° °

This Italian recipe is full of the warm, distinctive flavors of the Mediterranean.
Serve the dish with plain boiled rice and a green salad, or with lots of fresh rustic bread.

INGREDIENTS

4 red snapper, about 8 ounces
each, filleted
4 tablespoons olive oil
10 peppercorns, crushed
2 oranges, one peeled and sliced
and one squeezed
1 lemon
½ ounce/1 tablespoons butter
2 drained canned anchovy
fillets, chopped
4 tablespoons shredded fresh basil
salt and freshly ground
black pepper

SERVES 4

2 Halve the lemon. Remove the skin and pith from one half using a small, sharp knife, and slice the flesh thinly. Squeeze the juice from the other half.

3 Drain the fish, reserving the marinade and orange slices, and cook on a medium-hot barbecue for about 10–12 minutes, turning once and basting with the marinade.

4 Melt the butter in a pan with any remaining marinade. Add the chopped anchovy fillets and cook until they are completely soft. Stir in the orange and lemon juice and allow to simmer on the edge of the barbecue until slightly reduced. Stir in the basil and check the seasoning. Pour over the fish and garnish with the reserved orange slices and the lemon slices.

Place the fish fillets in a shallow dish in a single layer. Pour over the olive oil and sprinkle with the crushed peppercorns. Lay the orange slices on top of the fish. Cover the dish with plastic wrap, and leave to marinate in the refrigerator for 4 hours.

FISH PARCELS

° ° °

Sea bass is good for this recipe, but you could also use small whole trout
or a white fish fillet, such as cod or haddock.

INGREDIENTS

4 pieces sea bass fillet, or 4 small
sea bass, about 1 pound each
olive oil for brushing
2 shallots, thinly sliced
1 garlic clove, chopped
1 tablespoon capers
6 sun-dried tomatoes,
finely chopped
4 black olives, pitted and
thinly sliced
grated rind and juice of 1 lemon
1 teaspoon paprika
salt and freshly ground
black pepper

SERVES 4

2 Place a piece of fish in the center
of each piece of baking foil and season
well with plenty of salt and pepper.

3 Sprinkle over the shallots, chopped
garlic, capers, tomatoes, sliced olives
and grated lemon rind. Sprinkle with
the lemon juice and paprika.

4 Fold over the baking foil to enclose
the fish loosely, sealing the edges firmly
so that none of the juices can escape
during cooking. Place the parcels on a
moderately hot barbecue and cook for
about 8–10 minutes. To serve, place
each of the parcels on a plate and
loosen the tops to open.

Cook's Tip

These parcels can also be
baked in the oven: place them
on a baking sheet and cook
at 400°F for about
15–20 minutes.

1 Clean the fish if whole. Cut four
squares of double-thickness baking foil,
large enough to enclose the fish; brush
lightly with a little olive oil.

SPICED FISH BAKED THAI STYLE

Banana leaves make a perfect, natural wrapping for barbecue-cooked foods, but if they are not available you can use baking foil instead.

INGREDIENTS

4 red snapper or mullet, about
12 ounces each
banana leaves
1 lime
1 garlic clove, thinly sliced
2 scallions, sliced
2 tablespoons Thai red
curry paste
4 tablespoons coconut milk

SERVES 4

1 Clean the fish, removing the scales, and make several deep slashes in the side of each with a sharp knife. Place each fish on a layer of banana leaves.

2 Thinly slice half the lime and tuck t slices into the slashes in the fish, with the slivers of garlic. Sprinkle the slice scallions over the fish.

3 Grate the rind and squeeze the juice from the remaining half-lime and mix with the curry paste and coconut milk Spoon over the fish.

4 Wrap the leaves over the fish, to enclose them completely. Tie firmly with string and cook on a medium-ho barbecue for 15–20 minutes, turning occasionally. To serve, open up the parcels by cutting along the top edge with a knife and fanning out the leave

PORGY WITH ORANGE BUTTER SAUCE

Porgy is a revelation to anyone unfamiliar with its creamy rich flavor.
The fish has a firm white flesh that goes well with this rich butter sauce, sharpened with orange.

INGREDIENTS

2 porgies, about 12 ounces each,
scaled and gutted
2 teaspoons Dijon mustard
1 teaspoon fennel seeds
2 tablespoons olive oil
2 ounces watercress
6 ounces mixed lettuce leaves,
such as escarole and frisée

FOR THE ORANGE BUTTER SAUCE
2 tablespoons frozen orange
juice concentrate
6 ounces/3/4 cup sweet
butter, diced
salt and cayenne pepper

SERVES 2

Slash the porgies four times on either
de. Combine the mustard and fennel
eds, then spread over both sides of
e fish. Brush with olive oil and cook
a medium-hot barbecue for
)–12 minutes, turning once.

2 Place the orange juice concentrate in
a bowl and heat over a pan of
simmering water. Remove the pan from
the heat and gradually whisk in the
butter until creamy. Season well.

3 Dress the watercress and lettuce
leaves with the remaining olive oil,
and arrange with the fish on two plates.
Spoon the sauce over the fish and serve
with baked potatoes, if you like.

HALIBUT WITH FRESH TOMATO AND BASIL SALSA

Take care when cooking this dish as halibut has a tendency to break easily, especially when the skin has been removed. Season well to bring out the flavor of the fish and the taste of the sauce.

INGREDIENTS
4 halibut fillets, about
6 ounces each
3 tablespoons olive oil

FOR THE SALSA
1 medium tomato,
coarsely chopped
1/4 red onion, finely chopped
1 small jalapeño chile
2 tablespoons balsamic vinegar
10 large fresh basil leaves
1 tablespoon olive oil
salt and freshly ground
black pepper

SERVES 4

1 To make the salsa, mix together the chopped tomato, red onion, jalapeño chile and balsamic vinegar in a bowl. Slice the fresh basil leaves finely, using a sharp kitchen knife.

2 Stir the basil and the olive oil into the tomato mixture. Season to taste. Cover the bowl with plastic wrap and leave to marinate for 3 hours.

3 Rub the halibut fillets with oil and season. Cook on a medium barbecue for 8 minutes, basting with oil and turning once. Serve with the salsa.

Cod Fillet with Fresh Mixed-herb Crust

*Use fresh herbs and whole-wheat bread crumbs to make a delicious crisp crust for the fish.
Season the fish well and serve with large lemon wedges.*

INGREDIENTS

1 ounce/2 tablespoons butter
1 tablespoon fresh chervil
1 tablespoon fresh parsley, plus
extra sprigs to garnish
1 tablespoon fresh chives
6 ounces/3 cups bread crumbs
4 thick pieces of cod fillet, about
8 ounces each, skinned
1 tablespoon olive oil
lemon wedges, to garnish
salt and freshly ground
black pepper

SERVES 4

1 Melt the butter and chop all the herbs finely, using a sharp knife. Brush the cod fillets with melted butter and mix any remaining butter with the bread crumbs, fresh herbs and plenty of salt and freshly ground black pepper.

2 Press a quarter of the mixture onto each fillet, spreading evenly, and lightly sprinkle with olive oil. Cook on a medium barbecue for 10 minutes, turning once. Serve the fish garnished with lemon wedges and the sprigs of fresh parsley.

GRILLED SNAPPER WITH HOT MANGO SALSA

• • •

A ripe mango provides the basis for a deliciously rich fruity salsa. The dressing needs no oil and features the tropical flavors of cilantro, ginger and chile.

INGREDIENTS

12 ounces new potatoes
3 eggs
4 ounces green beans, trimmed
and halved
4 red snapper, about 12 ounces
each, cleaned, scaled and gutted
2 tablespoons olive oil
6 ounces mixed lettuce leaves,
such as frisée
2 cherry tomatoes
salt and freshly ground
black pepper

FOR THE SALSA

3 tablespoons chopped
fresh cilantro
1 medium-size ripe mango, peeled,
pitted and diced
1/2 red chile, seeded and chopped
1 inch fresh root ginger, grated
juice of 2 limes
generous pinch of celery salt

SERVES 4

1 Bring the potatoes to the boil in a large pan of salted water and simmer for 15–20 minutes. Drain.

2 Bring a second large pan of salted water to the boil. Put in the eggs and boil for 4 minutes, then add the beans and cook for a further 6 minutes, so that the eggs have had a total of 10 minutes. Drain and refresh the beans. Remove the eggs from the pan. Cool, then shell and cut into quarters.

3 Using a sharp knife, slash each snapper three times on either side. Brush with olive oil and cook on a medium-hot barbecue for 12 minutes, basting occasionally and turning once.

4 To make the salsa, place the chopped fresh cilantro in a food processor. Add the mango chunks, chile, grated ginger, lime juice and celery salt and process until smooth.

5 Dress the lettuce leaves with olive o and distribute them evenly among fo large plates.

6 Arrange the snapper on the lettuce and season. Halve the new potatoes and distribute them with the beans, tomatoes and quartered hard-boiled eggs over the salad. Serve immediatel with the salsa.

Variation

If fresh mangoes are unavailable, use canned ones, draining well. Sea bream are also good served with this hot mango salsa.

SMOKED HADDOCK WITH QUICK PARSLEY SAUCE

Make any herb sauce by this method, making sure it is thickened and seasoned well to complement the smoky flavor of the fish.

INGREDIENTS

*4 smoked haddock fillets, about
8 ounces each
3 ounces/6 tablespoons butter,
softened
2 tablespoons all-purpose flour
1/2 pint/1 1/4 cups milk
4 tablespoons chopped fresh parsley
salt and freshly ground black pepper*

SERVES 4

1 Smear the fish fillets on both sides with 4 tablespoons of the butter.

2 Beat the remaining butter and flour together to make a paste.

3 Cook the fish on a medium-hot barbecue for about 10 minutes, turning once. Meanwhile, to make the sauce, heat the milk in a pan to just below boiling point. Add the flour mixture in small spoonfuls, whisking constantly over the heat. Continue whisking until the sauce is smooth and thick.

4 Add the seasoning and chopped fresh parsley to the pan and stir well. Pour the parsley sauce over the haddock fillets to serve.

SALMON WITH RED ONION MARMALADE

· · ·

Salmon barbecues well but is most successful when it is at least 1-inch thick. The red onion marmalade is rich and delicious. Puréed blackcurrants work as well as crème de cassis.

INGREDIENTS

4 salmon steaks, about
6 ounces each
2 tablespoons olive oil
salt and freshly ground black pepper

FOR THE RED ONION MARMALADE
5 medium red onions, peeled
and finely sliced
2 ounces/4 tablespoons butter
6 fluid ounces/³⁄₄ cup red
wine vinegar
fluid ounces/¹⁄₄ cup crème de cassis
2 fluid ounces/¹⁄₄ cup grenadine
2 fluid ounces/¹⁄₄ cup red wine

SERVES 4

1 Use your hands to rub the olive oil into the salmon flesh and season well with plenty of salt and freshly ground black pepper.

2 Melt the butter in a large heavy pan and add the sliced onions. Sauté the onions gently for 5 minutes. until golden brown.

3 Stir in the vinegar, crème de cassis, grenadine and wine and continue to cook for about 10 minutes, until the liquid has almost entirely evaporated and the onions are glazed. Season well.

4 Brush the fish with a little more oil, and cook on a medium barbecue for about 6–8 minutes, turning once.

GRILLED SEA BASS WITH CITRUS FRUIT

Sea bass is a beautiful fish with a soft, dense texture and a delicate flavor. In this recipe it is complemented by citrus fruits and fruity olive oil.

INGREDIENTS

1 small grapefruit
1 orange
1 lemon
1 sea bass, about
3–3½ pounds, cleaned
and scaled
6 fresh basil sprigs
3 tablespoons olive oil
4–6 shallots, halved
4 tablespoons dry white wine
½ ounce/1 tablespoons butter
salt and freshly ground
black pepper
fresh dill, to garnish

SERVES 6

1 Using a vegetable peeler, remove the rind from the grapefruit, orange and lemon. Cut into thin julienne strips. Peel the pith from the fruits and, working over a bowl to catch the juices, cut out the segments from the grapefruit and the orange and set aside for the garnish. Slice the lemon thickly.

2 Season the cavity of the fish with salt and pepper and slash the flesh three times on each side. Reserving a few basil sprigs for the garnish, fill the cavity with the remaining basil, the lemon slices and half the julienne strips of citrus rind. Brush with olive oil and cook on a low–medium barbecue for about 20 minutes, basting occasionally and turning once.

3 Meanwhile, heat 1 tablespoon of the olive oil in a pan and cook the shallots gently until soft. Add the wine and 2–3 tablespoons of the fruit juice to the pan. Bring to the boil over a high heat, stirring. Stir in the remaining julienne strips of rind and boil for 2–3 minutes, then whisk in the butter.

4 When the fish is cooked, transfer it to a serving dish. Remove and discard the cavity stuffing. Spoon the shallots and sauce around the fish and garnish with fresh dill sprigs, the reserved basil and segments of grapefruit and orange.

GRILLED SEA BASS WITH FENNEL

The classic combination of sea bass and fennel works particularly well when the fish is cooked over charcoal. Traditionally fennel twigs are used, but this version of the recipe uses fennel seeds.

INGREDIENTS

*1 sea bass, about 3–3½ pounds,
cleaned and scaled
4 tablespoons olive oil
2 teaspoons fennel seeds
2 large fennel bulbs
4 tablespoons Pernod
salt and freshly ground
black pepper*

SERVES 6

1 Make four deep slashes in each side of the fish. Brush the fish with olive oil and season well with salt and freshly ground black pepper. Sprinkle the fennel seeds in the cavity and slashes of the fish. Cook on a low barbecue for 20 minutes, basting occasionally and turning once.

2 Meanwhile, trim and slice the fennel bulbs thinly, reserving any leafy fronds to use as a garnish. Brush the slices with olive oil and barbecue for about 8–10 minutes, turning occasionally, until tender.

3 Arrange the fennel slices on a serving plate. Lay the fish on top and garnish with the reserved fennel fronds.

4 When ready for eating, heat the Pernod in a small pan on the side of the barbecue, light it and pour it, flaming, over the fish. Serve at once.

MEXICAN SALMON

o o o

*The sauce for this dish is vibrant with hot, sweet and sour flavors
that permeate the fish before and during cooking.*

INGREDIENTS

1 small red onion
1 garlic clove
6 plum tomatoes
1 ounce/2 tablespoons butter
3 tablespoons tomato ketchup
2 tablespoons Dijon mustard
2 tablespoons dark brown sugar
1 tablespoon clear honey
1 teaspoon cayenne pepper
1 tablespoon ancho chili powder
1 tablespoon paprika
1 tablespoon Worcestershire sauce
4 salmon fillets, about
6 ounces each

SERVES 4

3 Melt the butter in a large, heavy pan
and gently cook the onion and garlic
until translucent.

4 Add the tomatoes to the pan and
simmer for 15 minutes.

5 Add the remaining ingredients,
excluding the salmon, and simmer for
a further 20 minutes. Pour the mixture
into a food processor and blend until
smooth. Leave to cool.

1 Using a sharp knife, finely chop
the red onion and finely dice the garlic.

2 Next, dice the plum tomatoes finely
and set them aside.

6 Brush the salmon with the sauce, and
chill for at least 2 hours. Cook on a hot
barbecue for 6 minutes, basting with
the sauce and turning once.

SALMON WITH TROPICAL FRUIT SALSA

• • •

*Fresh salmon really needs little adornment, but it does combine very well
with the exotic flavors in this colorful salsa.*

INGREDIENTS

4 salmon steaks or fillets, about
6 ounces each
finely grated rind and juice of
1 lime
1 small, ripe mango
1 small, ripe papaya
1 red chile
3 tablespoons chopped
fresh cilantro
salt and freshly ground
black pepper

SERVES 4

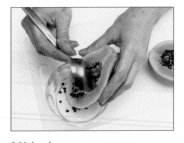

3 Halve the papaya, scoop out
the seeds with a spoon and remove the
peel. Finely chop the flesh and add it
to the mango chunks in the bowl.

5 Combine the mango, papaya, chile
and cilantro in a bowl and stir in the
remaining lime rind and juice. Season
to taste with plenty of salt and freshly
ground black pepper.

1 Place the salmon in a wide dish
and sprinkle over half the lime rind
and juice. Season with salt and pepper.

4 Cut the chile in half lengthwise.
Leave the seeds in to make the salsa hot
and spicy, or remove them for a milder
flavor. Finely chop the chile.

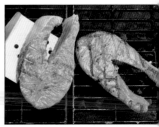

6 Cook the salmon on a medium
barbecue for about 5–8 minutes,
turning once. Serve with the fruit salsa.

2 Cut the mango in half, cutting either
side of the pit, and remove the stone.
Finely chop the mango flesh and place
the pieces in a bowl.

There are lots of ideas here for vegetable accompaniments to meat and fish dishes, as well as for substantial main dishes that everyone, vegetarian or not, will love. All vegetables can be cooked in foil parcels, but many are ideally suited to direct grilling on the barbecue.

VEGETARIAN
DISHES AND
VEGETABLES

~

RED BEAN AND MUSHROOM BURGERS

○ ○ ○

Vegetarians, vegans and meat-eaters alike will enjoy these healthy, low-fat veggie burgers.
With salad, pitta bread and Greek-style yogurt, they make a substantial meal.

INGREDIENTS

1 tablespoon olive oil
1 small onion, finely chopped
1 garlic clove, crushed
1 teaspoon ground cumin
1 teaspoon ground coriander
1/2 teaspoon ground turmeric
4 ounces/1 1/2 cups finely
chopped mushrooms
14-ounce can red kidney beans
2 tablespoons chopped
fresh cilantro
whole-wheat flour
olive oil, for brushing
salt and freshly ground
black pepper
strained plain yogurt

SERVES 4

1 Heat the olive oil in a frying pan and cook the chopped onion and garlic over a moderate heat, stirring, until softened. Add the spices and cook for a further minute, stirring constantly.

Cook's Tip

These burgers are not quite so firm as meat burgers, and will need careful handling on the barbecue.

2 Add the chopped mushrooms and cook, stirring, until softened and dry. Remove the pan from the heat and empty the contents into a large bowl.

3 Drain the beans thoroughly, place them in a bowl and mash with a fork.

4 Stir the kidney beans into the frying pan, with the chopped fresh cilantro, and mix thoroughly. Season the mixture well with plenty of salt and freshly ground black pepper.

5 Using floured hands, form the mixture into four flat burger shapes. If the mixture is too sticky to handle, mix in a little whole-wheat flour.

6 Lightly brush the burgers with olive oil and cook on a hot barbecue for 8–10 minutes, turning once, until golden brown. Serve with a spoonful of yogurt and a green salad, if you like.

GRILLED GOAT CHEESE PIZZA

*Pizzas cooked on the barbecue have a beautifully crisp and golden base. The combination
of goat cheese and red onion in this recipe makes for a flavorsome main course dish.*

2 Brush the dough round with olive oil
and place, oiled side down, on a
medium barbecue. Cook for about
6–8 minutes until firm and golden
underneath. Brush the uncooked side
with olive oil and turn the pizza over.

3 Mix together the tomatoes and
red pesto and quickly spread over
the cooked side of the pizza, to within
about ½ inch of the edge. Arrange the
onion, tomatoes and cheese on top and
sprinkle with salt and pepper.

4 Cook the pizza for 10 minutes more
until golden brown and crisp. Sprinkle
with fresh basil and serve.

INGREDIENTS

5 ounce packet pizza-base mix
olive oil, for brushing
¼ pint/⅔ cup bottled
strained tomatoes
2 tablespoons red pesto
1 small red onion, thinly sliced
8 cherry tomatoes, halved
4 ounces firm goat cheese, sliced
handful shredded fresh basil leaves
salt and freshly ground
black pepper

SERVES 4

1 Make up the pizza dough according
to the directions on the packet. Roll
out the dough on a lightly floured
surface to a round shape of about
10-inch diameter.

RED ONION GALETTES

If non-vegetarians are to eat these pretty puff pastry tarts, you can sprinkle some chopped anchovies over them before cooking them on the barbecue to add extra piquancy.

INGREDIENTS

4–5 tablespoons olive oil
1¼ pounds red onions, sliced
1 garlic clove, crushed
tablespoons chopped fresh mixed
herbs, such as thyme, parsley
and basil
8 ounces ready-made puff pastry
1 tablespoon sun-dried
tomato paste
freshly ground black pepper
fresh thyme sprigs, to garnish

SERVES 4

Ieat 2 tablespoons of oil in a frying
and add the onions and garlic. Cover
cook gently for 15–20 minutes,
ring occasionally, until soft but not
wned. Stir in the herbs.

Divide the pastry into four and
out each piece to a 6-inch round.
te the edges, prick all over with a
k and place on baking sheets.

3 Chill the rounds, on the baking
sheets, in the refrigerator for about
10 minutes. Mix 1 tablespoon of the
remaining oil with the tomato paste
and spread over the pastry rounds, to
within about ½ inch of the edge.

4 Spread the onion mixture over
the pastry and season with pepper.
Drizzle over a little oil, then place the
baking sheets on a medium barbecue
for 15 minutes, until the pastry is crisp.
Serve hot, garnished with thyme sprigs.

TOFU SATAY

. . .

Grill cubes of tofu until crispy, then serve with a Thai-style peanut sauce. Soak the satay sticks before use to prevent them from burning while on the barbecue.

INGREDIENTS

2 x 7-ounce packs smoked tofu
3 tablespoons light soy sauce
2 teaspoons sesame oil
1 garlic clove, crushed
1 yellow and 1 red bell pepper,
cut into squares
8–12 fresh bay leaves
sunflower oil, for brushing

FOR THE PEANUT SAUCE
2 scallions, chopped
2 garlic cloves, crushed
good pinch of chili powder, or a
few drops hot chili sauce
1 teaspoon sugar
1 tablespoon white wine vinegar
2 tablespoons light soy sauce
3 tablespoons crunchy peanut butter

SERVES 4–6

1 Cut the tofu into bitesize cubes and place in a large bowl. Add the soy sauce, sesame oil and crushed garlic and mix well. Cover and set aside to marinate for at least 20 minutes.

2 Beat all the peanut sauce ingredients together in a large bowl, using a wooden spoon, until well blended. Avoid using a food processor to blend the ingredients, as the texture should be slightly chunky.

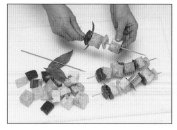

3 Drain the tofu and thread the cubes onto 8–12 satay sticks, alternating with the pepper squares and bay leaves. Larger bay leaves may need to be halved before threading.

4 Brush the satays with sunflower oil and cook on a hot barbecue or broiler, turning occasionally, until the tofu and peppers are browned and crisp. Serve hot with the peanut sauce.

142

SWEET AND SOUR VEGETABLES WITH PANEER

The Indian cheese used in this recipe, called paneer, can be bought from Asian stores, or you can use beancurd in its place. Paneer has a good firm texture and cooks very well on the barbecue.

INGREDIENTS

1 green and 1 yellow bell pepper,
cut into squares
8 cherry, or 4 medium, tomatoes
8 cauliflower florets
8 fresh or canned pineapple chunks
8 cubes paneer

FOR THE SEASONED OIL
1 tablespoon soya oil
2 tablespoons lemon juice
1 teaspoon salt
1 teaspoon freshly ground
black pepper
1 tablespoon clear honey
2 tablespoons chili sauce

SERVES 4

Thread the prepared vegetables, pineapple and paneer cubes onto four skewers, alternating the ingredients.

2 Mix together all the ingredients for the seasoned oil. If the mixture is a little too thick, add 1 tablespoon of water to loosen it. Brush the vegetables with the seasoned oil, ready for cooking.

3 Cook on a hot barbecue or broiler for 10 minutes, until the vegetables begin to char slightly, turning the skewers often and basting with the seasoned oil.

VEGETABLE KEBABS WITH PEPPERCORN SAUCE

Vegetables invariably taste good when cooked on the barbecue. You can include other
vegetables in these kebabs, depending on what is available at the time.

INGREDIENTS

24 mushrooms
16 cherry tomatoes
16 large fresh basil leaves
2 zucchini, cut into
16 thick slices
16 large fresh mint leaves
1 large red bell pepper, cut into
16 squares

TO BASTE
4 fluid ounces/1/2 cup melted butter
1 garlic clove, crushed
1 tablespoon crushed
green peppercorns

FOR THE GREEN PEPPERCORN SAUCE
2 ounces/1/4 cup butter
3 tablespoons brandy
8 fluid ounces/1 cup
heavy cream
1 teaspoon crushed green
peppercorns

SERVES 4

1 Carefully thread the vegetables onto eight bamboo skewers that you have soaked in water to prevent them from burning. Place the fresh basil leaves immediately next to the tomatoes, and wrap the mint leaves around the zucchini slices.

2 Mix the basting ingredients in a bowl and baste the kebabs thoroughly. Cook the skewers on a medium-hot barbecue, turning and basting regularly until the vegetables are just cooked – this should take about 5–7 minutes.

3 Heat the butter for the green peppercorn sauce in a frying pan, then add the brandy and light it. Whe the flames have died down, stir in the cream and the peppercorns. Cook for 2 minutes, stirring constantly. Serve th sauce with the kebabs.

CASSAVA AND VEGETABLE KEBABS

· · ·

This is an attractive and delicious assortment of African vegetables, marinated in a spicy garlic sauce, then roasted over hot coals. If cassava is unavailable, use sweet potato or yam instead.

INGREDIENTS

6 ounces cassava
1 onion, cut into wedges
1 eggplant, cut into
    bitesize pieces
1 zucchini, sliced
1 ripe plantain, sliced
1/2 red and 1/2 green bell
    pepper, sliced
16 cherry tomatoes
rice or couscous, to serve

FOR THE MARINADE

4 tablespoons lemon juice
4 tablespoons olive oil
3–4 tablespoons soy sauce
1 tablespoon tomato paste
1 green chile, seeded and
    finely chopped
1/2 onion, grated
2 garlic cloves, crushed
1 teaspoon apple pie spice
pinch of dried thyme

SERVES 4

eel the cassava and cut into bitesize
:es. Place in a large bowl, cover with
ing water and leave to blanch for
ut 5 minutes. Drain well.

lace all the prepared vegetables,
uding the cassava, in a large bowl
 mix with your hands so that all
vegetables are evenly distributed.

3 Blend the marinade ingredients and
pour over the vegetables. Cover and
leave to marinate for 1–2 hours.

4 Thread the vegetables, with the
cherry tomatoes, onto eight skewers
and cook on a hot barbecue for about
15 minutes until tender and browned.
Turn the skewers frequently and baste
them occasionally with the marinade.

5 Meanwhile, pour the remaining
marinade into a small pan and simmer
for about 10 minutes to reduce. Strain
the reduced marinade into a pitcher.
Serve the kebabs on a bed of rice or
couscous, with the sauce.

BAKED SQUASH WITH PARMESAN

Almost all types of squash are suitable for barbecue cooking, and they are extremely easy to deal with: simply wrap them in baking foil and place them in the hot embers until they soften.

INGREDIENTS

2 acorn or butternut squash,
about 1 pound each
1 tablespoon olive oil
2 ounces/4 tablespoons butter, melted
3 ounces/1 cup freshly grated
Parmesan cheese
4 tablespoons pine nuts, toasted
¹/₂ teaspoon freshly grated nutmeg
salt and freshly ground
black pepper

SERVES 4

2 Brush the cut surfaces with oil and sprinkle with salt and black pepper.

5 Dice the flesh, then stir in the melt butter. Add the Parmesan, pine nuts salt and pepper. Toss well to mix.

3 Wrap each squash in baking foil and place in the embers of the fire. Cook for 25–30 minutes, until tender. Turn the parcels occasionally so that the squash cook evenly.

6 Spoon the mixture back into the shells. Sprinkle with nutmeg and ser

1 Cut the squash in half and scoop out the seeds with a spoon.

4 Leave the squash until cool enough to handle. Unwrap the squash from the foil parcels and scoop out the flesh, leaving the skins intact.

Cook's Tip

Spaghetti squash can also be cooked in this way. Just scoop out the spaghetti-like strands and toss with butter and Parmesan cheese.

POTATO AND CHEESE POLPETTES

*These little morsels of potato and Greek feta cheese, flavored with dill and lemon juice, are
excellent when grilled on the barbecue, or they can be tossed in flour and fried in olive oil.*

INGREDIENTS

1¼ pounds potatoes
4 ounces feta cheese
4 scallions, chopped
3 tablespoons chopped fresh dill
1 egg, beaten
1 tablespoon lemon juice
2 tablespoons olive oil
salt and freshly ground
black pepper

SERVES 4

1 Boil the potatoes in their skins in
salted water until soft. Drain, then peel
while still warm. Place in a bowl and
mash. Crumble the feta cheese into the
potatoes and add the scallions, dill,
egg and lemon juice and season with
pepper and a little salt. Stir well.

2 Cover the mixture and chill until
firm. Divide the mixture into walnut-
size balls, then flatten them slightly.
Brush lightly with olive oil. Arrange
the polpettes on a grill rack and cook
on a medium barbecue, turning once,
until golden brown. Serve immediately

LOOFAH AND EGGPLANT RATATOUILLE

*Loofahs are edible gourds with spongy, creamy-white flesh. Like eggplant, their flavor is
intensified by roasting. Cooking the vegetables in a pan over the barbecue will retain their juices.*

INGREDIENTS

1 large eggplant
1 pound young loofahs or
sponge gourds
1 large red bell pepper, cut into
large chunks
8 ounces cherry tomatoes
8 ounces shallots
2 teaspoons ground coriander
4 tablespoons olive oil
2 garlic cloves, finely chopped
fresh cilantro sprigs
salt and freshly ground
black pepper

SERVES 4

Cut the eggplant into thick chunks
and sprinkle the pieces liberally with
salt to draw out the bitter juices. Leave
to drain for about 45 minutes, then
rinse under cold running water and pat
dry with paper towels.

Slice the loofahs into ¾-inch pieces.
Place the eggplant, loofah and pepper
pieces, together with the cherry
tomatoes and shallots, in a roasting
pan large enough to take all the
vegetables in a single layer.

3 Sprinkle the vegetables with the
ground coriander and oil. Sprinkle the
chopped garlic and fresh cilantro leaves
on top and season to taste.

4 Cook on the barbecue for about
25 minutes, stirring the vegetables
occasionally, until the loofah is golden
and the peppers are beginning to char.
As an alternative, you could thread the
vegetables on skewers and grill them.

BAKED STUFFED ZUCCHINI

∘ ∘ ∘

The tangy goat cheese stuffing contrasts well with the very delicate flavor of the zucchini in this recipe. Wrap the zucchini and bake them in the embers of the fire.

2 Insert pieces of goat cheese in the slits. Add a little chopped mint and sprinkle over the oil and black pepper

3 Wrap each zucchini in foil, place in the embers of the fire and bake for about 25 minutes, until tender.

INGREDIENTS

8 small zucchini, about
1 pound total weight
1 tablespoon olive oil, plus
extra for brushing
3–4 ounces goat cheese,
cut into thin strips
a few sprigs of fresh mint,
finely chopped, plus extra
to garnish
freshly ground black pepper

SERVES 4

1 Cut eight pieces of baking foil large enough to encase each zucchini, and lightly brush each piece with olive oil. Trim the zucchini and cut a thin slit along the length of each.

Cook's Tip

While almost any cheese can be used, mild cheeses such as Cheddar or mozzarella, will best allow the flavor of the zucchini to be appreciated.

VEGETABLE PARCELS WITH FLOWERY BUTTER

*Nasturtium leaves and flowers are edible and have a distinctive peppery flavor.
They make a pretty addition to summer barbecue dishes.*

INGREDIENTS

7 ounces baby carrots
9 ounces yellow patty-pan
squashes or zucchini
4 ounces baby corn cobs
1 onion, thinly sliced
2 ounces/4 tablespoons butter,
plus extra for greasing
finely grated rind of 1/2 lemon
6 young nasturtium leaves
4–8 nasturtium flowers
salt and freshly ground
black pepper

SERVES 4

rim the vegetables with a sharp
fe, leaving them whole unless they
very large – if necessary, cut them
o even-size pieces.

Divide the vegetables among four
uble-thickness squares of buttered
king foil and season well.

3 Mix the butter with the lemon
rind in a small bowl. Coarsely chop the
nasturtium leaves and add them to the
butter. Place a generous spoonful of the
butter on each pile of vegetables in the
squares of baking foil.

4 Fold over the foil and seal the edges
to make a neat parcel. Cook on
a medium-hot barbecue for 30 minutes
until the vegetables are tender. Open
the parcels and top each with one or
two nasturtium flowers. Serve at once.

GRILLED EGGPLANT PARCELS

These little Italian bundles of tomatoes, mozzarella cheese and basil, wrapped in slices of eggplant, taste delicious cooked on the barbecue.

INGREDIENTS
2 large, long eggplant
8 ounces mozzarella cheese
2 plum tomatoes
16 large fresh basil leaves
2 tablespoons olive oil
salt and freshly ground
black pepper

FOR THE DRESSING
4 tablespoons olive oil
1 teaspoon balsamic vinegar
1 tablespoon sun-dried
tomato paste
1 tablespoon lemon juice

FOR THE GARNISH
2 tablespoons toasted pine nuts
torn fresh basil leaves

SERVES 4

1 Remove the stalks from the eggplant and cut them lengthwise into thin slices using a mandolin or long-bladed knife – aim to get 16 slices in total, each about ¼-inch thick, disregarding the first and last slices.

2 Bring a large pan of salted water to the boil and cook the eggplant slices for about 2 minutes, until just softened. Drain the slices, then pat them dry on paper towels.

3 Cut the mozzarella cheese into eight slices. Cut each tomato into eight slices, not counting the first and last slices. Take two eggplant slices and arrange in a cross. Place a slice of tomato in the center, season, then add a basil leaf, followed by a slice of mozzarella, another basil leaf, another slice of tomato and more seasoning.

4 Fold the ends of the eggplant slices around the filling to make a neat parcel. Repeat with the rest of the assembled ingredients to make eight parcels. Chill the parcels in the refrigerator for about 20 minutes.

5 To make the tomato dressing, whisk together the olive oil, vinegar, sun-dried tomato paste and lemon juice. Season to taste with plenty of salt and freshly ground black pepper.

6 Brush the parcels with olive oil and cook on a hot barbecue for about 10 minutes, turning once, until golden. Serve hot, with the dressing, sprinkled with pine nuts and basil.

STUFFED TOMATOES AND PEPPERS

Colorful peppers and tomatoes make perfect containers for meat and vegetable stuffings. The smoky flavors in this dish are simply superb.

INGREDIENTS

2 large ripe tomatoes
1 green bell pepper
1 yellow or orange bell pepper
4 tablespoons olive oil, plus
extra for sprinkling
2 onions, chopped
2 garlic cloves, crushed
2 ounces/½ cup blanched
almonds, chopped
3 ounces/scant ½ cup long grain
rice, boiled and drained
2 tablespoons fresh mint,
coarsely chopped
2 tablespoons fresh parsley,
coarsely chopped
2 tablespoons golden raisins
3 tablespoons ground almonds
salt and freshly ground
black pepper
chopped mixed fresh herbs,
to garnish

SERVES 4

2 Halve the peppers, leaving the cores intact. Scoop out the seeds. Brush the peppers with 1 tablespoon olive oil and cook on a medium barbecue for 15 minutes. Place the peppers and tomatoes on a grill rack and season well with salt and pepper.

3 Cook the onions in the remaining olive oil for 5 minutes. Add the crushed garlic and chopped almonds to the pan and cook for a further minute.

4 Remove the pan from the heat and stir in the rice, chopped tomatoes, mint, parsley and golden raisins. Season well with salt and pepper and spoon the mixture into the tomatoes and peppers.

1 Cut the tomatoes in half and scoop out the pulp and seeds, using a teaspoon. Leave the tomatoes to drain on paper towels with the cut sides facing down. Roughly chop the tomato pulp and set it aside.

5 Sprinkle with the ground almonds and drizzle with a little extra olive oil. Cook on a medium barbecue for about 15 minutes. Garnish with fresh herbs.

COUSCOUS STUFFED PEPPERS

. . .

*Couscous makes a good basis for a stuffing, and in this recipe it is studded with raisins and
flavored with fresh mint. Charred peppers make the combination of flavors truly special.*

2 To cook the couscous, bring
8 fluid ounces/1 cup water to the bo[...]
Add the oil and salt, then remove fr[...]
the heat and add the couscous. Stir [...]
leave to stand, covered, for 5 minut[...]
Stir in the onion, raisins and mint.
Season well and stir in the egg yolk.

3 Use a teaspoon to fill the peppers
with the couscous mixture to about
three-quarters full (the couscous wil[...]
swell while cooking). Wrap each
pepper in a piece of oiled baking foi[...]

4 Cook on a medium barbecue for
20 minutes, until tender. Serve hot o[...]
cold, garnished with fresh mint leav[...]

INGREDIENTS

6 bell peppers
1 ounce/2 tablespoons butter
1 onion, finely chopped
1 teaspoon olive oil
½ teaspoon salt
6 ounces/1 cup couscous
1 ounce/2 tablespoons raisins
2 tablespoons chopped fresh mint
1 egg yolk
salt and freshly ground
black pepper
fresh mint leaves, to garnish

SERVES 4

1 Carefully slit each pepper with a
sharp knife and remove the cores and
seeds. Melt the butter in a small pan
and add the chopped onion. Cook until
soft but not browned.

CORN COBS IN A GARLIC BUTTER CRUST

*Whether you are catering for vegetarians or serving this with meat dishes, it will disappear
in a flash. The charred garlic butter crust adds a new dimension to the corn cobs.*

INGREDIENTS

6 ripe corn cobs
8 ounces/1 cup butter
2 tablespoons olive oil
2 garlic cloves, crushed
4 ounces/1 cup whole-wheat
bread crumbs
tablespoon chopped fresh parsley
salt and freshly ground
black pepper

SERVES 6

1 Pull off the husks and silks and boil
the corn cobs in a large pan of salted
water until tender. Drain the corn cobs
and leave to cool.

2 Melt the butter in a pan and add the
olive oil, crushed garlic, salt and freshly
ground black pepper, and stir to blend.
Pour the mixture into a shallow dish.
In another shallow dish blend the bread
crumbs and chopped fresh parsley. Roll
the corn cobs in the melted butter
mixture and then in the bread crumbs
until they are well coated.

3 Cook the corn cobs on a hot
barbecue for about 10 minutes, turning
frequently, until the bread crumbs are
golden brown.

STUFFED PARSLEYED ONIONS

These stuffed onions are a popular vegetarian dish served with fresh rustic bread and a crisp salad. They also make a very good accompaniment to meat dishes.

INGREDIENTS

4 large onions
4 tablespoons cooked rice
4 teaspoons finely chopped fresh parsley, plus extra to garnish
4 tablespoons strong Cheddar cheese, finely grated
2 tablespoons olive oil
1 tablespoon white wine
salt and freshly ground black pepper

SERVES 4

1 Cut a slice from the top of each onion and scoop out the center to leave a fairly thick shell. Combine all the remaining ingredients in a large bowl and stir to mix, moistening with enough white wine to bind the ingredients together well.

2 Use a spoon to fill the onions, then wrap each one in a piece of oiled baking foil. Bake in the embers of the fire for 30–40 minutes, until tender, turning the parcels often so they cook evenly. Serve the onions garnished with chopped fresh parsley.

STUFFED ARTICHOKE BOTTOMS

*The distinctive flavor of chargrilled globe artichokes is matched in this dish by
an intensely savory stuffing of mushrooms, cheese and walnuts.*

INGREDIENTS

8 ounces white mushrooms
1/2 ounce/1 tablespoons butter
2 shallots, finely chopped
2 ounces/1/4 cup soft cheese
2 tablespoons chopped walnuts
3 tablespoons grated
Gruyère cheese
4 large or 6 small artichoke
bottoms (from cooked artichokes,
leaves and choke removed, or
cooked frozen or canned
artichoke hearts)
salt and freshly ground
black pepper
fresh parsley sprigs, to garnish

SERVES 4

To make the duxelles for the stuffing,
t the mushrooms in a food processor
blender and pulse until they are
ely chopped.

Melt the butter in a frying pan
d cook the shallots over a medium
at for about 2–3 minutes until just
tened. Add the mushrooms, raise the
at slightly, and cook for 5–7 minutes
ore, stirring frequently, until all the
uid from the mushrooms has been
iven off and they are almost dry.
ason with plenty of salt and freshly
ound black pepper.

3 In a large bowl, combine the soft
cheese and cooked mushrooms. Add
the chopped walnuts and half the
grated Gruyère cheese, and stir well
to combine the mixture.

4 Divide the mixture among the
artichoke bottoms in an oiled baking
pan. Sprinkle over the remaining
cheese. Cook on the barbecue for
12 minutes, garnish and serve.

SPINACH WITH RAISINS AND PINE NUTS

∘ ∘ ∘

Raisins and pine nuts are frequent partners in Spanish recipes. In this recipe they are tossed with
wilted spinach and croûtons, and can be cooked quickly in a flameproof pan on the barbecue.

INGREDIENTS

2 ounces/⅓ cup raisins
1 thick slice rustic white bread
3 tablespoons olive oil
1 ounce/¼ cup pine nuts
1¼ pounds young spinach leaves,
stalks removed
2 garlic cloves, crushed
salt and freshly ground
black pepper

SERVES 4

1 Put the raisins in a bowl, cover with
boiling water and leave to soak for
10 minutes. Drain and set aside.

2 Cut the bread into cubes and discard
the crusts. Heat 2 tablespoons of the
olive oil in a large frying pan and fry
the bread until golden brown.

3 Heat the remaining oil and fry the
pine nuts, on the barbecue or hob, un[til]
beginning to color. Add the spinach
and garlic and cook quickly, turning
the spinach until it has just wilted. To[ss]
in the raisins and season lightly with
salt and pepper. Transfer to a serving
dish. Sprinkle with croûtons and serve[.]

GRILLED VEGETABLE TERRINE

◦ ◦ ◦

A colorful terrine, using all the vegetables associated with the Mediterranean, makes an elegant dish for outdoor eating. Cooking them on the barbecue adds to the flavor.

INGREDIENTS

large red bell peppers, quartered, cored and seeded
2 large yellow bell peppers, quartered, cored and seeded
1 large eggplant, sliced lengthwise
2 large zucchini, sliced lengthwise
6 tablespoons olive oil
1 large red onion, thinly sliced
3 ounces/1/2 cup raisins
1 tablespoon tomato paste
1 tablespoon red wine vinegar
14 fluid ounces/1²/3 cups tomato juice
1/2 ounce/2 tablespoons powdered gelatine
fresh basil leaves, to garnish

FOR THE DRESSING

5 tablespoons extra virgin olive oil
2 tablespoons red wine vinegar
salt and freshly ground black pepper

SERVES 6

Grill the peppers, skin-side down, on ot barbecue or broiler, until the as are beginning to blacken. Using gs, transfer to a bowl, cover and ve to cool.

rush the eggplant and zucchini slices h oil and cook until tender and den, turning occasionally.

eat the remaining oil in a pan, then the onion, raisins, tomato paste and wine vinegar. Cook until soft syrupy. Leave to cool in the pan.

'our half the tomato juice into a pan sprinkle with the gelatine. Dissolve tly over a very low heat, stirring.

5 Line an oiled 3 pint/7½ cup terrine pan with plastic wrap, leaving a little hanging over the sides. Place a layer of red bell peppers in the base and pour in enough of the tomato juice with gelatine to cover. Repeat with the eggplant, zucchini, yellow bell peppers and onion mixture, ending with another layer of red bell peppers and covering each layer with tomato juice and gelatine.

6 Add the remaining tomato juice to any left in the pan and pour into the terrine. Give it a sharp tap to eliminate air bubbles. Cover the terrine with plastic wrap and chill until set.

7 To make the dressing, whisk the oil and vinegar, and season with salt and black pepper. Turn out the terrine and serve in thick slices, drizzled with the dressing. Garnish with the basil leaves.

SUMMER VEGETABLES WITH YOGURT PESTO

° ° °

*Chargrilled vegetables make a meal on their own, or are delicious served as a
Mediterranean-style accompaniment to grilled meats and fish.*

INGREDIENTS

2 small eggplant
2 large zucchini
1 red bell pepper
1 yellow bell pepper
1 fennel bulb
1 red onion
olive oil, for brushing
salt and freshly ground
black pepper

FOR THE YOGURT PESTO
1/4 pint/2/3 cup strained
plain yogurt
3 tablespoons pesto

SERVES 4

1 Cut the eggplant into 1/2-inch slices.
Sprinkle with salt and leave to drain for
about 30 minutes. Rinse well in cold
running water and pat dry.

2 Use a sharp kitchen knife to cut
the zucchini in half lengthwise. Cut the
peppers in half, removing the seeds but
leaving the stalks in place.

3 Slice the fennel bulb and the red
onion into thick wedges, using a sharp
kitchen knife.

4 Stir the yogurt and pesto lightly
together in a bowl, to make a marbled
sauce. Spoon the yogurt pesto into a
serving bowl and set aside.

5 Arrange the vegetables on the hot
barbecue, brush generously with oli[...]
oil and sprinkle with plenty of salt a[...]
freshly ground black pepper.

6 Cook the vegetables until golden
brown and tender, turning occasiona[...]
The eggplant and peppers will take
6–8 minutes to cook, the zucchini,
onion and fennel 4–5 minutes. Serve
the vegetables as soon as they are
cooked, with the yogurt pesto.

Cook's Tip

Baby vegetables make
excellent candidates for grilling
whole, so look out for baby
eggplant and peppers, in particula[...]
There's no need to salt the eggplan[...]
if they're small.

WILD RICE WITH VEGETABLES

° ° °

Wild rice makes a special accompaniment to grilled vegetables in a simple vinaigrette dressing.
This recipe can be served as a side dish, but it also makes a tasty meal on its own.

INGREDIENTS

8 ounces/1 cup wild and long
grain rice mixture
1 eggplant, sliced
1 red, 1 yellow and 1 green bell
pepper, quartered, cored and seeded
2 red onions, sliced
8 ounces shiitake mushrooms
2 small zucchini, cut in
half lengthwise
olive oil, for brushing
2 tablespoons chopped fresh thyme

FOR THE DRESSING
6 tablespoons extra virgin olive oil
2 tablespoons balsamic vinegar
2 garlic cloves, crushed
salt and freshly ground
black pepper

SERVES 4

1 Put the wild and long grain rice mixture in a pan of cold salted water. Bring to the boil, then reduce the heat, cover and simmer for 30–40 minutes until the grains are tender (or follow the cooking instructions on the packet, if appropriate).

2 To make the dressing, mix together the olive oil, vinegar, crushed garlic and seasoning in a bowl or screw-topped jar until well blended.

3 Place the vegetables on a rack. Brush with oil and cook on a hot barbecue or broiler for 8–10 minutes, until tender and browned, turning them occasionally and basting with oil.

4 Drain the rice and toss in half the dressing. Tip into a serving dish and arrange the grilled vegetables on top. Pour over the remaining dressing and sprinkle over the chopped fresh thyme.

164

POTATO SKEWERS WITH MUSTARD DIP

*Potatoes cooked on the barbecue have a tasty flavor and crisp skin.
These skewers are served with a thick, garlic-rich dip.*

INGREDIENTS

2¼ pounds small new potatoes
7 ounces/2 cups shallots, halved
2 tablespoons olive oil
1 tablespoon sea salt

FOR THE MUSTARD DIP
4 garlic cloves, crushed
2 egg yolks
2 tablespoons lemon juice
½ pint/1¼ cups extra virgin
olive oil
2 teaspoons whole-grain mustard
salt and freshly ground
black pepper

SERVES 4

To make the mustard dip, place
the garlic, egg yolks and lemon juice
in a blender or food processor and
process for a few seconds until smooth.

With the motor running, add the oil,
until the mixture forms a thick cream.
Add the mustard and season.

3 Parboil the potatoes in salted boiling
water for about 5 minutes. Drain
thoroughly and then thread them onto
metal skewers with the shallots.

4 Brush with olive oil and sprinkle with
sea salt. Cook for 10–12 minutes over
a hot barbecue, turning often, until
tender. Serve with the mustard dip.

POTATO WEDGES WITH GARLIC AND ROSEMARY

Toss the potato wedges in fragrant, garlic-scented olive oil with chopped fresh rosemary before cooking them over the coals.

INGREDIENTS

1½ pounds medium old potatoes
1 tablespoon olive oil
2 garlic cloves, thinly sliced
4 tablespoons chopped
fresh rosemary
salt and freshly ground
black pepper

SERVES 4

1 Cut each potato into four wedges and parboil in boiling salted water for 5 minutes. Drain well.

2 Toss the potatoes in the olive oil with the garlic, rosemary and black pepper. Arrange on a grill rack.

3 Cook the potatoes on a hot barbecue for about 15 minutes, turning occasionally, until the wedges are crisp and golden brown.

166

SPANISH POTATOES

This is an adaptation of a traditional recipe for peppery fried potatoes. Cook the potatoes in a flameproof dish on the barbecue or in a pan on the stove, and serve them with grilled meats.

INGREDIENTS

1½ pounds small new potatoes
5 tablespoons olive oil
2 garlic cloves, sliced
½ teaspoon crushed chili
½ teaspoon ground cumin
2 teaspoons paprika
2 tablespoons red or white
wine vinegar
1 red or green bell pepper, sliced
coarse sea salt, to serve (optional)

SERVES 4

Cook the potatoes in a pan of boiling
~~sal~~ted water until almost tender. Drain
~~an~~d cut into chunks.

~~H~~eat the olive oil in a large frying
~~pa~~n or sauté pan and fry the potatoes,
~~tu~~rning them frequently, until golden.

3 Meanwhile, crush together the garlic, chili and cumin using a mortar and pestle. Mix with the paprika and wine vinegar to form a thick paste.

4 Add the garlic mixture to the potatoes with the sliced pepper and cook, stirring, for 2 minutes. Serve warm, or leave until cold. Sprinkle with coarse sea salt, if you like, to serve.

The powerful flavors of food cooked on the barbecue call for chunky salsas and tangy barbecue sauces. This chapter also includes some appetizing dips to go with bread sticks and crudités, and a selection of delicious marinades suitable for a wide variety of meat and fish.

SALSAS, DIPS AND MARINADES

CLASSIC TOMATO SALSA

. . .

This is the traditional tomato-based salsa that most people associate with spicy Mexican-inspired food. There are innumerable recipes for it, but the basics of onion, tomato, chile and cilantro are common to every one of them. Serve this salsa as a condiment with a wide variety of dishes.

INGREDIENTS

3–6 fresh Serrano chiles
1 large white onion
grated rind and juice of 2 limes,
plus strips of lime rind,
to garnish
8 ripe, firm tomatoes
large bunch of
fresh cilantro
1/4 teaspoon superfine sugar
salt

SERVES 6

2 Place the roasted chiles in a strong plastic bag and tie the top of the bag to keep the steam in. Set aside for about 20 minutes.

3 Meanwhile, chop the onion finely and put it in a bowl with the strips of lime rind and juice. The lime juice will soften the onion.

4 Remove the chiles from the bag and peel off the skins wearing rubber gloves. Cut off the stalks, slit the chiles and scrape out the seeds with a knife. Chop the flesh coarsely and set aside.

5 Cut a small cross in the base of each tomato. Place the tomatoes in a heatproof bowl and pour in boiling water to cover.

6 Leave the tomatoes in the water for 30 seconds, then lift them out using a slotted spoon and plunge them into bowl of cold water. Drain. The skins will have begun to peel back from th crosses. Remove the skins completely

7 Dice the peeled tomatoes and put them in a bowl. Add the chopped onion and lime mixture. Chop the fre cilantro finely.

8 Add the cilantro to the salsa, with the chiles, sugar and salt. Mix gently until the sugar has dissolved and all the ingredients are coated in lime juic Cover and chill for 2–3 hours to allo the flavors to blend. The salsa will keep for 3–4 days in the refrigerator. Garnish with the strips of lime rind ju before serving.

1 Use three chiles for a salsa of medium heat; up to six if you like it hot. To peel the chiles, spear them on a long-handled metal skewer and roast them over the flame of a gas burner until the skins blister and darken. Do not let the flesh burn. Alternatively, dry-fry them in a griddle pan until the skins are scorched.

Variations

Use scallions or mild red onions instead of the white onion. For a smoky flavor, use chipotle chiles instead of fresh Serrano chiles.

CHUNKY CHERRY TOMATO SALSA

* * *

Succulent cherry tomatoes and refreshing cucumber form the base of this delicious dill-seasoned salsa. Prepare up to 1 day in advance and store in the refrigerator until needed.

INGREDIENTS

1 ridge cucumber
1 teaspoon sea salt
1¼ pounds cherry tomatoes
grated rind and juice of 1 lemon
3 tablespoons chili oil
½ teaspoon dried chili flakes
2 tablespoons chopped fresh dill
1 garlic clove, finely chopped
salt and freshly ground
black pepper

SERVES 4

1 Trim the ends off the cucumber and cut it into 1-inch lengths, then cut each piece lengthwise into thin slices. Place in a colander and sprinkle with sea salt. Leave for 5 minutes.

2 Rinse the cucumber slices under co water and dry with paper towels.

3 Quarter the cherry tomatoes and place in a bowl with the cucumber.

4 Whisk together the lemon rind and juice, chili oil, chili flakes, dill and garlic. Season, then pour over the tomato and cucumber and toss well. Marinate for 2 hours before serving.

Cook's Tip

Try flavoring the salsa with other herbs, such as tarragon or mint.

SALSA VERDE

*There are many versions of this classic green salsa. Try this one sprinkled over
chargrilled squid, or with baked potatoes.*

INGREDIENTS
2–4 green chiles, halved
8 scallions
2 garlic cloves
2 ounces salted capers
sprig of fresh tarragon
bunch of fresh parsley
grated rind and juice of 1 lime
juice of 1 lemon
6 tablespoons olive oil
about 1 tablespoon green Tabasco
sauce, to taste
freshly ground black pepper
SERVES 4

eed the chiles and trim the scallions.
lve the garlic cloves. Place in a food
ocessor and pulse briefly.

Use your fingers to rub the excess salt
f the capers. Add them, with the
rragon and parsley, to the food
ocessor and pulse again until the
gredients are quite finely chopped.

3 Transfer the mixture to a large bowl.
Mix in the lime rind and juice, lemon
juice and olive oil, stirring lightly so the
citrus juice and oil do not emulsify.

4 Add green Tabasco sauce, a little
at a time, and black pepper to taste.
Chill the salsa in the refrigerator until
ready to serve, but do not prepare it
more than 8 hours in advance.

FIERY CITRUS SALSA

This unusual salsa makes a fantastic marinade for shellfish, and it is also delicious drizzled over meat that has been cooked on the barbecue.

INGREDIENTS

1 orange
1 green apple
2 fresh red chiles
1 garlic clove
8 fresh mint leaves
juice of 1 lemon
salt and freshly ground
black pepper

SERVES 4

1 Using a sharp knife, remove the peel and pith from the orange and, working over a bowl to catch the juices, cut out the segments. Squeeze any remaining juice into the bowl.

2 Use a sharp kitchen knife to peel the apple and slice it into wedges. Remove and discard the apple core.

3 Halve the chiles and remove the seeds, then place them in a blender or food processor with the orange segments and juice, apple wedges, garlic and mint.

4 Process until smooth. With the motor running, gradually pour in the lemon juice. Season to taste with salt and freshly ground black pepper and serve the salsa immediately.

BARBECUE-COOKED CORN SALSA

Serve this succulent salsa with grilled gammon or pork, or with smoked meats. The chargrilled corn cob makes the salsa particularly flavorsome.

INGREDIENTS

2 corn cobs
2 tablespoons melted butter
4 tomatoes
6 scallions, chopped
1 garlic clove, finely chopped
2 tablespoons lemon juice
2 tablespoons olive oil
red Tabasco sauce, to taste
salt and freshly ground
black pepper

SERVES 4

3 Skewer the tomatoes and hold over the barbecue or grill for about 2 minutes, turning, until the skin splits and wrinkles. Slip off the skins and dice the flesh. Add to the corn with the scallions and chopped garlic.

4 Stir the lemon juice and olive oil together, adding Tabasco, salt and black pepper to taste. Pour over the salsa, stir well, cover and leave to marinate at room temperature for 1–2 hours before serving.

...emove the husks and silks from the ...n cobs. Brush with the melted butter ... gently cook on the barbecue or ...iler for 20 minutes, turning ...asionally, until tender and charred.

...o remove the kernels, stand each ... upright on a chopping board and ... a large, heavy knife to slice down ... length of the cob. Put the kernels ... mixing bowl.

MANGO SALSA

∘ ∘ ∘

This has a fresh, fruity taste and is perfect with chargrilled fish. The bright colors make it an attractive addition to any barbecue party.

INGREDIENTS
2 fresh red Fresno chiles
2 ripe mangoes
½ white onion
small bunch of fresh cilantro
grated rind and juice of
1 lime

SERVES 4

1 To peel the chiles, spear them on a long-handled metal skewer and roast them over the flame of a gas burner until the skins blister and darken. Do not let the flesh burn. Alternatively, dry-fry them in a griddle pan until the skins are scorched.

2 Place the roasted chiles in a strong plastic bag and tie the top of the bag to keep the steam in. Leave for 20 minutes.

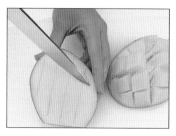

3 Meanwhile, put one of the mangoes on a board and cut off a thick slice close to the flat side of the pit. Turn the mango around and repeat on the other side. Score the flesh on each thick slice with criss-cross lines at ½-inch intervals, taking care not to cut through the skin. Repeat with the second mango.

4 Fold the mango halves inside out so that the mango flesh stands proud of the skin, in neat dice. Carefully slice these off the skin and into a bowl. Cut off the flesh adhering to each stone, dice it and add it to the bowl.

5 Remove the roasted chiles from the bag and carefully peel off the skins. Cut off the stalks, then slit the chiles and scrape out the seeds.

Cook's Tip
Mangoes, in season, are readily available nowadays, but are usually sold unripe. Keep in a warm room for 24 hours or until they are just soft to the touch. Do not allow them to ripen beyond this point.

6 Chop the white onion and the cilantro finely and add them to the diced mango. Chop the chile flesh finely and add it to the mixture in the bowl, together with the lime rind and juice. Stir well to mix, cover and chill in the refrigerator for at least 1 hour before serving. The salsa will keep for 2–3 days in the refrigerator.

ROASTED TOMATO AND CILANTRO SALSA

Roasting the tomatoes gives a greater depth to the taste of this salsa, which also benefits from the warm, rounded flavor of roasted chiles.

INGREDIENTS

1¼ pounds tomatoes
2 fresh Serrano chiles
1 onion
juice of 1 lime
large bunch of
fresh cilantro
salt

SERVES 6

eheat the oven to 400°F. Cut the
atoes into quarters and place them
roasting pan. Add the chiles.
st for 45–60 minutes, until the
atoes and chiles are charred
softened.

2 Place the chiles in a plastic bag. Tie the top of the bag to keep the steam in and set aside for 20 minutes. Leave the tomatoes to cool slightly, then remove the skins and dice the flesh.

3 Chop the onion finely, then place in a bowl and add the lime juice and the chopped tomatoes.

4 Remove the chiles from the bag and peel off the skins. Cut off the stalks, then slit the chiles and scrape out the seeds with a sharp knife. Chop the chiles coarsely and add them to the onion mixture. Mix well.

5 Chop the cilantro and add most of it to the salsa. Season with salt, cover and chill in the refrigerator for at least 1 hour before serving, sprinkled with the remaining cilantro. This salsa will keep in the refrigerator for 1 week.

BARBECUE SAUCE

· · ·

Brush this sauce liberally over chicken drumsticks, chops or kebabs before cooking on the barbecue, or serve as a hot or cold accompaniment to hot dogs and burgers.

INGREDIENTS

2 tablespoons vegetable oil
1 large onion, chopped
2 garlic cloves, crushed
14-ounce can tomatoes
2 tablespoons Worcestershire sauce
1 tablespoon white wine vinegar
3 tablespoons clear honey
1 teaspoon mustard powder
½ teaspoon chili seasoning or
    mild chili powder
salt and freshly ground
    black pepper

SERVES 4

3 Pour into a food processor or blender and process until smooth.

4 Press through a strainer if you like Adjust the seasoning to taste.

1 Heat the vegetable oil in a large pan and cook the onions and garlic until soft and golden.

2 Stir in the remaining ingredients and simmer gently, uncovered, for about 15–20 minutes, stirring occasionally. Remove the pan from the heat and leave to cool slightly.

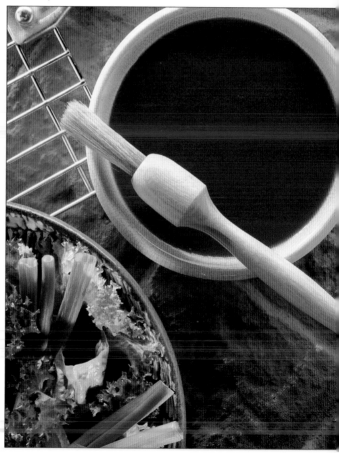

GUACAMOLE

*Nachos or tortilla chips are the traditional accompaniments for this classic Mexican dip,
but it also tastes great served on the side with burgers or kebabs.*

INGREDIENTS

2 ripe avocados
2 red chiles, seeded
1 garlic clove
1 shallot
2 tablespoons olive oil,
plus extra to serve
juice of 1 lemon
salt
fresh flat leaf parsley, to garnish

SERVES 4

1 Halve the avocados, flick out the pits, using the point of a sharp knife, and use a dessert spoon to scoop the flesh into a large bowl.

2 Mash the flesh well, using a potato masher or a large fork, so that the avocado is a fairly smooth consistency.

3 Finely chop the chiles, garlic clove and shallot, then stir into the mashed avocado with the olive oil and lemon juice. Add salt to taste and mix well.

4 Spoon the mixture into a serving bowl. Drizzle over a little more olive oil and sprinkle with flat leaf parsley leaves. Serve immediately. Guacamole can be prepared up to 8 hours in advance and stored in the refrigerator, sprinkled with lemon juice and covered with plastic wrap.

179

CARAMELIZED ONION RELISH

Slow, gentle cooking reduces the onions to a soft, sweet relish.
It makes a tasty addition to many barbecue menus.

2 Heat the butter and oil together in a large pan. Add the onions and sugar and cook very gently for 30 minutes over a low heat, stirring occasionally, until reduced to a soft rich brown caramelized mixture.

3 Coarsely chop the capers and stir them into the caramelized onions. Leave to cool completely.

4 Stir in the chopped fresh parsley and add salt and ground black pepper to taste. Cover with plastic wrap and chill in the refrigerator until ready to serve.

INGREDIENTS

3 large onions
2 ounces/4 tablespoons butter
2 tablespoons olive oil
2 tablespoons light brown sugar
2 tablespoons pickled capers
2 tablespoons chopped
fresh parsley
salt and freshly ground black pepper
SERVES 4

1 Peel the onions and halve them vertically, through the core, using a sharp knife. Slice them thinly.

PARSLEY BUTTER

This butter, or one of the variations below, makes a subtle accompaniment to barbecued food, particularly fish with a delicate flavor.

INGREDIENTS

4 ounces/½ cup softened butter
tablespoons chopped fresh parsley
½ teaspoon lemon juice
cayenne pepper
lt and freshly ground black pepper

SERVES 4

eat the butter until creamy, then t in the parsley, lemon juice and enne pepper, and season lightly.

2 Spread the butter ¼-inch thick on to foil and chill, then cut into shapes with a knife or fancy cutter.

3 Alternatively, form the butter into a roll, wrap in plastic wrap or foil and chill. Cut off slices as required.

Variations

LEMON OR LIME BUTTER
Add 1 tablespoon finely grated lemon or lime rind and 1 tablespoon juice to the butter.

HERB BUTTER
Replace the parsley with 2 tablespoons chopped fresh mint, chives or tarragon.

GARLIC BUTTER
Add 2 crushed garlic cloves to the butter with 1–2 tablespoons chopped fresh parsley.

ANCHOVY BUTTER
Add 6 anchovy fillets, drained of oil and mashed with a fork, to the butter. Season with pepper only.

MUSTARD BUTTER
Add 2 teaspoons English mustard and 2 tablespoons chopped chives to the butter.

These butters will keep in the refrigerator for several days, and will also freeze, wrapped in plastic wrap or foil to avoid any loss of flavor.

THOUSAND ISLAND DIP

This creamy dip can be served with grilled shrimp laced onto bamboo skewers
or with a simple mixed seafood salad.

INGREDIENTS
4 sun-dried tomatoes in oil
4 tomatoes
1/4 pint/2/3 cup soft
farmer's cheese
4 tablespoons mayonnaise
2 tablespoons tomato paste
2 tablespoons chopped fresh parsley
grated rind and juice of 1 lemon
red Tabasco sauce, to taste
1 teaspoon Worcestershire or
soy sauce
salt and freshly ground black pepper

SERVES 4

1 Drain the sun-dried tomatoes on paper towels to remove excess oil, then finely chop.

2 Skewer each fresh tomato in turn on a metal fork and hold in a gas flame for 1–2 minutes, until the skin wrinkles and splits. Slip off and discard the skins, then halve the tomatoes and scoop out the seeds with a teaspoon. Finely chop the tomato flesh.

3 Beat the soft farmer's cheese, then gradually beat in the mayonnaise an tomato paste until blended.

4 Stir in the chopped parsley and su dried tomatoes, then add the choppe tomatoes and their seeds, and mix w

5 Add the lemon rind and juice and Tabasco to taste. Stir in Worcestersh or soy sauce, and salt and pepper. Transfer the dip to a bowl, cover an chill until ready to serve.

MELLOW GARLIC DIP

Two whole heads of garlic may seem too much but, once cooked, the taste is sweet and mellow.
Serve with crunchy bread sticks and potato snacks.

2 When cool enough to handle, separate the garlic cloves and peel. Place on a chopping board and sprinkle with salt. Mash the garlic with a fork until puréed.

3 Place the garlic in a large bowl and stir in the mayonnaise, yogurt and whole-grain mustard. Mix well.

INGREDIENTS

2 whole garlic heads
1 tablespoon olive oil
4 tablespoons mayonnaise
5 tablespoons strained
plain yogurt
1 teaspoon whole-grain mustard
salt and freshly ground black pepper

SERVES 4

1 Slice the tops from the heads of garlic, using a sharp knife. Brush with olive oil and wrap in foil. Cook on a medium-hot barbecue for 25 minutes, turning occasionally.

4 Check the seasoning, adding more salt and pepper to taste, then spoon the dip into a serving bowl. Cover and chill in the refrigerator until ready to serve.

CREAMY EGGPLANT DIP

• • •

*Spread this velvet-textured dip thickly onto slices of French bread toasted on the barbecue,
then top with slivers of sun-dried tomato to make wonderful Italian-style crostini.*

INGREDIENTS

1 large eggplant
2 tablespoons olive oil
1 small onion, finely chopped
2 garlic cloves, finely chopped
4 tablespoons chopped fresh parsley
5 tablespoons crème fraîche
red Tabasco sauce, to taste
juice of 1 lemon, to taste
salt and freshly ground
black pepper

SERVES 4

3 Peel the eggplant and mash the flesh
with a large fork or potato masher to
make a pulpy purée.

4 Stir in the onion and garlic, parsle
and crème fraîche. Add Tabasco, lem
juice, and season to taste. Serve war

1 Cook the whole eggplant on a
medium barbecue or broiler for about
20 minutes, turning occasionally, until
the skin is blackened and the eggplant
soft. Cover the eggplant with a clean
dish towel and set aside to cool for
about 5–6 minutes.

2 Heat the oil in a frying pan and cook
the chopped onion and garlic for about
5 minutes, until soft but not browned.

FAT-FREE SAFFRON DIP

*Serve this mild dip with fresh vegetable crudités – it is particularly good with
florets of cauliflower, asparagus tips and baby carrots and corn.*

INGREDIENTS

1 tablespoon boiling water
small pinch of saffron threads
7 ounces/scant 1 cup fat-free
fromage frais or farmer's cheese
10 fresh chives
10 fresh basil leaves
salt and freshly ground
black pepper

SERVES 4

our the boiling water into a bowl
d add the saffron threads. Leave to
ep for 3 minutes.

eat the fromage frais or cheese in a
ge bowl until smooth. Stir in the
fron liquid with a wooden spoon.

Cook's Tip

If you don't have any saffron, add
a squeeze of lemon or lime juice.

3 Snip the chives into the dip. Tear the
basil leaves into small pieces and stir
them in. Mix thoroughly.

4 Add salt and freshly ground black
pepper to taste. Serve the dip with fresh
vegetable crudités, if you like.

SPICY YOGURT MARINADE

Use this marinade for chicken, lamb or pork, and marinate the meat, covered and chilled, for 24–36 hours to develop a mellow spicy flavor.

INGREDIENTS

1 teaspoon coriander seeds
2 teaspoons cumin seeds
6 cloves
2 bay leaves
1 onion, quartered
2 garlic cloves
2-inch piece of fresh
root ginger,
coarsely chopped
1/2 teaspoon chili powder
1 teaspoon ground turmeric
1/4 pint/2/3 cup plain yogurt
juice of 1 lemon

SERVES 6

1 Spread the coriander and cumin seeds, cloves and bay leaves over the base of a large frying pan and dry-fry over a moderate heat until the bay leaves are crisp.

2 Leave the spices to cool, then grind coarsely with a mortar and pestle.

3 Finely chop the onion, garlic and ginger in a blender or food processor. Add the ground spices, chili, turmeric, yogurt and lemon juice.

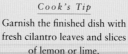

Cook's Tip
Garnish the finished dish with fresh cilantro leaves and slices of lemon or lime.

4 If you are marinating cuts of chick or large pieces of meat, make several deep slashes to allow the flavors to penetrate. Arrange the pieces in a sin layer and pour over the marinade. Cover and leave in the refrigerator to marinate for at least 24 hours.

ORANGE AND GREEN PEPPERCORN MARINADE

° ° °

This is an excellent light marinade for delicately flavored whole fish, such as sea trout,
bass or bream. The beauty of the fish is perfectly set off by the softly colored marinade.

INGREDIENTS

1 red onion
2 small oranges
6 tablespoons light olive oil
2 tablespoons cider vinegar
2 tablespoons green peppercorns in
brine, drained
2 tablespoons chopped fresh parsley
salt and sugar

FOR 1 MEDIUM-SIZE FISH

With a sharp knife, slash the fish
4 times on each side.

2 Cut a piece of foil big enough to
wrap the fish and use to line a large
dish. Peel and slice the onion and
oranges. Lay half the slices on the foil,
place the fish on top and cover with
the remaining onion and orange.

3 Mix the remaining marinade
ingredients and pour over the fish.
Cover and leave to marinate for
4 hours, occasionally spooning the
marinade over the fish.

4 Fold the foil loosely over the fish and
seal the edges securely. Bake on a
medium barbecue for 15 minutes for
1 pound, plus 15 minutes over.

GINGER AND LIME MARINADE

° ° °

This fragrant marinade will guarantee a mouth-watering aroma from the barbecue. Shown here on shrimp and monkfish kebabs, it is just as delicious with chicken or pork.

INGREDIENTS

3 limes
1 tablespoon green cardamom pods
1 onion, finely chopped
1-inch piece of fresh root
ginger, grated
1 large garlic clove, crushed
3 tablespoons olive oil

SERVES 4–6

3 Mix all the marinade ingredients together and pour over the meat or fish. Stir in gently, cover and leave in a cool place to marinate for 2–3 hours.

4 Drain the meat or fish when you a[re] ready to cook it on the barbecue. Ba[ste] the meat occasionally with the marinade, while cooking.

1 Finely grate the rind from one lime and squeeze the juice from all of them.

2 Split the cardamom pods and remove the seeds. Crush the seeds with a mortar and pestle or the back of a heavy-bladed knife.

SUMMER HERB MARINADE

∘ ∘ ∘

Make the best use of summer herbs in this marinade. Try any combination of herbs, depending on what you have on hand, and use with veal, chicken, pork, lamb or salmon.

INGREDIENTS

large handful of fresh herb sprigs,
e.g. chervil, thyme, parsley, sage,
chives, rosemary, oregano
6 tablespoons olive oil
3 tablespoons tarragon vinegar
1 garlic clove, crushed
2 scallions, chopped
salt and freshly ground
black pepper

SERVES 4

3 Place the meat or fish in a bowl and pour over the marinade. Cover and leave to marinate in a cool place for 4–6 hours.

4 Drain the meat or fish when you are ready to cook it on the barbecue. Use the marinade to baste the meat occasionally while cooking.

Discard any coarse stalks or damaged leaves from the herbs, then chop them finely.

Add the chopped herbs to the remaining marinade ingredients in a large bowl. Stir to mix thoroughly.

At the end of a barbecue, it's a lovely idea to use the lingering

fire to make a delicious fruity dessert. Even those who thought

they couldn't eat another bite will be beguiled. Accompany

grilled fruit with a spicy sauce, crisp toasted brioche or freshly

made griddle cakes.

DESSERTS

CHARGRILLED APPLES ON CINNAMON TOASTS

. . .

This simple, scrumptious dessert is best made with an enriched bread such as brioche,
but any light, sweet bread will do.

INGREDIENTS

4 sweet, eating apples
juice of ½ lemon
4 individual brioches or muffins
4 tablespoons melted butter
2 tablespoons golden
superfine sugar
1 teaspoon ground cinnamon
whipped cream, to serve

SERVES 4

2 Cut the brioches or muffins into thick slices. Brush the slices with melted butter on both sides.

4 Place the apple and brioche slices a medium-hot barbecue and cook th for about 3–4 minutes, turning once until they are beginning to turn gold brown. Do not allow to burn.

1 Core the apples and use a sharp knife to cut them into 3–4 thick slices. Sprinkle the apple slices with lemon juice and set them aside.

3 Mix together the superfine sugar and ground cinnamon in a small bowl to make the cinnamon sugar. Set aside.

5 Sprinkle half the cinnamon sugar over the apple slices and brioche toa and cook for a further minute on the barbecue, until the sugar is sizzling a the toasts are a rich golden brown.

6 To serve, arrange the apple slices o the toasts and sprinkle them with the remaining cinnamon sugar. Serve ho with whipped cream.

PINEAPPLE WEDGES WITH RUM BUTTER GLAZE

° ° °

Fresh pineapple is even more full of flavor when cooked on the barbecue, and this spiced rum glaze makes it into a very special dessert.

INGREDIENTS

1 medium pineapple
2 tablespoons dark brown sugar
1 teaspoon ground ginger
4 tablespoons melted butter
2 tablespoons dark rum

SERVES 4

3 Soak 4 bamboo skewers in water for 15 minutes to prevent them from scorching on the barbecue. Push a skewer through each wedge, into the stalk, to hold the chunks in place.

4 Mix together the sugar, ginger, bu[tter] and rum and brush over the pineap[ple.] Cook the wedges on the barbecue f[or] 4 minutes; pour the remaining glaze over the top and serve.

1 With a large, sharp knife, cut the pineapple lengthwise into four wedges. Cut out and discard the central core.

2 Cut between the flesh and skin, to release the skin, but leave the flesh in place. Slice the flesh across and lengthwise to make thick chunks.

Cook's Tip

For an easier version, simply remove the skin and then cut the whole pineapple into thick slices and cook as above.

ʙAKED BANANAS WITH SPICY VANILLA FILLING

. . .

Bananas are ideal for barbecue cooking, since they bake in their skins and need no preparation at all. This flavored butter adds richness; children may prefer melted chocolate, jam or honey.

INGREDIENTS

4 bananas
6 green cardamom pods
1 vanilla bean
finely grated rind of 1 small orange
2 tablespoons brandy or orange juice
4 tablespoons light brown sugar
3 tablespoons butter
crème fraîche or strained plain
yogurt, to serve

SERVES 4

1 Place the bananas, in their skins, on a hot barbecue and leave for about 6–8 minutes, turning occasionally, until they are turning brownish black.

2 Meanwhile, split the cardamom pods and remove the seeds. Crush lightly with a mortar and pestle.

3 Split the vanilla bean lengthwise and scrape out the tiny seeds. Mix them with the cardamom seeds, orange rind, brandy or juice, brown sugar and butter into a thick paste.

4 Using a sharp knife, slit the skin of each banana, then open out the skin and spoon in a little of the paste. Serve the bananas immediately with a spoonful of crème fraîche or yogurt.

ORANGES IN MAPLE AND COINTREAU SYRUP

. . .

This is one of the most delicious ways to eat an orange, and a luxurious way to round off a barbecue. For a children's or alcohol-free version, omit the liqueur.

INGREDIENTS

4 teaspoons butter, plus extra, melted, for brushing
4 medium oranges
2 tablespoons maple syrup
2 tablespoons Cointreau or Grand Marnier liqueur
crème fraîche, fromage frais or mascarpone cheese, to serve

SERVES 4

1 Cut four double-thickness squares of baking foil, large enough to wrap each of the oranges. Brush the center of each square of foil with plenty of melted butter.

2 Remove some shreds of orange rind, to decorate. Blanch these, dry them and set them aside. Peel the oranges, removing all the white pith and catching the juice in a bowl.

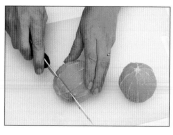

3 Slice the oranges crosswise into thick slices. Reassemble them and place each orange on a square of baking foil.

4 Tuck the baking foil up securely around the oranges to keep them in shape, leaving the foil open at the to[p]

5 Mix together the reserved orange juice, maple syrup and liqueur and spoon the mixture over the oranges.

6 Add a pat of butter to each parcel and close the foil at the top to seal in the juices. Place the parcels on a hot barbecue for 10–12 minutes, until hot. Serve with crème fraîche, fromag[e] frais or mascarpone cheese, topped with the shreds of orange rind.

NECTARINES WITH MARZIPAN AND MASCARPON

∘ ∘ ∘

A luscious dessert that no one can resist – dieters may prefer to use low-fat soft cheese or ricotta instead of mascarpone.

INGREDIENTS

4 firm, ripe nectarines or peaches
3 ounces/½ cup marzipan
5 tablespoons mascarpone cheese
3 macaroons, crushed

SERVES 4

1 Cut the nectarines or peaches in half and remove the pits.

2 Divide the marzipan into eight pieces, roll into balls, using your fingers, and press one piece of marzipan into the stone cavity of each nectarine half.

Cook's Tip

Either nectarines or peaches can be used for this recipe. If the pit does not pull out easily when you halve the fruit, use a small, sharp knife to cut around it.

3 Spoon the mascarpone cheese on top of the fruit halves. Sprinkle the crushed macaroon cookies over the mascarpone cheese.

4 Place the half-fruits on a hot barbecue for 3–5 minutes, until they are hot and the mascarpone starts to melt. Serve immediately.

GRILLED STRAWBERRY CROISSANTS

∘ ∘ ∘

The combination of crisp croissants, ricotta cheese and sweet strawberry conserve makes for a deliciously simple, sinful dessert, which is like eating warm cream cakes!

INGREDIENTS

4 croissants
4 ounces/1/2 cup ricotta cheese
4 ounces/1/2 cup strawberry
conserve or jam

SERVES 4

3 Top the ricotta with a generous spoonful of strawberry conserve and replace the top half of the croissant.

4 Place the filled croissants on a hot barbecue and cook for 2–3 minutes, turning once. Serve immediately.

On a chopping board, split the croissants in half and open them out.

Spread the bottom half of each croissant with a generous layer of the ricotta cheese.

Cook's Tip

As an alternative to croissants, try biscuits, brioches or muffins, toasted on the barbecue.

GRIDDLE CAKES WITH MULLED PLUMS

∘ ∘ ∘

These delectably light little pancakes are fun to make on the barbecue. They are served with a rich, spicy plum sauce, and you could offer cream or yogurt, too.

INGREDIENTS

1¼ pounds red plums
6 tablespoons light
  brown sugar
1 cinnamon stick
2 whole cloves
1 piece star anise
6 tablespoons apple juice

FOR THE GRIDDLE CAKES
2 ounces/½ cup all-purpose flour
2 teaspoons baking powder
pinch of salt
2 ounces/½ cup fine cornmeal
2 tablespoons light
  brown sugar
1 egg, beaten
½ pint/1¼ cups milk
2 tablespoons corn oil

SERVES 6

2 Bring to the boil, then reduce the heat, cover the pan and simmer gently for 8–10 minutes, stirring occasionally, until the plums are soft. Remove the spices and keep the plums warm on the side of the barbecue.

3 For the griddle cakes, sift the plain flour, baking powder and salt into a large mixing bowl and stir in the cornmeal and muscovado sugar.

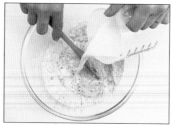

4 Make a well in the center of the ingredients and add the egg, then beat in the milk. Beat thoroughly with a whisk or wooden spoon to form a smooth batter. Beat in half the oil.

5 Heat a griddle or a heavy frying pa[n] on a hot barbecue. Brush with the remaining oil, then drop tablespoon[s] of batter onto it, allowing them to spread. Cook the griddle cakes for about a minute, until bubbles start to appear on the surface and the underside is golden brown.

6 Turn the cakes over and cook the other side for a further minute, or un[til] golden. Serve the cakes hot from the griddle with a spoonful of mulled plums and cream or yogurt, if you li[ke].

1 Halve, pit and quarter the plums. Place them in a flameproof pan, with the sugar, spices and apple juice.

Cook's Tip

If you prefer, make the griddle cakes in advance, on the stovetop, and then simply heat them for a few seconds on the barbecue to serve with the plums.

FRUIT KEBABS WITH CHOCOLATE FONDUE

Fondues are always lots of fun, and the delicious ingredients used here – fresh fruit, chocolate and marshmallow – mean that this recipe will be a popular choice with children and adults alike.

2 Mix together the butter, lemon juice and ground cinnamon and brush the mixture generously over the fruits.

3 For the fondue, place the chocolate, cream and marshmallows in a small pan and heat gently, without boiling, stirring constantly until the mixture melted and is smooth.

4 Cook the kebabs on a medium-hot barbecue for about 2–3 minutes, turning once, or until the fruit is golden. Stir the vanilla extract into the fondue. Empty the fondue into a small bowl and serve immediately, with the fruit kebabs.

INGREDIENTS

2 bananas
2 kiwi fruit
12 strawberries
1 tablespoon melted butter
1 tablespoon lemon juice
1 teaspoon ground cinnamon
8 ounces semisweet chocolate
4 fluid ounces/½ cup
light cream
8 marshmallows
½ teaspoon vanilla extract

SERVES 4

1 Peel the bananas and cut into thick chunks. Peel the kiwi fruit and quarter them. Thread the bananas, kiwi fruit and strawberries onto four wooden skewers. (Soak the skewers in water for 15 minutes beforehand to prevent them from scorching on the barbecue.)

SPICED PEAR AND BLUEBERRY PARCELS

This fruity combination makes a delicious dessert for a hot summer's evening.
You could substitute other berry fruits for the blueberries if you like.

INGREDIENTS

4 firm, ripe pears
2 tablespoons lemon juice
1 tablespoon melted butter
5 ounces/1¼ cups blueberries
4 tablespoons light brown sugar
freshly ground black pepper

SERVES 4

3 Cut four squares of double-thickness foil, large enough to wrap the pears, and brush them with melted butter. Place two pear halves on each, cut sides upwards. Gather the foil up around them, to hold them level.

4 Mix the blueberries and sugar together and spoon them over the pears. Sprinkle with black pepper. Seal the edges of the foil over the pears and cook on a fairly hot barbecue for 20–25 minutes.

eel the pears thinly. Cut them in lengthwise. Scoop out the core n each half, using a teaspoon and arp kitchen knife.

rush the pears with lemon juice, to vent them from discoloring.

Cook's Tip

To assemble in advance, line with a ayer of waxed paper, as the acid in the juice may react with the foil and taint the flavor.

PUMPKIN IN BROWN SUGAR

Rich, sticky and sweet, this warming dessert looks very attractive, tastes wonderful and is not at all difficult to prepare.

INGREDIENTS

butter, for greasing
1 small pumpkin,
about 1¾ pounds
12 ounces/1½ cups soft dark brown sugar
6 tablespoons water
1 teaspoon ground cloves
12 cinnamon sticks, each about 4-inch in length
fresh mint sprigs, to decorate
thick yogurt or crème fraîche, to serve

SERVES 6

1 Cut six large, double-thickness squares of foil and lightly grease with butter. Using a sharp knife, halve the pumpkin, cut into wedges and remove the seeds and fibers. Divide the wedges among the foil squares, placing them in a single layer skin-side down. Fill the hollows with the sugar.

2 Carefully sprinkle the water over wedges, taking care not to wash all sugar out of the hollows. Sprinkle o the ground cloves and add two cinnamon sticks to each parcel. Folc the sides of the foil, then tuck in an fold over the edges to make loosely wrapped, but secure, parcels.

3 Cook the parcels on a low barbec turning them occasionally, for abou 30 minutes, or until the pumpkin is tender and the sugar and water have formed a syrup.

4 Carefully unwrap the foil parcels and transfer the pumpkin to a warn platter and pour the hot syrup over. Decorate each portion with mint anc the cinnamon sticks and serve with thick yogurt or crème fraîche.

BAKED APPLES IN HONEY AND LEMON

° ° °

Tender baked apples with a classic flavoring of lemon and honey make a simple dessert.
Serve with custard or a spoonful of whipped cream, if you like.

INGREDIENTS

4 medium cooking apples
1 tablespoon clear honey
grated rind and juice of 1 lemon
1 tablespoon butter, melted

SERVES 4

...move the cores from the apples, ...ing them whole. Cut four squares ...ouble-thickness baking foil, to ...p the apples, and brush with butter.

...ith a cannelle or sharp knife, ...lines through the apple skin at ...lar intervals.

3 Mix together the honey, lemon rind, juice and butter in a small bowl.

4 Spoon the mixture into the apples and wrap in foil, sealing the edges securely. Cook on a hot barbecue for 20 minutes, until the apples are tender.

POACHED PEARS IN MAPLE AND YOGURT SAUC

° ° °

This elegant dessert is easier to make than it looks – poach the pears on the stove or barbecue when you cook the main course, and have the cooled syrup ready to add just before serving.

INGREDIENTS

6 firm pears
1 tablespoon lemon juice
8 fluid ounces/1 cup sweet white
wine or cider
thinly pared rind of 1 lemon
1 cinnamon stick
2 tablespoons maple syrup
1/2 teaspoon arrowroot
1/4 pint/2/3 cup strained
plain yogurt

SERVES 6

1 Peel the pears, leaving them whole and with stalks. Brush with lemon juice to prevent them from discoloring. Use a potato peeler or small knife to scoop out the core from the base of each pear.

2 Place the pears in a wide, heavy p and pour over the wine, with enoug cold water almost to cover the fruit Add the lemon rind and cinnamon stick, and bring to the boil on the stove or, using a flameproof pan, o the barbecue. Reduce the heat, cove and simmer for 30 minutes, or unti tender. Lift out the pears carefully.

3 Boil the remaining liquid, uncove until reduced to about 4 fluid ounc 1/2 cup. Strain and add the maple sy Blend a little of the liquid with the arrowroot. Return to the pan and cook, stirring, until thick and clear. Leave to cool.

4 Slice each pear, leaving the slices attached at the stem end, and fan o on serving plates. Stir 2 tablespoons the cooled syrup into the yogurt and spoon around the pears. Drizzle the pears with the remaining syrup and serve immediately.

CHOCOLATE MINT TRUFFLE PHYLLO PARCELS

These exquisite little parcels are utterly irresistible: there will be no leftovers. The use of fresh mint in the recipe gives a wonderfully refreshing flavor.

2 Cut the phyllo pastry sheets into 3-inch squares and cover with a damp cloth to prevent them drying out.

3 Brush a square of phyllo with melted butter, lay on a second sheet, brush again and place a spoonful of filling in the middle of the top sheet. Bring in all four corners and twist to form a purse shape. Repeat to make 18 parcels.

4 Place the phyllo parcels on a griddle or baking sheet, well brushed with melted butter. Cook on a medium-hot barbecue for about 10 minutes, until the phyllo pastry is crisp. Leave to cool, then dust lightly with sifted confectioners' sugar and then with sifted cocoa powder.

INGREDIENTS

1 tablespoon chopped fresh mint
3 ounces/³⁄₄ cup ground almonds
2 ounces semisweet
chocolate, grated
4 ounces/¹⁄₂ cup crème fraîche
2 eating apples, peeled and grated
9 large sheets phyllo pastry
3 ounces/¹⁄₃ cup butter, melted
confectioners' sugar, to dust
unsweetened cocoa powder,
to dust

MAKES 18 PARCELS

1 Mix the chopped fresh mint, almonds, grated chocolate, crème fraîche and grated apple in a large mixing bowl. Set aside.

Al fresco meals – whether in the garden, on the beach or in a grassy meadow – are a great pleasure both to organize and to experience. This section offers inspirations for special summer meals and garden parties, including some original and delicious ideas for party drinks.

OUTDOOR
ENTERTAINING

VEGETABLES WITH TAPENADE AND HERB AIOLI

° ° °

A beautiful platter of summer vegetables served with one or two interesting sauces makes a really delicious and informal appetizer, which is perfect for picnics, since it can all be prepared in advance.

INGREDIENTS

2 red bell peppers, cut into strips
2 tablespoons olive oil
8 ounces new potatoes
4 ounces green beans
8 ounces baby carrots
8 ounces young asparagus
12 quail eggs
fresh herbs, to garnish
coarse salt, for sprinkling

FOR THE TAPENADE
6 ounces/1½ cups pitted
black olives
2-ounce can anchovy
fillets, drained
2 tablespoons capers
4 fluid ounces/½ cup olive oil
finely grated rind of 1 lemon
1 tablespoon brandy (optional)
freshly ground black pepper

FOR THE HERB AIOLI
5 garlic cloves, crushed
2 egg yolks
1 teaspoon Dijon mustard
2 teaspoons white wine vinegar
8 fluid ounces/1 cup light olive oil
3 tablespoons chopped mixed fresh
herbs, such as chervil, parsley
and tarragon
2 tablespoons chopped watercress
salt and freshly ground
black pepper

SERVES 6

1 To make the tapenade, finely chop the olives, anchovies and capers and beat together with the oil, lemon rind and brandy, if using. (Alternatively, lightly process the ingredients in a blender or food processor.)

2 Season with pepper and blend in a little more oil if the mixture seems very dry. Transfer to a serving dish.

3 To make the aioli, beat together the garlic, egg yolks, mustard and vinegar. Gradually blend in the olive oil, a drop at a time, whisking well until thick and smooth.

4 Stir in the mixed herbs and chopped watercress. Season with salt and pepper to taste, adding a little more vinegar if necessary. Cover with plastic wrap and chill until ready to serve.

Cook's Tip
Any leftover tapenade is delicious tossed with pasta or spread onto warm toast. If you are making this dish as part of a picnic, leave the vegetables to cool before packing in an airtight container. Pack the quail eggs in their original box.

5 Brush the peppers with oil and co[ok] on a hot barbecue or under a hot broiler until just beginning to char.

6 Cook the potatoes in a large pan of boiling, salted water until tender. Add the beans and carrots and blan[ch] for 1 minute. Add the asparagus an[d] cook for a further 30 seconds. Drai[n] the vegetables. Cook the quail eggs in boiling water for 2 minutes.

7 Arrange all the vegetables, eggs and sauces on a serving platter. Gar[nish] with fresh herbs and serve with coa[rse] salt, for sprinkling.

FALAFEL

◦ ◦ ◦

*These North African fritters are traditionally made using dried fava beans, but chickpeas are
more easily available. Serve in warmed pitta bread, with salad and garlic-flavored yogurt.*

INGREDIENTS

5 ounces/³⁄₄ cup dried chickpeas
1 large onion, coarsely chopped
2 garlic cloves, coarsely chopped
*4 tablespoons coarsely chopped
fresh parsley*
1 teaspoon cumin seeds, crushed
1 teaspoon coriander seeds, crushed
¹⁄₂ teaspoon baking powder
oil, for deep-frying
*salt and freshly ground
black pepper*

SERVES 4

1 Put the chickpeas in a large bowl and
cover with plenty of cold water. Leave
to soak overnight.

2 Drain the chickpeas and cover with
fresh water in a pan. Bring the
chickpeas to the boil, reduce the heat
and simmer for about 1¹⁄₂–2 hours, or
until soft. Drain thoroughly.

3 Place in a food processor with the
onion, garlic, parsley, cumin, coriander
and baking powder. Season to taste.
Process to form a firm paste.

4 Shape the mixture into walnut-siz
balls, using your hands, and flatten
them slightly. In a deep pan, heat
2 inches of oil until a little of the
mixture sizzles on the surface. Fry t
falafel in batches until golden. Drai
on paper towels and serve.

Cook's Tip

Although they can be fried
in advance, falafel are at their
best served warm. Wrap them in
foil or pack them in an insulated
container to take them on picnics
or keep them warm on the edge
of the barbecue until needed.

HUMMUS BI TAHINA

Blending chickpeas with garlic, lemon and oil makes a deliciously creamy purée to serve as a dip with crudités or warmed pitta bread.

INGREDIENTS

ounces/³⁄₄ cup dried chickpeas
juice of 2 lemons
2 garlic cloves, sliced
tablespoons olive oil, plus extra
to serve
¹⁄₄ pint/²⁄₃ cup tahini paste
salt and freshly ground
black pepper
flat leaf parsley, to garnish
cayenne pepper, to serve

SERVES 4–6

t the chickpeas in a large bowl and
r with plenty of cold water. Leave
ak overnight.

2 Drain the chickpeas and cover with fresh water in a pan. Bring the chickpeas to the boil, then reduce the heat and simmer for about 1¹⁄₂–2 hours or until soft. Drain thoroughly.

3 Process the chickpeas to a purée in a food processor. Add the lemon juice, garlic, oil, cayenne pepper and tahini and blend until creamy.

4 Season the chickpea purée with plenty of salt and freshly ground black pepper and transfer to a serving dish. Drizzle the purée with olive oil and sprinkle lightly with cayenne pepper. Serve the dip garnished with a few flat leaf parsley sprigs.

Cook's Tip

If you do not have time to soak dried chickpeas, canned chickpeas can be used instead. Allow two 14-ounce cans and drain them thoroughly.

TOMATO AND CHEESE TARTS

° ° °

These crisp little tartlets look impressive but are actually very easy to make.
They are best eaten fresh from the oven.

INGREDIENTS

3 sheets phyllo pastry
1 egg white
6 ounces/3/4 cup cream cheese
handful fresh basil leaves
4 small tomatoes, sliced
salt and freshly ground
black pepper

MAKES 12

1 Preheat the oven to 400°F. Brush the sheets of phyllo pastry lightly with egg white and cut into 4-inch squares.

2 Layer the squares in twos, in 12 muffin pans. Spoon the cream cheese into the pastry cases. Season with ground black pepper and top with fresh basil leaves.

3 Arrange the tomatoes on the tarts, season and bake for 10–12 minutes, until the pastry is golden. Serve warm

Cook's Tip
Use halved cherry tomatoes
for the tarts, if you like.

Tandoori Chicken Sticks

These aromatic chicken pieces are traditionally baked in the special clay oven known as a tandoor. They are equally delicious served hot or cold, and make irresistible barbecue food.

INGREDIENTS

pound boneless, skinless chicken
breast portions

FOR THE HERB YOGURT
8 fluid ounces/1 cup
plain yogurt
2 tablespoons whipping cream
1/2 cucumber, peeled, seeded and
finely chopped
1–2 tablespoons fresh chopped
cilantro or mint
salt and freshly ground
black pepper

FOR THE MARINADE
fluid ounces/3/4 cup plain yogurt
1 teaspoon garam masala
1/4 teaspoon ground cumin
1/4 teaspoon ground coriander
1/4 teaspoon cayenne pepper
1 teaspoon tomato paste
1–2 garlic cloves, finely chopped
1-inch piece of fresh root ginger,
finely chopped
grated rind and juice
of 1/2 lemon
1–2 tablespoons chopped fresh
cilantro or mint

MAKES ABOUT 25

2 To prepare the marinade, place all the ingredients in a food processor and process until smooth. Pour into a shallow dish.

3 Freeze the chicken for 5 minutes to firm it. Slice in half horizontally. Cut the slices into 3/4-inch strips and add to the marinade. Toss to coat well. Cover with plastic wrap and chill for 6–8 hours or overnight.

4 Drain the chicken pieces and arrange on a rack, scrunching up the chicken slightly to make wavy shapes. Cook on a hot barbecue for 4–5 minutes until brown and cooked through, turning once. Alternatively, arrange on a foil-lined baking sheet and cook under a hot broiler. Serve hot, threaded on toothpicks or short skewers, with the herb yogurt dip. For a picnic, cool and pack into a box.

For the herb yogurt, combine all the gredients in a bowl. Season, cover d chill until ready to serve.

HAM PIZZETTAS WITH MELTED BRIE AND MANGO

° ° °

These individual little pizzas are topped with an unusual but very successful combination of smoked ham, Brie and juicy chunks of fresh mango.

INGREDIENTS

8 ounces/2 cups white bread flour
¼ ounce envelope rapid-rise dried yeast
¼ pint/⅔ cup warm water
4 tablespoons olive oil

FOR THE TOPPING

1 ripe mango
5 ounces smoked ham, sliced extra thin
5 ounces Brie cheese, diced
12 yellow cherry tomatoes, halved
salt and freshly ground black pepper

SERVES 6

1 In a large bowl, stir together the flour and yeast, with a pinch of salt. Make a well in the center and stir in the water and 3 tablespoons of the olive oil. Stir until thoroughly mixed.

Cook's Tip

It's important to flatten out the dough rounds quite thinly and to cook them fairly slowly, or they will not cook evenly. To save time, you could use an 11-ounce packet of pizza dough mix.

2 Turn the dough out onto a lightly floured surface and knead it for about 5 minutes, or until smooth.

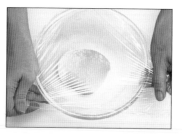

3 Return the dough to the bowl and cover it with a damp cloth or oiled plastic wrap. Leave the dough to rise in a warm place for about 30 minutes or until it is doubled in size and springy to the touch.

4 Divide the dough into six and roll each piece into a ball. Flatten out with your hand and use your knuckles to press each piece of dough to a round shape of about 6 inches in diameter, with a raised lip around the edge.

5 Halve, pit and peel the mango and cut it into small dice. Arrange with the ham on top of the pizzettas. Top with cheese and tomatoes and sprinkle with salt and ground black pepper.

6 Drizzle the remaining oil over the pizzettas. Place them on a medium-hot barbecue and cook for 8 minutes, until golden brown and crisp underneath.

OYSTER AND BACON BROCHETTES

° ° °

Six oysters per person make a good appetizer, served with the seasoned oyster liquor to trickle over the skewers. Alternatively, serve nine per person as a main course, accompanied by a salad.

INGREDIENTS

36 oysters
18 thin-cut strips rindless
fatty bacon
1 tablespoon paprika
1 teaspoon cayenne pepper
freshly ground black pepper
celery leaves and fresh red chiles,
to garnish

FOR THE SAUCE

1/2 fresh red chile, seeded and very
finely chopped
1 garlic clove, crushed
2 scallions, very finely chopped
2 tablespoons finely chopped
fresh parsley
liquor from the oysters
juice of 1/4–1/2 lemon,
to taste
salt and freshly ground
black pepper

SERVES 4–6

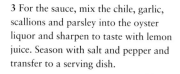

2 Push the knife in and cut the muscle, holding the shell closed. Tip the liquor into the bowl. Cut the oyster free. Discard the drained shells.

3 For the sauce, mix the chile, garlic, scallions and parsley into the oyster liquor and sharpen to taste with lemon juice. Season with salt and pepper and transfer to a serving dish.

4 Cut each bacon strip across the middle. Season the oysters lightly w paprika, cayenne and freshly groun black pepper and wrap each one in a bacon strip, then thread them on skewers. Cook on a hot barbecue f about 5 minutes, turning frequently until the bacon is crisp and brown. Garnish with celery leaves and red chiles and serve with the sauce.

1 Open the oysters over a bowl to catch their liquor for the sauce. Wrap your left hand (if you are right-handed) in a clean dish towel and cup the deep shell of each oyster in your wrapped hand. Work the point of a strong, short-bladed knife into the hinge between the shells and twist firmly.

TURKEY ROLLS WITH GAZPACHO SAUCE

This Spanish-style recipe uses quick-cooking turkey steaks, but you could also cook veal scallops in the same way.

INGREDIENTS

4 turkey breast cutlets
1 tablespoon red pesto
4 chorizo sausages
1 tablespoon olive oil
salt and freshly ground
black pepper

FOR THE GAZPACHO SAUCE
1 green bell pepper, chopped
1 red bell pepper, chopped
3-inch piece cucumber
1 medium tomato
1 garlic clove
3 tablespoons olive oil
1 tablespoon red wine vinegar

SERVES 4

o make the gazpacho sauce, place
peppers, cucumber, tomato, garlic,
blespoons of the olive oil and the
gar in a food processor and process
l almost smooth. Season to taste
salt and ground black pepper.

the turkey breast cutlets are quite
k, place them between two sheets
lastic wrap and beat them with the
of a rolling pin or a meat pounder,
latten them slightly.

3 Spread the red pesto over the turkey,
place a chorizo sausage on each piece
and roll up firmly.

4 Slice the rolls thickly and thread them
onto skewers. Brush with olive oil and
cook on a medium barbecue for about
10–12 minutes, turning once. Serve
with the gazpacho sauce.

CHICKEN, MUSHROOM AND CILANTRO PIZZA

Shiitake mushrooms add an earthy flavor to this colorful pizza, while fresh chile and chile-flavored olive oil give it a hint of spiciness. Cook the pizza on the barbecue or in the oven.

INGREDIENTS

3 tablespoons olive oil
12 ounces skinless chicken breast
fillets, cut into thin strips
8 scallions, sliced
1 fresh red chile, seeded
and chopped
1 red bell pepper, cut into strips
3 ounces fresh shiitake
mushrooms, sliced
3–4 tablespoons chopped
fresh cilantro
1 pizza base, about
10–12 incjes diameter
1 tablespoon chili oil
5 ounces mozzarella cheese
salt and freshly ground
black pepper

SERVES 3–4

2 Pour off any excess oil, then set aside to let the chicken mixture cool.

3 Stir the fresh cilantro into the cooled chicken mixture in the wok.

4 Brush all over the pizza base with chili oil.

5 Spoon over the chicken mixture a drizzle over the remaining olive oil.

1 Heat 2 tablespoons of olive oil in a wok or large frying pan. Add the chicken, scallions, chile, red pepper and mushrooms and stir-fry over a high heat for 2–3 minutes until the chicken is firm but still slightly pink inside. Season to taste.

6 Grate the mozzarella cheese and sprinkle it over the pizza base. Cook the pizza on a medium-hot barbecue for 15–20 minutes, until the base is crisp and golden and the cheese is bubbling. Serve the pizza immediately.

MEDITERRANEAN QUICHE

° ° °

*This quiche forms the ideal base for a hearty picnic feast. The strong Mediterranean flavors of
tomatoes, peppers and anchovies complement the cheese pastry beautifully.*

INGREDIENTS

FOR THE PASTRY
8 ounces/2 cups all-purpose flour
pinch of salt
pinch of dry mustard
4 ounces/1/2 cup butter, chilled
and diced
2 ounces/1/2 cup grated
Gruyère cheese
salt

FOR THE FILLING
2-ounce can anchovy fillets, drained
2 fluid ounces/1/4 cup milk
2 tablespoons French mustard
3 tablespoons olive oil
2 large Spanish onions, sliced
1 red bell pepper, very
finely sliced
3 egg yolks
12 fluid ounces/11/2 cups
heavy cream
1 garlic clove, crushed
6 ounces/11/2 cups grated sharp
Cheddar cheese
2 large tomatoes, thickly sliced
2 tablespoons chopped fresh basil,
to garnish

SERVES 6–8

2 Add the Gruyère cheese and process
again briefly. Add enough iced water to
make a stiff dough: the dough will be
ready when it forms a ball. Wrap the
dough in plastic wrap and chill in the
refrigerator for 30 minutes.

3 Meanwhile, make the filling.
Soak the anchovies in the milk for
about 20 minutes to make them less
salty. Pour off the milk. Heat the olive
oil in a frying pan and cook the onions
and red pepper until they soften.

4 In a bowl, beat the egg yolks, do▮
cream, garlic and grated Cheddar
cheese together.

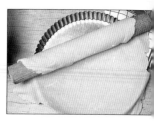

5 Preheat the oven to 400°F. Roll o▮
the chilled pastry and line a 9-inch
loose-based quiche pan. Spread the
mustard over and chill for a further
15 minutes.

6 Arrange the tomatoes in a layer i▮
pastry crust. Top with the onion an▮
pepper mixture and the anchovy fill▮
Pour over the egg mixture. Bake for
30 minutes. Serve warm or at room
temperature, sprinkled with fresh b▮

Cook's Tip
Leave the quiche in its pan if yo▮
are packing it for a picnic.

1 To make the pastry, place the flour,
salt and mustard in a food processor,
add the butter and process the mixture
until it resembles fine bread crumbs.

CHICKEN AND APRICOT PHYLLO PIE

• • •

The filling for this pie has a Middle Eastern flavor – minced chicken combined with apricots, bulgur wheat, nuts and spices. It both looks and tastes spectacular.

INGREDIENTS

3 ounces/¹/₂ cup bulghur wheat
3 ounces/6 tablespoons butter
1 onion, chopped
1 pound ground chicken
2 ounces/¹/₄ cup ready-to-eat dried
apricots, finely chopped
1 ounce/¹/₄ cup blanched
almonds, chopped
1 teaspoon ground cinnamon
¹/₂ teaspoon ground allspice
2 fluid ounces/¹/₄ cup strained
plain yogurt
2 tablespoons chopped fresh chives
2 tablespoons chopped fresh parsley
6 large sheets phyllo pastry
salt and freshly ground
black pepper

SERVES 6

1 Preheat the oven to 400°F. Put the bulghur wheat in a large bowl with ¹/₂ cup boiling water. leave the wheat to soak for 5 minutes, until the water is absorbed.

2 Heat 2 tablespoons of the butter in a pan and cook the onion and chicken until pale golden. Stir in the apricots, almonds and bulghur wheat and cook for a further 2 minutes. Remove from the heat and stir in the cinnamon, allspice, yogurt, half the chives and the parsley. Season to taste.

3 Melt the remaining butter. Unroll the phyllo pastry and cut into 10-inch round shapes. Keep the pastry rounds covered with a clean, damp dish towel to prevent them from drying out.

4 Line a 9-inch loose-based quiche pan with three pastry rounds, brushing each one with melted butter as you layer them. Spoon in the chicken mixture and cover with three more pastry rounds, brushed with butter as before.

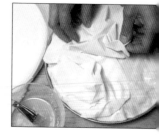

5 Crumple the remaining rounds a[nd] place on top of the pie. Brush with remaining butter. Bake the pie for 30 minutes, until the pastry is golde[n] brown and crisp. Serve hot or cold, garnished with the remaining chives[.]

CHICKEN WITH FRESH HERBS AND GARLIC

A whole chicken can be roasted on a spit on the barbecue. This marinade keeps the flesh moist and delicious, and the fresh herbs add summery flavors.

INGREDIENTS

1/2 pounds free-range chicken
finely grated rind and juice of
1 lemon
1 garlic clove, crushed
2 tablespoons olive oil
2 fresh thyme sprigs
2 fresh sage sprigs
6 tablespoons sweet
butter, softened
salt and freshly ground
black pepper

SERVES 4

on the chicken well. Mix the
rind and juice, crushed garlic
ive oil together and pour them
he chicken. Leave to marinate
refrigerator for at least 2 hours.

Cook's Tip

oasting the chicken in the oven,
reheat the oven to 450°F and
educe the heat to 375°F after
minutes. If you are roasting a
hicken to serve cold, cooking
it in foil helps to keep it
cculent – open the foil for the
last 20 minutes to brown
the skin, then close it as the
chicken cools.

2 Place the herbs in the cavity of the
bird and smear the butter over the skin.
Season well. Cook the chicken on a spit
on the barbecue for 1½–1¾ hours,
basting with the marinade, until the
juices run clear when the thigh is
pierced with a skewer. Leave the bird
to rest for 15 minutes before carving.

PEPPER STEAK

• • •

*This easy, rather indulgent, bistro classic can be put together in a matter of minutes for an
intimate summer supper in the garden. The creamy sauce helps to balance the heat of the pepper.*

INGREDIENTS

2 tablespoons black peppercorns
2 tenderloin or boneless sirloin
steaks, about 8 ounces each
½ ounce/1 tablespoons butter
2 teaspoons olive oil
3 tablespoons brandy
¼ pint/⅔ cup
whipping cream
1 garlic clove, finely chopped
salt

SERVES 2

1 Place the black peppercorns in
a sturdy plastic bag. Crush the
peppercorns with a rolling pin or
meat pounder until they are crushed
to medium-coarse pepper.

2 Put the steaks on a chopping bo
and trim away any excess fat, usin
sharp kitchen knife. Press the pep
firmly onto both sides of the meat
to coat it completely.

3 Melt the butter with the olive oi
in a heavy frying pan over a medi
high heat. Add the meat and cook
for 6–7 minutes, turning once, un
cooked to your liking. Transfer th
steaks to a warmed platter or plat
and cover to keep warm.

4 Pour in the brandy to deglaze th
frying pan. Bring the brandy to th
and cook until it has reduced by h
scraping the base of the frying pan
then add the whipping cream and
garlic. Bubble gently over a low-
medium heat for about 4 minutes,
until the cream has reduced by ab
one-third. Stir any accumulated ju
from the meat into the sauce, tast
add salt to taste. Serve the steaks
with the sauce.

PORK WITH MARSALA AND JUNIPER

· · ·

Sicilian marsala wine gives savory dishes a rich, fruity and alcoholic tang. The pork is fully complemented by the flavor of the sauce in this quick and luxurious dish.

INGREDIENTS

1 ounce dried cèpe or porcini
mushrooms
4 pork scallops
2 teaspoons balsamic vinegar
8 garlic cloves
½ ounce/1 tablespoons butter
3 tablespoons marsala
several rosemary sprigs
10 juniper berries, crushed
salt and freshly ground
black pepper

SERVES 4

the dried mushrooms in a
bowl and just cover with hot
. Leave to stand for 20 minutes
ow the mushrooms to soak.

2 Brush the pork with 1 teaspoon of
the vinegar and season with salt and
pepper. Put the garlic cloves in a pan of
boiling water and cook for 10 minutes,
until soft. Drain and set aside.

3 Melt the butter in a large frying pan.
Add the pork and cook quickly until
browned on the underside. Turn the
meat over and cook for 1 minute more.

4 Add the marsala, rosemary sprigs,
drained mushrooms, 4 tablespoons of
the mushroom water, the garlic cloves,
juniper berries and the remaining
balsamic vinegar.

5 Simmer gently for 3–5 minutes, until
the pork is cooked through. Season
lightly and serve hot.

STUFFED ROAST LOIN OF PORK

○ ○ ○

This recipe uses fruit and nuts as a stuffing for roast pork in the Catalan style. It is full of flavor and is very good served cold, making an excellent centerpiece for a summer buffet or a picnic.

INGREDIENTS

4 tablespoons olive oil
1 onion, finely chopped
2 garlic cloves, chopped
2 ounces/1 cup fresh bread crumbs
4 ready-to-eat dried figs, chopped
8 pitted green olives, chopped
4 tablespoons sliced almonds
1 tablespoon lemon juice
1 tablespoon chopped fresh parsley
1 egg yolk
2 pounds boned loin of pork
salt and freshly ground
black pepper

SERVES 4

1 Preheat the oven to 400°F, or prepare the barbecue. Heat 3 tablespoons of the oil in a pan, add the onion and garlic, and cook gently until softened. Remove the pan from the heat and stir in the bread crumbs, figs, olives, almonds, lemon juice, chopped fresh parsley and egg yolk. Season to taste with salt and ground black pepper.

2 Remove any string from the pork and unroll the belly flap, cutting away any excess fat or meat to enable you to do so. Spread the stuffing over the flat piece and roll it up, starting from the thick side. Tie at intervals with string.

3 Pour the remaining olive oil into a roasting pan and put in the pork, or arrange on the spit of the barbecue. Roast for 1 hour and 15 minutes, or until the juices run clear from the meat.

4 Remove the pork from the oven the spit and, if serving hot, let it re 10 minutes before carving into thi slices. If serving cold, wrap the me foil to keep it moist until you carv

LAMB CASSEROLE WITH GARLIC AND BEANS

. . .

This recipe has a Spanish influence and makes a substantial meal, served with potatoes.
Fava beans add color and texture to the dish.

INGREDIENTS

3 tablespoons olive oil
3–3½ pounds lamb fillet, cut
into 2-inch cubes
1 large onion, chopped
5 large garlic cloves, unpeeled
1 bay leaf
1 teaspoon paprika
fluid ounces/½ cup dry sherry
4 ounces shelled fresh or
frozen fava beans
blespoons chopped fresh parsley
salt and freshly ground
black pepper

SERVES 6

3 Add the garlic, bay leaf, paprika and sherry. Season to taste and bring to the boil. Cover and simmer gently for 1½ hours, until tender.

4 Add the fava beans to the casserole and simmer for a further 10 minutes. Stir in the chopped fresh parsley just before serving.

at 2 tablespoons olive oil in a large proof casserole. Add half the meat rown well on all sides. Transfer late. Brown the rest of the meat same way and remove from asserole.

at the remaining oil in the pan, he onion and cook for about nutes until soft. Return the meat casserole.

RED MULLET WITH LAVENDER

Cook a fish dish with a difference by adding lavender to red mullet for a wonderful aromatic flavor. Sprinkle some lavender flowers on the coals too, to give a delightful perfumed ambience.

INGREDIENTS

*4 red mullet or snapper, scaled,
gutted and cleaned
2 tablespoons olive oil*

*FOR THE MARINADE
3 tablespoons fresh lavender
flowers or 1 tablespoon dried
lavender leaves, coarsely chopped
coarsely chopped rind of 1 lemon
4 scallions, chopped
salt and freshly ground
black pepper*

SERVES 4

1 Place the fish in a shallow dish. Mix the ingredients for the marinade and pour over the fish. Cover with plastic wrap and leave in the refrigerator to marinate for 3 hours.

2 Remove the fish from the marinade and brush it with olive oil. Cook the fish on a hot barbecue for about 10–15 minutes, turning once and basting with olive oil as it cooks.

SALMON STEAKS WITH OREGANO SALSA

∘ ∘ ∘

*This combination of salmon with piquant tomato works incredibly well. The barbecue gives the
salmon an exquisite flavor. Served hot or cold, this is an ideal dish for a summer lunch.*

INGREDIENTS

1 tablespoon butter
4 salmon steaks, about
8 ounces each
fluid ounces/¹/₂ cup white wine
freshly ground black pepper

FOR THE SALSA
2 teaspoons chopped fresh
oregano, plus sprigs to garnish
4 scallions
ounces ripe tomatoes, peeled
ablespoons extra virgin olive oil
¹/₂ teaspoon superfine sugar
1 tablespoon tomato paste

SERVES 4

1 Butter four squares of double-
thickness baking foil. Put a salmon
steak on each and add a little wine and
a grinding of black pepper. Wrap the
salmon steaks loosely in the squares,
sealing the edges securely. Cook on a
medium-hot barbecue for 10 minutes,
until just tender. If serving the steaks
hot, keep them warm.

2 Put the chopped fresh oregano in a
food processor and chop it very finely.
Add the scallions, tomatoes and
remaining salsa ingredients. Pulse until
chopped but not a smooth purée.

3 Serve the salmon hot or cold with the
salsa, garnished with a few fresh sprigs
of oregano.

HERBAL PUNCH

∘ ∘ ∘

This refreshing party drink will have people coming back for more, and it is an original non-alcoholic choice for drivers and children.

INGREDIENTS

³/₄ pint/2 cups clear honey
7 pints water
³/₄ pint/2 cups freshly squeezed
lemon juice
3 tablespoons fresh rosemary
leaves, plus extra to decorate
3¹/₂ pounds/8 cups
sliced strawberries
³/₄ pint/2 cups freshly squeezed
lime juice
3 pints/7¹/₂ cups sparkling
mineral water
ice cubes
3–4 scented geranium leaves

SERVES 30 PLUS

1 Combine the honey, 4 cups water, one-eighth of the lemon juice and the fresh rosemary leaves in a pan. Bring to the boil, stirring, until the honey is dissolved. Remove from the heat and leave to stand for about 5 minutes. Strain into a large punch bowl and set aside to cool.

2 Press the strawberries through a strainer into the punch bowl, add rest of the water and lemon juice, the lime juice and sparkling mineral water. Stir gently to combine the ingredients. Add the ice cubes just 5 minutes before serving, and float the geranium and rosemary leaves on the surface.

MINT CUP

Mint is a perennially popular flavoring, and this delicate cup is a wonderful mixture with an intriguing taste. It is the perfect summer drink to serve with meals outdoors.

INGREDIENTS

handful fresh mint leaves
1 tablespoon sugar
crushed ice
1 tablespoon lemon juice
6 fluid ounces/³/4 cup
grapefruit juice
1 pint/2¹/2 cups chilled
tonic water
mint sprigs and lemon slices,
to decorate

SERVES 4–6

1 Crush the mint leaves with the sugar and put into a pitcher. Fill the pitcher to the top with crushed ice.

2 Add the lemon juice, grapefruit juice and tonic water. Stir gently to combine the ingredients and decorate with mint sprigs and slices of lemon.

STRAWBERRY AND MINT CHAMPAGNE
· · ·

This is a simple concoction that makes a bottle of champagne or sparkling white wine go much further. It tastes very special on a hot summer's evening.

INGREDIENTS
1¼ pounds strawberries
6–8 fresh mint leaves
1 bottle champagne or sparkling
white wine
fresh mint sprigs, to decorate

SERVES 4–6

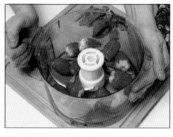

2 Put through a fine strainer into a large bowl. Half fill a glass with the mixture and top up with champagne or sparkling wine. Decorate with a sprig of fresh mint.

1 Purée the strawberries and fresh mint leaves in a food processor.

MELON, GINGER AND BORAGE CUP
· · ·

Melon and ginger complement each other magnificently. If you prefer, you can leave out the powdered ginger – the result is milder but equally delicious.

INGREDIENTS
½ large honeydew melon
1¾ pints/4 cups ginger ale
powdered ginger, to taste
borage sprigs with flowers,
to decorate

SERVES 6–8

1 Discard the seeds from the half melon and scoop the flesh into a food processor. Blend the melon to a purée.

2 Pour the purée into a large pitcher and top up with ginger ale. Add powdered ginger to taste. Pour into glasses and decorate with borage.

SENSATIONAL
SALADS

o   o   o

In these health-conscious days and with the increasing
availability of exotic vegetables and produce from around the
world, salads have become the fashion item in restaurants and
on dining tables everywhere. This second part of the book is
devoted to a mouthwatering selection of salads – from
the subtle flavor combination of goat cheese and figs to the
flamboyant luxury of fresh lobster, and from the charming
simplicity of salad leaves combined with fresh herbs to the
carnival colors of brown rice and tropical fruit.

This section starts with a detailed guide to ingredients –
vegetables, fruit, salad leaves, herbs, spices, vinegars, oils and
flavorings. The introductory pages also include step-by-step
recipes for the most popular salad dressings and a time-saving
selection of instant dressings and dips.

The recipes that follow cover all courses, occasions and
seasons, from light meals and appetizers to glamorous dishes
for special occasions, and from raw and cooked side salads to
main meals for a midweek family supper. The final chapter
features fruit salads, and you may be surprised to discover how
many different ways this popular dessert can be prepared.

Salads add refreshing flavors and textures to any meal, as well
as an appetizing splash of color, but they are also a valuable
source of vitamins, minerals and other nutrients – all year
around. Nothing could make it easier to eat five portions of
vegetables and fruit each day, which is recommended by
nutritionists, than this mouthwatering collection of recipes.

SALAD VEGETABLES

◦ ◦ ◦

The salad vegetable is any type of vegetable that earns its keep in a salad by virtue of freshness and flavor. Vegetables for a salad can be raw or lightly cooked. If cooked, they are best served at room temperature to bring out their full flavor. Here is a selection of the most commonly used and popular salad vegetables.

Avocado

This has a smooth, buttery flesh when ripe and is an asset to many salads, of which guacamole is perhaps the best known. Avocados can also be served on their own as an appetizer, with a simple, light vinaigrette dressing or a spoonful of lemon mayonnaise, or even just a squeeze of lemon juice and salt.

Baby Corn Cobs

Baby corn cobs can be eaten whole, may be lightly cooked or raw, and should be served warm or at room temperature for maximum flavor.

Carrots

These should be young, slender and sweet to taste. Either cooked or raw, they bring flavor and color to a salad.

Celery

A useful salad vegetable, celery is grown all year around for its robust, earthy flavor. The crisp stems should be neither stringy nor tough. Celery partners well with cooked ham, apple and walnut in Waldorf salad and is also used as a crudité with dips.

Cucumbers

A common salad ingredient that turns up, invited or not, in salad bowls everywhere. The quality of this vegetable is best appreciated in strongly flavored salads.

Fennel

The bulb (or Florence) variety has a strong, aniseed flavor and looks like a squat head of celery. Because the flavor can be dominant, it may be blanched in boiling water for 6 minutes before use in a salad.

Garlic

Strong to taste, garlic is essential to the robust cooking of South America, the Mediterranean and Asia. It should be used carefully, as it can mask other flavors, but it is a vital part of salad preparation. To impart a very gentle hint of garlic rub around the inside of your salad bowl with a cut clove. Another way to moderate the strength of fresh garlic is to store a few crushed cloves in a bottle of olive oil, and use the oil sparingly in dressings.

Green Beans

The varieties are too numerous to mention here, but they all have their merits as salad vegetables. To appreciate the sweet flavor of young tender green beans, cook them for 6 minutes and then refresh immediately under cold running water so that the crispness and color are retained. An essential ingredient of salade Niçoise, green beans are an ideal crudité and also partner well with a spicy tomato sauce.

Mushrooms

These provide a rich tone to many salads and are eaten both raw and cooked. The oyster mushroom, which grows wild but is also cultivated, has a fine flavor and texture. White mushrooms are widely available and are often used raw, thinly sliced, in a mixed salad.

Cremini mushrooms are similar to white mushrooms but have slightly more flavor.

Onions

Several varieties are suited to salads. The strongest is the small, brown onion, which should be chopped finely and used sparingly. Less strong are the large, white Spanish and Bermuda onions, which have a sweeter, milder flavor and may be used coarsely chopped. Red onions are also sweet and mild in flavor and add a colorful touch to salads.

Potatoes

A staple carbohydrate ingredient to add bulk to a salad or provide a main element. Waxy varieties are the most suitable for potato salads, and some types have been specially developed as salad potatoes.

Scallions

These have a milder flavor than the common onion and give a gentle bite to many popular salads.

Tomatoes

Technically a fruit rather than a vegetable, tomatoes are valued for their flavor and color. Dwarf varieties usually ripen more quickly than large ones, have a better flavor and texture and are often less watery.

Zucchini

These can be bitter to the taste and are usually cooked before being combined with other young vegetables. Smooth in texture when cooked, they blend very well with tomatoes, eggplant, bell peppers and different kinds of onions. Use baby zucchini for a sweeter flavor if you want to serve raw zucchini as a crudité.

SALAD FRUIT

· · ·

The contents of the fruit bowl offer endless possibilities for sweet and savory salads.

Apples
This versatile fruit offers a unique flavor and crunchy texture to both sweet and savory salads.

Apricots
You can use apricots raw, dried or lightly poached.

Bananas
These bring a special richness to fruit salads, although their flavor can often interfere with more delicate fruit.

Blackberries
With a very short season, wild blackberries have more flavor than cultivated.

Blueberries
These tight-skinned berries combine well with the sharpness of fresh oranges.

Cherries
Cherries should be firm and glossy and are a deliciously sweet and colorful ingredient in many kinds of fruit salad.

Cranberries
Too sharp to eat raw but very good for cooking.

Dates
Fresh dates are sweet and juicy, dried ones have a more intense flavor. Both kinds work well in fresh fruit salads.

Figs
Green- or purple-skinned fruit, with sweet, pinkish-red flesh. Eat whole or peeled.

Gooseberries
Dessert types can be eaten raw, but cooking varieties are more widely available.

Grapefruit
These can have yellow, green or pink flesh; the pink-fleshed or ruby varieties are the sweetest.

Grapes
Large Muscat varieties, in season from late summer to autumn, are the most coveted and also the most expensive.

Kiwi Fruit
Available all year around.

Kumquats
Tiny relatives of the orange, they can be eaten raw or cooked.

Lemons and Limes
Both these indispensable citrus fruits are used for flavor, and to prevent fruit, such as apples, pears and avocados, from turning brown.

Lychees
A small fruit with a hard pink skin and sweet, juicy flesh.

Mangoes
Tropical fruit with an exotic flavor and golden-orange flesh, that is wonderful in sweet or savory salads.

Melons
These grow in abundance from mid- to late summer and provide a resource of freshness and flavor. Melon is at its most delicious served icy cold.

Nectarines
A relative of the peach with a smoother skin.

Oranges
At their best during winter, they can be segmented and added to sweet and savory salads.

Papaya
These fruits of the tropics have a distinctive, sweet flavor. When ripe they are yellow–green.

Peaches
Choose white peaches for the sweetest flavor, and yellow for a more aromatic taste.

Pears
Perfect for savory salads, and with strong blue cheese and toasted pecan nuts.

Physalis
These small, fragrant, pleasantly tart orange berries are wrapped in a paper cape.

Pineapples
Ripe pineapples resist firm pressure in the hand and have a sweet smell.

Plums
There are many dessert and cooking varieties.

Raspberries
Much-coveted soft fruits that partner well with ripe mango, passion fruit and strawberries.

Rhubarb
Technically a vegetable, it is too tart to eat raw.

Star Fruit
When sliced, this makes a pretty shape perfect for garnishes.

Strawberries
A popular summer fruit, especially served with cream.

LETTUCES AND LEAVES

o o o

One particular aspect of lettuce that sets it apart from any other vegetable is that you can buy it in only one form – fresh.

Lettuce has been cultivated for thousands of years. In Egyptian times it was sacred to the fertility god Min. It was then considered a powerful aphrodisiac, yet for the Greeks and the Romans it was thought to have quite the opposite effect, making one sleepy and generally soporific. Chemists today confirm that lettuce contains a hypnotic similar to opium, and in herbal remedies lettuce is recommended for insomniacs.

There are hundreds of different varieties of lettuce. Today an increasing choice is available so that the salad bowl can become a riot of color, taste and texture with no other ingredient than a selection of leaves.

Boston

These are the classic round lettuces. They have a pale heart and floppy, loosely packed leaves. They have a pleasant flavor as long as they are fresh. Choose the lettuce with the best heart by picking it up at the bottom and gently squeezing to check there is a firm center. Many more varieties are now available.

Lollo Rosso

Both lollo rosso and lollo biondo are similar in shape, but the latter is a paler green without any purple edges. Both are non-hearting lettuce. Although they do not have a lot of flavor, they look superb and are often used to form a nest of leaves on which to place the rest of a salad. They hold a large amount of dressing.

Romaine

The romaine lettuce was known in antiquity. It has two names, romaine, used in the United States and France, and Cos, derived from the Greek island where it was found. Romaine is considered to have the best flavor and is the correct lettuce for use in the famous American Caesar salad.

Escarole

This is one of the more robust lettuces in terms of flavor and texture. Like the closely related frisée, escarole has a distinctive bitter flavor. Served with a judicious mixture of other leaves and a well-flavored dressing, escarole and frisée will give your salad a pleasant "bite."

Oak Leaf Lettuce

Also known as feuille de chêne and salad bowl, oak leaf lettuce, together with lollo rosso and lollo biondo, is another member of the loosehead lettuce group. Oak leaf lettuce has a very gentle flavor. It is an extremely decorative leaf and makes a beautiful addition to any salad, and a lovely garnish.

Bibb

These attractive little lettuces look like something between a baby cos and a tightly-furled butterhead. They have firm hearts and quite a distinct flavor. They have tight centers and can be sliced whole, and the quarters used for carrying slivers of smoked fish or anchovy as a simple appetizer.

Chinese Cabbage

This has pale green, crinkly leaves with long, wide, white ribs. Its shape is a little like a very fat head of celery, which gives rise to another of its names, celery cabbage. It has a crunchy texture, and since it is available all year around, it makes a useful winter salad component.

Radicchio

This is a variety developed from Belgian endive. It looks like a lettuce with deep wine-red leaves and cream ribs and owes its splendid foliage to careful shading from the light. If it is grown in the dark, the leaves are marbled pink. Its bitter flavor contrasts well with green salads.

Mâche

Also known as corn salad this is a popular winter leaf that does not actually belong to the lettuce family, but is terrific in salads. Called lamb's lettuce in England, mâche has small, attractive, dark green, delicate leaves and grows in pretty little sprigs. Its flavor is mild and nutty.

Watercress

Perhaps the most robustly flavored of all the salad ingredients, a handful of watercress is all you need to perk up a dull or boring salad. It has a distinctive "raw" flavor, peppery and slightly pungent, and this, together with its shiny leaves, make it a popular and attractive garnish.

Arugula

This has a wonderful peppery flavor and is excellent in a mixed green salad. It was eaten by the Greeks and Romans as an aphrodisiac. Since it has such a striking flavor a little goes a long way; just a few leaves will transform a green salad and liven up a sandwich.

HERBS

. . .

For as long as salads have drawn on the qualities of fresh produce, sweet herbs have played an important part in providing individual character and flavor. When herbs are used in a salad, they should be as full of life as the salad leaves they accompany. Dried herbs are no substitute for fresh ones and should be kept for cooked dishes, such as casseroles. Salad herbs are distinguished by their ability to release flavor without lengthy cooking.

Most salad herbs belong finely chopped in salad dressings and marinades, while the robust flavors of rosemary, thyme and fennel branches can be used on the barbecue to impart a smoky herb flavor. Ideally salad herbs should be picked just before use, but if you cannot use them immediately keep them in water to retain their freshness. Parsley, mint and cilantro will keep for up to a week in this way if also covered with a plastic bag and placed in the refrigerator.

Basil

Remarkable for its fresh, pungent flavor unlike that of any other herb, basil is widely used in Mediterranean salads, especially Italian recipes. It has a special affinity with tomatoes. Basil leaves are tender and delicate and should be gently torn or snipped with scissors, rather than chopped with a knife, which will bruise them.

Chives

These belong to the onion family and have a mild onion flavor. The slender, green stems and soft mauve flowers are both edible. Chives are an indispensable flavoring for potato salads.

Cilantro

The chopped leaves of this pungent, distinctively flavored herb are popular in Middle Eastern and Asian salads.

Lavender

This soothingly fragrant herb is edible and may be used in both sweet and savory salads, because it combines well with thyme, garlic, honey and orange.

Mint

This much-loved, easy-to-grow herb is widely used in Greek and Middle Eastern salads, such as tzatziki and tabbouleh. It is also a popular addition to fruit salads. Garden mint is the most common variety; others include spearmint, pineapple mint and the round-leafed apple mint.

Above: Clockwise from top left; thyme, cilantro, parsley, chives, lavender, rose, mint and basil.

Parsley

Flat and curly leaf parsley are both used for their fresh, green flavor. Flat leaf parsley is said to have a stronger taste. Freshly chopped parsley is used by the handful in salads and dressings.

Rose

Although it is not technically a herb, the sweet-scented rose can be used to flavor fresh fruit salads. It combines well with blackberries and raspberries.

Thyme

An asset to salads featuring rich, earthy flavors, this herb has a penetrating flavor.

SPICES

. . .

Spices are the aromatic seasonings found in the seed, bark, fruit and sometimes flowers of certain plants and trees. Spices are highly valued for their warm, inviting flavors, and thankfully their price is relatively low. The flavor of a spice is contained in the volatile oils of the seed, bark or fruit; so, like herbs, spices should be used as fresh as possible. Whole spices keep better than ground ones, which tend to lose their freshness within 3–4 months.

Not all spices are suitable for salad-making, although many allow us to explore the flavors of other cultures. Some of the recipes in this book use curry spices, but only in moderation so as not to spoil the delicate salad flavors.

Caraway
These savory-sweet-tasting seeds are widely used in German and Austrian cooking and feature strongly in many Jewish dishes. The small ribbed seeds are similar in appearance and taste to cumin. The flavor combines especially well with German mustard in a dressing for frankfurter salad.

Cayenne pepper
A type of chili powder, this is the dried and finely ground fruit of a very hot chile pepper. It is an important seasoning in South American cooking and is often used when seasoning fish and seafood. Cayenne pepper can be blended with paprika if it is too hot and should be used with care.

Celery salt
A combination of ground celery seed and salt, this is used for seasoning vegetables and has a special affinity with carrots.

Cumin seeds
Often associated with Asian and North African cooking, cumin can be bought ground or as small, slender seeds. It combines well with coriander seeds.

Curry paste
Prepared curry paste consists of a blend of Indian spices preserved in oil. It may be added to dressings, and is particularly useful in this respect for showing off the sweet qualities of fish and shellfish.

Paprika
This spice is made from a variety of sweet red pepper. It is mild in flavor, and adds color.

Pepper
Undoubtedly the most popular spice used in the West, pepper features in the cooking of almost every nation. Peppercorns can be

Above: Flavorsome additions to salads include (clockwise from top left) celery salt, caraway seeds, curry paste, saffron threads, peppercorns and cayenne pepper.

white, black, green or red and should always be freshly milled rather than bought already ground. Red or pink peppercorns are not actually a pepper, but a South American berry.

Saffron
The world's most expensive spice, made from the dried stigma of a crocus, real saffron has a tobacco-rich smell and gives a sweet yellow tint to liquids used for cooking. It can be used in creamy dressings and brings out the richness of fish and shellfish dishes. There are many powdered imitations, which provide color without the flavor of the real thing.

OILS, VINEGARS AND FLAVORINGS

• • •

Oils

Oil is the main ingredient of most dressings and provides an important richness to salads. Neutral oils, such as sunflower, safflower or peanut, are ideally used as a background for stronger oils. Sesame, walnut and hazelnut oils are the strongest and should be used sparingly. Olive oil is prized for its clarity of flavor and clean richness. The most significant producers of olive oil are Italy, France, Spain and Greece. These and other countries produce two main grades of olive oil: estate-grown extra-virgin olive oil; and semi-fine olive oil, which is of a good, basic standard.

Olive oils

Oils from different countries have distinctive characteristics.

French olive oils are subtly flavored and provide a well-balanced lightness to dressings.

Greek olive oils are typically strong in character. They are often green with a thick texture and are unsuitable for mayonnaise.

Italian olive oils are noted for their vigorous Mediterranean flavors. Tuscan oils are noted for their well-rounded, spicy flavor. Sicilian oils tend to be lighter in texture, although they are often stronger in flavor.

Spanish olive oils are typically fruity and often have a nutty quality with a slight bitterness.

Nut oils

Hazelnut and walnut oils are valued for their strong, nutty flavor. Tasting richly of the nuts from which they are pressed, both are usually blended with neutral oils for salad dressings.

Seed oils

Peanut oil, safflower and sunflower oil are valued for their clean, neutral flavor.

Salad Flavorings

Capers

These are the pickled flower buds of a bush native to the Mediterranean. Their strong, sharp flavor is well suited to richly flavored salads.

Lemon and lime juice

The juice of lemons and limes is used to impart a clean acidity to oil dressings. They should be used in moderation.

Mustard

Mustard has a tendency to bring out the flavor of other ingredients. It also acts as an emulsifier in dressings and allows oil and vinegar to merge for a short period of time. The most popular mustards for use in salads are French, especially Dijon, German, English and whole-grain.

Above: Top left to right: Italian virgin olive oil, Spanish olive oil, Italian olive oil, safflower oil, hazelnut oil, walnut oil, peanut oil, French olive oil, Italian olive oil, white wine vinegar. Left to right bottom; lemon, olives, limes, capers and mustard.

Olives

Black and green olives belong in salads with a Mediterranean flavor. Black olives are generally sweeter and juicier than green ones.

Vinegars

White wine vinegar

This should be used in moderation to balance the richness of an oil. A good-quality white wine vinegar will serve most purposes.

Balsamic vinegar

Sweeter than other vinegars, only a few drops of balsamic vinegar are necessary to enhance a salad or dressing. It is also a good substitute for lemon juice. The best types are more than 12 years old.

MAKING HERBED OILS AND VINEGARS

∘ ∘ ∘

Many herbed oils and vinegars are available commercially, but you can very easily make your own. Pour the oil or vinegar into a sterilized jar and add your flavoring. Allow to steep for 2 weeks, then strain and decant into an attractive bottle that has also been sterilized properly. Add a seal and an identifying label.

Flavored vinegars should be used within 3 months, and herb-flavored oils within 10 days. Fresh herbs for flavoring oils and vinegars should be rinsed clean and patted completely dry with kitchen paper before you use them.

Tarragon Vinegar

Steep tarragon in cider vinegar, then decant. Insert 2 or 3 long sprigs of tarragon into the bottle.

Rosemary Vinegar

Steep a sprig of fresh rosemary in red wine vinegar, then decant. Pour the vinegar into a sterilized, dry bottle and add a few long stems of rosemary as decoration.

Lemon and Lime Vinegar

Steep strips of lemon and lime rind in white wine vinegar, then decant. Pour into a sterilized, clean bottle and add fresh strips of rind for color.

Raspberry Vinegar

Pour vinegar into a pan with 1 tablespoon of pickling spices and heat gently for 5 minutes. Pour the hot mixture over the raspberries in a bowl and then add 2 fresh sprigs of lemon thyme. Cover and leave the mixture to steep for two days in a cool, dark place. Strain the liquid and pour the flavored vinegar into a sterilized bottle and seal.

Dill and Lemon Oil

Steep a handful of fresh dill and a large strip of lemon rind in virgin olive oil, then decant. Use for salads containing fish or shellfish.

Mediterranean Herb Oil

Steep fresh rosemary, thyme and marjoram in virgin or extra virgin olive oil, then decant.

Basil and Chili Oil

Steep basil and 3 chiles in virgin olive oil, then decant. Add to tomato and mozzarella salads.

Warning

There is some evidence that oils containing fresh herbs and spices can grow harmful molds, especially once the bottle has been opened and the contents are not fully covered by the oil. To protect against this, it is recommended that the herbs and spices are removed once their flavor has passed into the oil.

From left: Tarragon Vinegar, Rosemary Vinegar, Raspberry Vinegar, Lemon and Lime Vinegar.

VEGETABLE PREPARATION

Shredding Cabbage

Cabbage features in many salad recipes, such as coleslaw, and this method for shredding can be used for all varieties.

1 Use a large knife to cut the cabbage into quarters.

2 Cut the hard core from each quarter and discard; this part is not really edible when raw.

3 Slice each quarter to form fine shreds. Shredded cabbage will keep for several hours in the refrigerator, but do not dress it until you are ready to serve.

Chopping an Onion

Chopped onions are used in many recipes and, whether they are very finely or coarsely chopped, the method is the same; just vary the gap between cuts.

1 Cut off the stalk end of the onion and cut in half through the root, leaving the root intact. Remove the skin and place the halved onion, cut-side down, on the board. Make lengthwise vertical cuts into the onion, taking care not to cut right through to the root.

2 Make two or three horizontal cuts from the stalk end through to the root, but without cutting all the way through. Space the cuts at about ¼-inch intervals.

3 Turn the onion onto its side. Cut the onion across from the stalk end to the root, again at about ¼-inch intervals. The onion will fall away in small squares. Cut further apart for larger squares.

Preparing Garlic

Don't worry if you don't have a garlic press: instead, try this method, which gives wonderful, juicy results.

1 Break off the clove of garlic, place the flat side of a large knife on top and strike with your fist. Remove all the papery outer skin. Begin by finely chopping the clove.

2 Sprinkle over a little table salt and, using the flat side of a large knife blade, work the salt into the garlic, until the clove softens and releases its juices. Use the garlic pulp as required.

Preparing Chiles

Chiles add a distinct flavor, but remove the fiery-hot seeds.

1 Always protect your hands, as chiles can irritate the skin; wear rubber gloves and never rub your eyes after handling chiles. Halve the chile lengthwise and remove and discard the seeds.

2 Slice, finely chop and use as required. Wash the knife and board thoroughly in hot, soapy water. Always wash your hands thoroughly after preparing chiles.

Peeling Tomatoes

If you have the time, peel tomatoes before adding them to dressings. This avoids including rolled-up, tough pieces of tomato skin.

Make a cross in each tomato with a sharp knife and place in a bowl.

Pour over enough boiling water to cover, and leave to stand for about 30 seconds. The skins should start to come away. Slightly unripe tomatoes may take a little longer.

Drain the tomatoes and peel off the skin with a sharp knife. Don't leave the tomatoes in the boiling water for too long.

Chopping Herbs

Chop fresh herbs just before you use them.

1 Remove the leaves and place on a clean, dry board.

2 Chop the herbs, as finely or as coarsely as required, by holding the tip of the blade of a large, sharp knife on the board and rocking the handle up and down.

Cutting Julienne Strips

Julienne strips of carrots, celery, cucumber and other vegetables make attractive garnishes and salad ingredients.

1 Peel the vegetable and use a large knife to cut it into 2-inch lengths. Cut a thin sliver from one side of the first piece so that it sits flat on the board.

2 Cut each piece into thin slices lengthwise. Stack the slices of vegetable and then cut through them again to make fine strips.

Preparing Scallions

Scallions make such a crisp and tasty addition to salads that they are worth the effort of preparation.

1 Trim off the root of the scallion with a sharp knife. Peel away any damaged or tough leaves.

2 For an intense flavor and an attractive green color cut the dark green part into thin sticks.

3 For a milder flavor just use the white part of the scallion, discard the root and slice thinly on a slight diagonal.

FRUIT PREPARATION

· · ·

Citrus Fruit

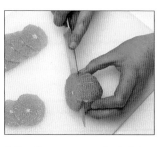

1 For slices, cut across the fruit in slices with a serrated knife.

1 To peel, cut a slice from the top and from the base. Set the fruit base down on a work surface.

2 Cut off the peel lengthwise in thick strips. Remove the colored rind and all the white pith (which has a bitter taste). Cut following the curve of the fruit.

1 To remove the thin, colored rind, use a vegetable peeler to shave off the rind in wide strips, taking none of the white pith. Use these strips whole or cut them into fine shreds with a sharp knife.

2 Alternatively, rub the fruit against the fine holes of a metal grater, turning the fruit so that you take just the rind and not the white pith. Or use a special tool, called a citrus zester, to take fine threads of rind. The shallow angle of the blade cuts into the outer surface of the rind only. Finely chop the threads for tiny pieces.

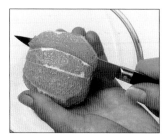

1 For segments, hold the fruit over a bowl to catch the juice. Working from the side of the fruit to the center, slide the knife down first one side of a separating membrane and then the other. Continue cutting out all the segments.

Fresh Currants

1 Pull small bunches of fruit through the prongs of a fork to remove red, black or white currants from the stalks. This prevents squashing them.

Apples and Pears

1 For whole fruit, use an apple corer to stamp out the whole core from stalk end to base.

1 For halves, use a melon baller to scoop out the core. Cut out the stal and base with a sharp knife.

2 For rings, remove the core and seeds. Set the fruit on its side and cu across into rings, as required.

1 For slices, cut the fruit in half and remove the core and seeds. Se one half, cut-side down, and cut it across into neat slices. Repeat wit the other half.

Fresh Dates

Halve the fruit lengthwise and lift out the pit.

Papayas and Melons

Halve the fruit. Scoop out the seeds from the central hollow, then scrape away any fibers. For slices, follow the pear technique.

Kiwi Fruit, Carambola

Cut the fruit across into neat slices; discard the ends.

Pineapples

1 To peel the pineapple, set the pineapple on its base, hold it at the top and cut thick slices of skin from top to bottom. Dig out any "eyes" that remain with the point of the knife.

2 For chunks, halve the peeled fruit lengthwise and then cut into quarters. Cut each quarter into spears and cut out the core. Cut each spear into chunks.

3 For rings, cut the peeled fruit across into slices and cut or stamp out the core.

Keeping Fresh Color

If exposed to the air for long, the cut flesh of fruits such as apples, bananas and avocados starts to turn brown. So if cut fruit has to wait before being served, sprinkle the cut surfaces with lemon juice, or immerse hard fruits in water and lemon juice, but do not soak or the fruit may become soggy.

Mangoes

1 Cut lengthwise on either side of the pit. Then cut from the two thin ends of the stone.

2 Remove the skin and cut the flesh into slices or cubes.

Peaches, Nectarines, Apricots and Plums

1 Cut the fruit in half, cutting around the indentation. Twist the halves apart. Lift out the pit, or lever it out with the tip of a knife. Or cut the unpeeled fruit into wedges, removing the pit. Set each wedge peel-side down and slide the knife down to peel.

SALAD DRESSINGS

Although the ingredients of a salad are important, the true secret of a perfect salad is a good dressing.

A French dressing made from the very best olive oil and vinegar can rescue even the dullest selection of lettuce leaves, while a homemade mayonnaise is impressive.

If you are a confident and experienced salad dresser you might feel able simply to add olive oil and vinegar directly to your salad just before serving, but the safest way of creating a perfect dressing is to prepare it in advance. Homemade dressings can be stored in the refrigerator for up to a week and will improve in flavor. Here is a selection of favorites.

Thousand Islands Dressing

This creamy dressing is great with green salads and grated carrot, hot potato, pasta and rice salads.

INGREDIENTS

4 tablespoons sunflower oil
1 tablespoon orange juice
1 tablespoon lemon juice
2 teaspoons grated lemon rind
1 tablespoon finely chopped onion
1 teaspoon paprika
1 teaspoon Worcestershire sauce
1 tablespoon finely chopped
fresh parsley
salt and ground black pepper

MAKES ABOUT
4 FLUID OUNCES/½ CUP

Put all the ingredients into a screw-top jar and season to taste with salt and pepper. Replace the lid and shake well.

French Dressing

This is the most popular dressing.

INGREDIENTS

6 tablespoon extra virgin olive oil
1 tablespoon white wine vinegar
1 teaspoon French mustard
pinch of superfine sugar

MAKES ABOUT
4 FLUID OUNCES/½ CUP

1 Place the extra virgin olive oil and white wine vinegar in a clean screw-top jar.

2 Add the French mustard and superfine sugar.

3 Replace the lid and shake the jar well to mix.

French Herb Dressing

The delicate scents and flavors of fresh herbs combine especially well in a French dressing. Use just one herb or a selection.

INGREDIENTS

4 tablespoons extra virgin olive oil
2 tablespoons sunflower oil
1 tablespoon lemon juice
4 tbsp finely chopped fresh herbs
(parsley, chives, tarragon
and marjoram)
pinch of superfine sugar

MAKES ABOUT
4 FLUID OUNCES/½ CUP

1 Place the extra virgin olive oil and sunflower oil in a clean screw-top jar.

2 Add the lemon juice, chopped herbs and sugar.

3 Replace the lid and shake the jar well to mix.

Mayonnaise

For consistent results, make sure that both egg yolks and oil are at room temperature before combining. Homemade mayonnaise is made with raw egg yolks and may therefore be considered unsuitable for young children, pregnant mothers and the elderly.

INGREDIENTS
2 egg yolks
1 teaspoon French mustard
¼ pint/⅔ cup extra virgin olive oil
¼ pint/⅔ cup peanut or sunflower oil
2 teaspoons white wine vinegar
salt and ground black pepper

MAKES ABOUT
½ PINT/1¼ CUPS

1 Place the egg yolks and mustard in a food processor and process until smoothly blended.

2 Add the olive oil through the feeder tube, a little at a time, while the processor is still running. When the mixture is thick, add the peanut or sunflower oil in a slow, steady stream.

3 Add the vinegar and season to taste with salt and pepper.

Yogurt Dressing

This is a less rich version of a classic mayonnaise and is much easier to make. It can be used as a low-fat substitute. Change the herbs as you wish, or leave them out.

INGREDIENTS
¼ pint/⅔ cup plain yogurt
2 tablespoons mayonnaise
2 tablespoons milk
1 tablespoon chopped fresh parsley
1 tablespoon chopped fresh chives

MAKES ABOUT
7 FLUID OUNCES/SCANT 1 CUP

Put all the ingredients in a bowl. Season to taste and mix well.

Blue Cheese and Chive Dressing

Blue cheese dressings have a strong, robust flavor and are well suited to winter salad leaves such as escarole, Belgian endive and radicchio.

INGREDIENTS
3 ounces blue cheese (Stilton, Bleu d'Auvergne or Gorgonzola)
¼ pint/⅔ cup plain yogurt
3 tablespoons olive oil
2 tablespoons lemon juice
1 tablespoon chopped fresh chives
ground black pepper

MAKES ABOUT
12 FLUID OUNCES/1½ CUPS

1 Remove the rind from the cheese and combine the cheese with a third of the yogurt in a bowl.

2 Add the remainder of the yogurt, the olive oil and the lemon juice and mix well.

3 Stir in the chopped chives and season the dressing to taste with ground black pepper.

Basil and Lemon Mayonnaise

This luxurious dressing is flavored with lemon juice and two types of fresh basil. It can be served with all kinds of leafy salads, crudités or coleslaws. The dressing will keep in an airtight jar for up to a week in the refrigerator.

INGREDIENTS

2 extra large egg yolks
1 tablespoon lemon juice
¼ pint/⅔ cup extra virgin olive oil
¼ pint/⅔ cup sunflower oil
4 garlic cloves
handful of fresh green basil
handful of fresh opal basil
salt and ground black pepper

MAKES ABOUT
½ PINT/1¼ CUPS

1 Place the egg yolks and lemon juice in a blender or food processor and process briefly.

2 In a pitcher, stir together both oils. With the machine running, pour in the oil very slowly, a little at a time.

3 Once half of the oil mixture has been added and the dressing has successfully emulsified, the remaining oil can be incorporated more quickly in a continuous steady stream. Continue processing until a thick, creamy mayonnaise has formed.

4 Peel and crush the garlic cloves and add to the mayonnaise. Alternatively, place the cloves on a chopping board and sprinkle with salt, then flatten them with the heel of a heavy-bladed knife and chop the flesh. Flatten the garlic again to make a coarse purée, then add to the mayonnaise.

5 Remove the basil stalks and tear both types of leaves into small pieces. Stir into the mayonnaise.

6 Add salt and pepper to taste, then transfer the mayonnaise to a serving dish. Cover and chill until ready to serve.

INSTANT DRESSINGS AND DIPS

° ° °

you need an instant dressing
dip, try one of these quick
cipes. Most of them use
antry ingredients.

Creamy Black Olive Dip

ir a little black olive paste into
carton of extra-thick heavy cream
ntil smooth and well blended.
dd salt, ground black pepper and
squeeze of lemon juice to taste.
rve chilled.

Crème Fraîche Dressing with Scallions

inely chop a bunch of scallions
nd stir into a carton of crème
aîche. Add a dash of chili sauce
nd a squeeze of lime juice and
ason with salt and ground
lack pepper.

Yogurt and Mustard Dip

Iix a small carton of creamy,
rained plain yogurt with
-2 teaspoons whole-grain
ustard. Serve with crudités.

Herb Mayonnaise

iven up ready-made French-style
ayonnaise with a handful of
hopped fresh herbs.

Tomato and Horseradish Dip

ring a little tang to bottled
trained tomatoes by adding some
orseradish sauce or 1–2 teaspoons
reamed horseradish and salt and
epper to taste.

Pesto Dip

Stir 1 tablespoon ready-made red
or green pesto into a carton of sour
cream. Serve with crisp crudités
or wedges of oven-roasted
Mediterranean vegetables.

Spiced Yogurt Dressing

Stir a little curry paste and chutney
into a carton of yogurt.

Sun-dried Tomato Dip

Stir 1–2 tablespoons sun-dried
tomato paste into a carton of
strained plain yogurt. Season with
salt and black pepper.

*Above: Top row: Creamy Black
Olive Dip, Crème Fraîche Dressing
with Scallions. Second row: Herb
Mayonnaise, Sun-dried Tomato
Dip. Third row: Yogurt and
Mustard Dip, Soft Cheese and
Chive Dip, Spiced Yogurt Dressing.
Fourth row: Pesto Dip, Tomato
and Horseradish Dip.*

Soft Cheese and Chive Dip

Mix a tub of soft cheese with
2–3 tablespoons chopped fresh
chives and season to taste with salt
and ground black pepper. If the dip
is too thick, stir in a little milk. Use
as a dressing for all kinds of salads,
especially winter coleslaws.

Salads are the most versatile accompaniments to hot and cold

dishes – in both summer and winter – and are ideal for serving

at a barbecue. They are perfect for picnics and make effortless

appetizers when you are entertaining.

LIGHT AND SIDE
SALADS

CRUDITÉS

. . .

A colorful selection of raw vegetables, or crudités, may be served with drinks or as small appetizers. The term "crudités" is used both for small pieces of vegetables served with a tasty dip and for a selection of vegetable salads presented in separate dishes. By choosing contrasting colors, you can make a beautiful presentation of raw or lightly cooked vegetables, attractively arranged on a platter or in baskets and served with a tangy dip, such as aioli (garlic mayonnaise) or tapenade (olive paste). Allow 3–4 ounces of each vegetable per person.

Aioli

Put four crushed garlic cloves (or more or less, to taste) in a small bowl with a pinch of salt and crush with the back of a spoon. Add two egg yolks and beat for 30 seconds with an electric mixer until creamy. Beat in 8 fluid ounces/1 cup extra virgin olive oil, one drop at a time, until the mixture thickens. As it begins to thicken, the oil can be added in a thin, steady stream until the mixture is thick. Thin the sauce with a little lemon juice and season to taste with salt and pepper. Chill for up to 2 days; bring to room temperature and stir before serving.

Tapenade

Put 7 ounces pitted black olives, 6 canned anchovy fillets, 2 tablespoons rinsed capers, 1–2 garlic cloves, 1 teaspoon fresh thyme leaves, 1 tablespoon Dijon mustard, the juice of ½ lemon, freshly ground black pepper and, if you like, 1 tablespoons brandy in a food processor fitted with the metal blade. Process for 15–30 seconds until smooth, then scrape down the sides of the bowl. With the machine running, slowly add 4–6 tablespoons extra virgin olive oil to make a smooth, firm paste. Store in an airtight container.

Raw Vegetable Platter

INGREDIENTS

2 red and 2 yellow bell peppers, seeded and sliced lengthwise
8 ounces fresh baby corn cobs, blanched
1 Belgian endive head (red or white), trimmed and leaves separated
6–8 ounces thin asparagus, trimmed and blanched
1 small bunch radishes with small leaves
6 ounces cherry tomatoes
12 quail eggs, boiled for 3 minutes, drained, refreshed and peeled
aioli or tapenade, to serve

SERVES 6–8

Arrange the prepared vegetables on a large serving plate together with the quail eggs. Cover with a damp dish towel until ready to serve. Serve with aioli or tapenade for dipping.

Tomato and Cucumber Salad

INGREDIENTS

1 medium cucumber, peeled and thinly sliced
5–6 ice cubes
2 tablespoons white wine vinegar
6 tablespoons crème fraîche or sour cream
2 tablespoons chopped fresh mint
4 or 5 ripe tomatoes, sliced
salt and freshly ground black pepper

SERVES 4–6

Place the cucumber in a bowl, sprinkle with a little salt and 1 tablespoon of the vinegar and toss with the ice cubes. Chill for 1 hour to crisp, then rinse, drain and pat dry. Return to the bowl, add the cream, pepper and mint and stir to mix well. Arrange the tomato slices on a serving plate, sprinkle with the remaining vinegar and spoon the cucumber slices into the center.

Carrot and Parsley Salad

INGREDIENTS

1 garlic clove, crushed
grated rind and juice of 1 orange
2–3 tablespoons peanut oil
1 pound carrots, cut into very fine julienne strips
2–3 tablespoons chopped fresh parsley
salt and freshly ground black pepper

SERVES 4–6

Rub a bowl with the garlic and leave in the bowl. Add the orange rind and juice and season. Whisk in the oil until blended, then remove the garlic. Add the carrots and half of the parsley and toss well. Garnish with the remaining parsley.

LETTUCE AND HERB SALAD

∘ ∘ ∘

Stores now sell many different types of lettuce leaves all year, so try to use a mixture.

INGREDIENTS

^{1}/$_2$ cucumber
mixed lettuce leaves
1 bunch watercress, about
4 ounces
1 Belgian endive head, sliced
3 tablespoons chopped fresh herbs

FOR THE DRESSING
1 tablespoon white wine vinegar
1 teaspoon prepared mustard
5 tablespoons olive oil
salt and freshly ground
black pepper

SERVES 4

3 Either toss the cucumber, lettuce, watercress, Belgian endive and herbs together in a bowl, or arrange them in the bowl in layers.

4 Stir the dressing, then pour over the salad and toss lightly to coat the salad vegetables and leaves. Serve immediately.

1 To make the dressing, mix the vinegar and mustard together, then whisk in the oil and seasoning.

2 Peel the cucumber, if you like, then halve it lengthwise and scoop out the seeds. Thinly slice the flesh. Tear the lettuce leaves by hand into bitesize pieces.

MINTED MELON AND GRAPEFRUIT COCKTAIL

° ° °

Melon is always a popular and refreshing appetizer.

INGREDIENTS

1 small Charentais melon,
about 2¼ pounds
2 pink grapefruit
1 yellow grapefruit
1 teaspoon Dijon mustard
1 teaspoon raspberry or
sherry vinegar
1 teaspoon clear honey
1 tablespoon chopped fresh mint
fresh mint sprigs, to garnish

SERVES 4

1 Halve the melon and remove the seeds with a teaspoon. With a melon baller, carefully scoop the flesh into balls.

2 With a sharp knife, peel the pink and yellow grapefruit and cut away all the white pith. Carefully remove the segments by cutting between the membranes, holding the fruit over a bowl to catch any juice.

3 Whisk the Dijon mustard, raspberry or sherry vinegar, honey, chopped mint and reserved grapefruit juice together in a mixing bowl. Add the melon balls and grapefruit segments and mix well. Cover and chill in the refrigerator for 30 minutes.

4 Ladle into four serving dishes, garnish each one with a sprig of fresh mint and serve.

BLACK AND ORANGE SALAD

○ ○ ○

This dramatically colorful salad, with its piquant, spicy dressing, is very unusual. It is a feast for the eyes as well as for the taste buds.

INGREDIENTS

3 oranges
4 ounces/1 cup pitted black olives
1 tablespoon chopped
fresh cilantro
1 tablespoon chopped
fresh parsley

FOR THE DRESSING
2 tablespoons olive oil
1 tablespoon lemon juice
1/2 teaspoon paprika
1/2 teaspoon ground cumin

SERVES 4

1 With a sharp knife, cut away the peel and pith from the oranges and divide the fruit into segments.

2 Place the oranges in a salad bowl and add the black olives, cilantro and parsley.

3 Blend together the olive oil, lemon juice, paprika and cumin. Pour the dressing over the salad and toss gently. Chill for about 30 minutes and serve.

ROCKET AND CILANTRO SALAD

○ ○ ○

Unless you have a plentiful supply of rocket, you may well have to use extra spinach or another green leaf.

INGREDIENTS

4 ounces or more
arugula leaves
4 ounces young spinach leaves
1 large bunch fresh cilantro,
about 1 ounce
2–3 fresh parsley sprigs

FOR THE DRESSING
1 garlic clove, crushed
3 tablespoons olive oil
2 teaspoons white wine vinegar
pinch of paprika
cayenne pepper
salt

SERVES 4

1 Place the rocket and spinach leaves in a salad bowl. Chop the cilantro and parsley and sprinkle them over the top.

2 In a small pitcher, blend together the garlic, olive oil, vinegar, paprika, cayenne pepper and salt to taste.

3 Pour the dressing over the salad and serve immediately.

CAESAR SALAD

. . .

There are many stories about this salad's origin. The most likely is that it was invented by Caesar Cardini in his Mexican restaurant in the 1920s.

INGREDIENTS

3 slices day-old bread,
¹/₂-inch thick
4 tablespoons garlic oil
2 ounces piece Parmesan cheese
1 romaine lettuce
salt and freshly ground
black pepper

FOR THE DRESSING
2 egg yolks, as fresh as possible
1 ounce canned anchovy fillets,
drained and coarsely chopped
¹/₂ teaspoon French mustard
4 fluid ounces/¹/₂ cup olive oil
1 tablespoon white wine vinegar

SERVES 4

1 To make the dressing, combine the egg yolks, anchovies, mustard, oil and vinegar in a screw-top jar and shake well.

2 Remove the crusts from the bread with a serrated knife and cut into 1-inch fingers.

3 Heat the garlic oil in a large frying-pan, add the pieces of bread and fry until golden brown all over. Remove from the pan, sprinkle with salt and leave to drain on paper towels.

Cook's Tip

The classic dressing for Caesar Salad is made with raw egg yolks. Make sure that you use only the freshest eggs, bought from a reputable supplier. Expectant mothers, young children and the elderly are not advised to eat raw egg yolks. You could omit them from the salad dressing and grate hard-boiled yolks on top of the salad instead.

4 Cut thin shavings from the Parmesan cheese with a swivel-bade vegetable peeler.

5 Wash the lettuce leaves and spin dry or pat dry with paper towels o. a clean dish towel. Place in a salad bowl or on individual plates, smother with the dressing, and sprinkle with the garlic croûtons and Parmesan cheese shavings. Season to taste with salt and pepper and serve immediately.

TURKISH SALAD

. . .

This is a perfect combination of textures and flavors.

INGREDIENTS

1 cos or romaine lettuce heart
1 green bell pepper
1 red bell pepper
1/2 cucumber
4 tomatoes
1 red onion
8 ounces feta cheese, crumbled
black olives, to garnish

FOR THE DRESSING
3 tablespoons olive oil
3 tablespoons lemon juice
1 garlic clove, crushed
1 tablespoon chopped fresh parsley
1 tablespoon chopped fresh mint
salt and freshly ground
black pepper

SERVES 4

1 Chop the lettuce into bitesize pieces. Seed the peppers, remove and discard the cores and cut the flesh into thin strips. Chop the cucumber and slice or chop the tomatoes. Cut the onion in half, then slice finely.

2 Place the chopped lettuce, peppers, cucumber, tomatoes and onion in a large salad bowl. Sprinkle the crumbled feta over the top and toss together lightly.

3 To make the dressing, blend together the olive oil, lemon juice and garlic in a small bowl. Stir in the chopped parsley and mint and season with salt and black pepper to taste. Alternatively, put all the ingredients in a screw-top jar and shake well.

4 Pour the dressing over the salad and toss lightly. Garnish with a handful of black olives and serve the salad immediately.

PERSIAN SALAD

. . .

This very simple salad can be served with almost any dish. Don't add the dressing until just before you are ready to serve.

INGREDIENTS

4 tomatoes
1/2 cucumber
1 onion
1 romaine lettuce heart

FOR THE DRESSING
2 tablespoons olive oil
juice of 1 lemon
1 garlic clove, crushed
salt and freshly ground
black pepper

SERVES 4

1 Cut the tomatoes and cucumber into small cubes. Finely chop the onion and tear the lettuce heart into pieces.

2 Place the prepared tomatoes, cucumber, onion and lettuce in a large salad bowl and mix them lightly together.

3 To make the dressing, pour the olive oil into a small bowl. Add the lemon juice, garlic and seasoning and blend together well.

4 Pour the dressing over the salad and toss lightly to mix. Sprinkle with extra black pepper to taste and serve immediately.

SPINACH AND MUSHROOM SALAD

o o o

This nutritious salad goes well with strongly flavored dishes. If served alone as a light lunch, it could be dressed with a French vinaigrette and served with warm French bread.

INGREDIENTS

10 baby corn cobs
2 medium tomatoes
4 ounces/1½ cups mushrooms
1 medium onion cut into rings
20 small spinach leaves
1 ounce salad cress (optional)
salt and freshly ground
black pepper

SERVES 4

1 Halve the baby corn cobs lengthwise and slice the tomatoes.

2 Trim the mushrooms and cut them into thin slices.

3 Arrange the corn cobs, tomatoes, mushrooms, onions, spinach and cress, if using, attractively in a large bowl. Season with salt and pepper to taste and serve.

NUTTY SALAD

o o o

A delicious salad with a tangy bite to it that can be served as an accompaniment to a main meal, or as an appetizer.

INGREDIENTS

1 medium onion, cut into 12 rings
4 ounces/¾ cup canned red kidney
beans, drained
1 medium green zucchini, sliced
1 medium yellow zucchini, sliced
2 ounces pasta shells, cooked
2 ounces/½ cup cashew nuts
1 ounce/¼ cup peanuts
lime wedges and fresh cilantro
sprigs, to garnish

FOR THE DRESSING
4 fluid ounces/½ cup fromage frais
or farmer's cheese
2 tablespoons plain yogurt
1 fresh green chile, chopped

1 tablespoon chopped
fresh cilantro
½ teaspoon crushed
black peppercorns
½ teaspoon crushed dried
red chili
1 tablespoon lemon juice
2.5ml/½ teaspoon salt

SERVES 4

1 Arrange the onion rings, red kidney beans, green and yellow zucchini slices and pasta shells in a salad dish, ready for serving. Sprinkle the cashew nuts and peanuts over the top.

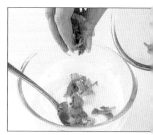

2 In a separate bowl, blend together the fromage frais, yogurt, green chile, cilantro and salt and beat well using a fork.

3 Sprinkle the crushed black pepper, red chili and lemon juice over the dressing. Garnish the salad with the lime wedges and cilantro sprigs and serve with the dressing in a separate bowl or poured over the salad.

FRESH CEPES SALAD

° ° °

To capture the just-picked flavor of a cèpe, this delicious salad is enriched with an egg yolk and walnut oil dressing.

INGREDIENTS

*12 ounces fresh cèpes
6 ounces mixed salad leaves, including batavia, young spinach and frisée
2 ounces/1/2 cup broken walnut pieces, toasted
2-ounce piece Parmesan cheese
salt and freshly ground black pepper*

FOR THE DRESSING
*2 egg yolks
1/2 teaspoon French mustard
5 tablespoons peanut oil
3 tablespoons walnut oil
2 tablespoons lemon juice
2 tablespoons chopped fresh parsley
pinch of superfine sugar*

SERVES 4

1 To make the dressing, place the egg yolks in a screw-top jar with the mustard, peanut and walnut oils, lemon juice, parsley and sugar. Shake well.

2 Trim the cèpes and cut them into thin slices.

3 Place the cèpes in a large salad bowl and combine with the dressing. Leave for 10–15 minutes for the flavors to mingle.

4 Wash and dry the salad leaves, then add them to the salad bowl and toss them with the cèpes.

5 Turn the cèpes out onto four large serving plates. Season well with salt and pepper, sprinkle with the toasted walnuts and shavings of Parmesan cheese, then serve.

CLASSIC GREEK SALAD

. . .

If you have ever visited Greece, you'll know that this salad makes a delicious first course.

INGREDIENTS

1 romaine lettuce
½ cucumber, halved lengthwise
4 tomatoes
8 scallions, sliced
black olives
4 ounces feta cheese

FOR THE DRESSING
6 tablespoons white wine vinegar
¼ pint/⅔ cup extra virgin
olive oil
salt and freshly ground
black pepper

SERVES 4

Tear the lettuce leaves into pieces and place in a large bowl. Slice the cucumber and add to the bowl.

Cut the tomatoes into wedges and put them into the bowl.

Cook's Tip

The salad can be assembled in advance and chilled, but should be dressed only just before serving. Keep the dressing at room temperature as chilling deadens the flavor.

3 Add the scallions to the bowl together with the black olives, and toss well.

4 Cut the feta cheese into cubes and add to the salad.

5 Put the vinegar, olive oil and seasoning into a small bowl and whisk well. Pour the dressing over the salad and toss to combine. Serve with extra black olives and chunks of bread, if you like.

271

ORANGE AND RED ONION SALAD WITH CUMIN

. . .

Cumin and fresh mint give this refreshing salad a very Middle Eastern flavor. Small, seedless oranges are the most suitable type, if available.

INGREDIENTS

6 oranges
2 red onions
1 tablespoon cumin seeds
1 teaspoon coarsely ground
black pepper
1 tablespoon chopped fresh mint
6 tablespoons olive oil
salt
fresh mint sprigs and black olives,
to serve

SERVES 6

1 Slice the oranges thinly, working over a bowl to catch any juice. Then, holding each orange slice in turn over the bowl, cut around with kitchen scissors to remove the peel and pith. Reserve the juice. Slice the onions thinly and separate out into rings.

2 Arrange the orange and onion slices in layers in a shallow dish, sprinkling each layer with cumin seeds, black pepper, chopped mint, olive oil and salt to taste. Pour ove the reserved orange juice.

3 Leave the salad to marinate in a cool place for about 2 hours. Sprinkle over the mint sprigs and black olives and serve.

SPANISH SALAD WITH CAPERS AND OLIVES

. . .

Make this refreshing salad in the summer when tomatoes are at their sweetest.

INGREDIENTS

4 tomatoes
1/2 cucumber
1 bunch scallions, trimmed
and chopped
1 bunch watercress
8 stuffed olives
2 tablespoons drained capers

FOR THE DRESSING
2 tablespoons red wine vinegar
1 teaspoon paprika
1/2 teaspoon ground cumin
1 garlic clove, crushed
5 tablespoons olive oil
salt and freshly ground
black pepper

SERVES 4

1 Peel the skin from the tomatoes and finely dice the flesh. Put them in a salad bowl.

2 Peel the cucumber, dice the flesh finely and add it to the tomatoes. Add half the chopped scallions to the salad bowl and mix lightly. Break the watercress into small sprigs. Add to the tomato mixture, with the stuffed olives and capers.

3 To make the dressing, mix the wine vinegar, paprika, cumin and garlic in a bowl. Whisk in the olive oil and season with salt and peppe to taste. Pour the dressing over the salad and toss lightly to combine. Serve the salad immediately with the remaining scallions.

CARROT AND ORANGE SALAD

· · ·

The ingredients of this fresh-tasting salad could have been made for each other.

INGREDIENTS

1 pound carrots
2 large oranges
1 tablespoon olive oil
2 tablespoons lemon juice
pinch of sugar (optional)
2 tablespoons toasted pine nuts
salt and freshly ground
black pepper

SERVES 4

1 Peel the carrots and grate them into a large bowl.

2 Peel the oranges with a sharp knife and cut into segments, catching the juice in a small bowl.

Variation

Substitute shelled chopped pistachio nuts for the toasted pine nuts, if you like.

3 Blend together the olive oil, lemon juice and orange juice. Season with a little salt and pepper to taste and stir in a pinch of sugar if you like.

4 Toss the orange segments together with the carrots and pour the dressing over them. Sprinkle the salad with the pine nuts just before serving.

SPINACH AND ROAST GARLIC SALAD

° ° °

*Don't worry about the amount
of garlic in this salad. During
roasting, the garlic becomes
sweet and subtle and loses its
pungent taste.*

INGREDIENTS

*12 garlic cloves, unpeeled
4 tablespoons extra virgin olive oil
1 pound baby spinach leaves
2 ounces/1/2 cup pine nuts,
lightly toasted
juice of 1/2 lemon
salt and freshly ground
black pepper*

SERVES 4

1 Preheat the oven to 375°F.
Place the garlic cloves separately
in a small roasting pan, add
2 tablespoons of the olive oil and
toss thoroughly to coat. Roast for
about 15 minutes, until the garlic
cloves are slightly charred around
the edges.

2 While still warm, tip the garlic
into a salad bowl. Add the spinach,
pine nuts, lemon juice, remaining
olive oil and a little salt. Toss well
and add black pepper to taste.
Serve immediately, inviting guests
to squeeze the softened garlic purée
out of the skin to eat.

MIXED GREEN SALAD

∘ ∘ ∘

A good combination of leaves for this salad would be arugula, radicchio, mâche and frisée, with herbs such as chervil, basil and parsley.

INGREDIENTS

1 garlic clove, peeled
2 tablespoons red wine vinegar
1 teaspoon Dijon mustard (optional)
5–8 tablespoons extra virgin olive oil
7–8 ounces mixed salad leaves and herbs
salt and freshly ground black pepper

SERVES 4–6

1 Rub a large salad bowl with the garlic clove. Leave the garlic clove in the bowl.

2 Add the vinegar, salt and pepper to taste and mustard, if using. Stir to mix the ingredients and dissolve the salt, then gradually whisk in the olive oil.

3 Remove the garlic clove and stir the vinaigrette to combine.

4 Add the salad leaves to the bowl and toss well. Serve the salad immediately before it starts to wilt.

Variation

Try young dandelion leaves when they are in season, but be sure to pick them far away from traffic routes and agricultural crop spraying.

APPLE AND CELERIAC SALAD

∘ ∘ ∘

Celeriac, despite its coarse appearance, has a sweet and subtle flavor. In this salad it is served raw, allowing its unique taste and texture to emerge.

INGREDIENTS

1½ pounds celeriac, peeled
2–3 teaspoons lemon juice
1 teaspoon walnut oil (optional)
1 eating apple
3 tablespoons mayonnaise
2 teaspoons Dijon mustard
1 tablespoon chopped fresh parsley
salt and freshly ground black pepper

SERVES 3–4

1 Using a food processor or coarse cheese grater, shred the celeriac. Alternatively, cut it into very thin julienne strips.

2 Place the prepared celeriac in a bowl and sprinkle with the lemon juice and the walnut oil, if using. Stir well to mix.

3 Peel the apple if you like. Cut the apple into quarters and remove the core. Slice the apple quarters thinly crosswise and toss together with the celeriac.

4 Mix together the mayonnaise, mustard and parsley and season with salt and pepper to taste. Add the dressing to the celeriac mixture and stir well. Chill for several hours until ready to serve.

Cook's Tip

The bumpy skin of celeriac is too tough for a vegetable peeler. Use a sharp knife.

BELGIAN ENDIVE, FRUIT AND NUT SALAD

. . .

*The mildly bitter taste of the
Belgian endive combines well
with the sweetness of the fruit
and the creamy curry sauce.*

INGREDIENTS

*3 tablespoons mayonnaise
1 tablespoon strained
plain yogurt
1 tablespoon mild curry paste
6 tablespoons light cream
¹/₂ iceberg lettuce
2 Belgian endive heads
2 ounces/¹/₂ cup cashew nuts
2 ounces/1¹/₄ cups flaked coconut
2 red eating apples
3 ounces/¹/₃ cup currants*

SERVES 4

1 Mix the mayonnaise, yogurt,
curry paste and light cream in a
small bowl. Cover with plastic
wrap and chill in the refrigerator
until required.

2 Tear the lettuce into pieces and
put into a mixing bowl.

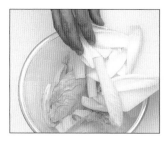

3 Cut the root end off each head of
Belgian endive, separate the leaves
and add them to the lettuce.
Preheat the broiler.

4 Spread out the cashew nuts on a
baking sheet and broil for
2 minutes, until golden. Tip into a
bowl and set aside. Spread out the
coconut on a baking sheet. Grill for
1 minute, until golden.

5 Quarter the apples and cut out
the cores. Thinly slice the apples
and add them to the lettuce with
the toasted coconut and cashew
nuts and the currants.

6 Spoon the dressing over the
salad, toss lightly and serve.

Variation

For an even more colorful
salad, use 1 head Belgian
endive and 1 head radicchio,
and substitute 1 green
eating apple for 1 of
the red ones.

Cook's Tip

Watch the coconut flakes and
cashew nuts with great care
when they are under the
broiler, as they brown very fast
and can burn easily.

FENNEL, ORANGE AND ROCKET SALAD

° ° °

This light and refreshing salad is an ideal accompaniment to serve with spicy or rich foods.

INGREDIENTS

2 oranges
1 fennel bulb
4 ounces arugula leaves
2 ounces/½ cup black olives

FOR THE DRESSING
2 tablespoons extra virgin olive oil
1 tablespoon balsamic vinegar
1 small garlic clove, crushed
salt and freshly ground
black pepper

SERVES 4

1 With a vegetable peeler, cut thin strips of rind from the oranges, making sure that you leave the pith behind. Cut the rind into thin julienne strips. Cook in a small pan of boiling water for a few minutes, then drain.

2 Peel the oranges, removing all the white pith. Slice them into thin rounds and discard any seeds.

3 Cut the fennel bulb in half lengthwise with a sharp knife. Slice across the bulb as thinly as possible, using a food processor fitted with a slicing disk. Alternatively, use a mandolin.

4 Combine the oranges and fennel in a serving bowl and toss with the arugula leaves. Mix together the oil, vinegar and garlic and season to taste with salt and pepper. Pour over the salad, toss well and leave to stand for a few minutes. Sprinkle with the olives and strips of orange and serve.

EGGPLANT, LEMON AND CAPER SALAD

° ° °

This cooked vegetable relish is delicious served as an accompaniment to cold meats, with pasta, or simply on its own with some good, rustic bread. Make sure the eggplant is well cooked until it is meltingly soft.

INGREDIENTS

1 large eggplant, about 1½ pounds
4 tablespoons olive oil
grated rind and juice of 1 lemon
2 tablespoons capers, rinsed
12 pitted green olives
2 tablespoons chopped fresh
flat leaf parsley
salt and freshly ground
black pepper

SERVES 4

1 Cut the eggplant into 1-inch cubes. Heat the olive oil in a large, heavy frying pan and cook the eggplant cubes over a medium heat for about 10 minutes, tossing regularly, until golden and softened. You may need to do this in two batches. Drain the eggplant on paper towels and sprinkle with a little salt.

2 Place the eggplant cubes in a large serving bowl. Toss with the lemon rind and juice, capers, olives and chopped parsley, and season well with salt and pepper. Serve at room temperature.

Cook's Tip

This will taste even better when made the day before. It will store, covered, in the refrigerator for up to 4 days.

APPLE COLESLAW

. . .

There are many variations of
this Dutch salad; this recipe
combines the sweet flavors of
apple and carrot with celery
salt. Coleslaw is traditionally
served with ham.

INGREDIENTS

1 pound white cabbage
1 medium onion
2 eating apples, peeled and cored
6 ounces carrots, peeled
¼ pint/⅔ cup mayonnaise
1 teaspoon celery salt
freshly ground black pepper

SERVES 4

1 Discard the outside leaves of the
white cabbage if they are dirty or
damaged. Cut the cabbage into
2-inch wedges, then remove the
stem sections.

2 Feed the cabbage wedges and the
onion through a food processor
fitted with a slicing blade. Change
to a grating blade and grate the
apples and carrots. Alternatively
use a vegetable slicer and a hand
grater for the apples and carrots.

3 Combine all the salad ingredients
in a large serving bowl. Fold in the
mayonnaise and season with the
celery salt and black pepper.

Variation

For a richer coleslaw, add
½ cup grated Cheddar cheese.
You may find you will need
smaller portions, since the
cheese makes a more
filling dish.

CARROT, RAISIN AND APRICOT COLESLAW

° ° °

This colorful salad combines cabbage, carrots and dried fruit.

INGREDIENTS

*12 ounces white cabbage,
finely shredded
8 ounces carrots, grated
1 red onion, thinly sliced
3 celery sticks, sliced
6 ounces/generous 1 cup raisins
3 ounces/³/4 cup dried apricots,
chopped*

FOR THE DRESSING
*4 fluid ounces/¹/2 cup mayonnaise
6 tablespoons plain yogurt
2 tablespoons chopped fresh herbs
salt and freshly ground
black pepper*

SERVES 6

Put the cabbage and carrots in a large bowl.

2 Add the sliced onion, sliced celery, raisins and chopped apricots and mix well.

3 In a small bowl, mix together the mayonnaise, yogurt and chopped herbs and season to taste with salt and black pepper.

4 Add the mayonnaise dressing to the coleslaw ingredients and toss together to mix. Cover with plastic wrap and chill in the refrigerator before serving.

Variation

Substitute other dried fruit, such as golden raisins and ready-to-eat dried pears or peaches.

283

FENNEL COLESLAW

. . .

The flavor of fennel plays a major role in this coleslaw.

INGREDIENTS

6 ounces fennel
2 scallions, plus extra
to garnish
6 ounces white cabbage
4 ounces celery
6 ounces carrots
2 ounces/scant 1/2 cup
golden raisins
1/2 tsp caraway seeds
1 tablespoon chopped fresh parsley
3 tablespoons extra virgin olive oil
1 teaspoon lemon juice

SERVES 4

3 Stir in the chopped parsley, olive oil and lemon juice and mix all the ingredients very thoroughly. Cover and chill for 3 hours to allow the flavors to mingle. Shred the scallion for the garnish and sprinkle it over the coleslaw before serving.

1 Using a sharp knife, cut the fennel bulb and scallions into thin slices.

2 Slice the cabbage and celery thinly and cut the carrots into fine strips. Place them in a serving bowl together with the sliced fennel and scallions. Add the sultanas and caraway seeds and toss lightly to mix.

BEANSPROUT AND DAIKON SALAD

. . .

Ribbon-thin slices of fresh, crisp vegetables and beansprouts are served with an Asian dressing.

INGREDIENTS

8 ounces/1 cup beansprouts
1 cucumber
2 carrots
1 small daikon
1 small red onion, thinly sliced
1 inch fresh root ginger, cut into
thin matchsticks
1 red chile, seeded and thinly sliced
1 bunch fresh cilantro

FOR THE ASIAN DRESSING
1 tablespoon rice wine vinegar
1 tablespoon light soy sauce
1 tablespoon Thai fish sauce
1 garlic clove, finely chopped
1 tablespoon sesame oil
3 tablespoons peanut oil
2 tablespoons sesame seeds,
lightly toasted

SERVES 4

First make the dressing. Place all the dressing ingredients in a bottle or screw-top jar and shake well.

Cook's Tip

The dressing may be made in advance and will keep well for a couple of days if stored in the refrigerator or a cool place.

2 Wash the beansprouts and drain thoroughly in a colander. If you like, blanch them in boiling water for 1 minute, drain, refresh under cold water and drain again.

3 Peel the cucumber, cut in half lengthwise and scoop out the seeds. Peel the cucumber flesh into long ribbon strips using a vegetable peeler or mandolin.

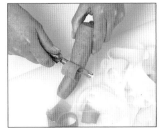

4 Peel the carrots and daikon into long strips in the same way as for the cucumber.

5 Place the carrots, radish and cucumber in a large, shallow serving dish, add the onion, ginger, chile and cilantro and toss to mix. Pour the dressing over the salad just before serving and toss lightly again.

TZATZIKI

. . .

Tzatziki is a Greek cucumber salad dressed with yogurt, mint and garlic. It is typically served with grilled lamb and chicken, but is also good with salmon and trout.

INGREDIENTS

1 cucumber
1 teaspoon salt
3 tablespoons finely chopped fresh mint, plus a few sprigs to garnish
1 garlic clove, crushed
1 teaspoon superfine sugar
7 fluid ounces/scant 1 cup strained plain yogurt
paprika, to garnish (optional)

SERVES 4

1 Peel the cucumber. Reserve a little to use as a garnish, if you like, and cut the remainder in half, lengthwise. Remove the seeds with a teaspoon and discard. Slice the cucumber thinly and combine with the salt. Set aside for about 15–20 minutes. The salt will soften the cucumber and draw out any bitter juices.

2 Place the chopped mint, garlic, sugar and yogurt in a bowl. Stir well to combine.

3 Rinse the cucumber in a strainer under cold running water to wash away the salt. Drain well and combine with the yogurt mixture in a serving bowl. Decorate with sprigs of mint. Garnish with paprika, if you like.

Cook's Tip

If preparing tzatziki in a hurry, do not salt the cucumber. The cucumber will have a more crunchy texture, and will be slightly less sweet.

MARINATED CUCUMBER SALAD

. . .

*lovely cooling salad, with the
istinctive flavor of fresh dill.*

INGREDIENTS

*2 medium cucumbers
1 tablespoon salt
3¹/2 ounces/¹/2 cup sugar
6 fluid ounces/³/4 cup hard cider
1 tablespoon cider vinegar
3 tablespoons chopped fresh dill
freshly ground black pepper*

SERVES 4–6

Slice the cucumbers thinly and
ace them in a colander, sprinkling
lt between each layer. Put the
olander over a bowl and leave to
rain for 1 hour.

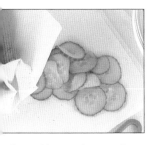

Thoroughly rinse the cucumber
nder cold running water to
emove excess salt, then pat dry
ith paper towels.

3 Gently heat the sugar, cider and
vinegar in a pan, until the sugar
has dissolved. Remove from the
heat and leave to cool. Put the
cucumber slices in a bowl, pour
over the cider mixture and leave to
marinate for 2 hours.

4 Drain the cucumber well and
discard the marinade. Sprinkle the
cucumber with the dill and pepper
to taste. Mix well and transfer to a
serving dish. Cover with plastic
wrap and chill in the refrigerator
until ready to serve.

Cook's Tip

The salad would be a perfect
accompaniment for poached
fresh salmon.

FLOWER GARDEN SALAD

. . .

Dress a colorful mixture of salad leaves with olive oil and lemon juice, then top it with crispy bread crostini.

INGREDIENTS

3 thick slices day-old bread
4 fluid ounces/½ cup extra virgin olive oil
1 garlic clove, halved
½ small romaine lettuce
½ small oak-leaf lettuce
1 ounce arugula leaves
1 ounce fresh flat leaf parsley
a small handful of young dandelion leaves
juice of 1 lemon
a few nasturtium leaves and flowers
pansy and pot marigold flowers
sea salt flakes and freshly ground black pepper

SERVES 4–6

3 Tear all the salad leaves into bitesize pieces and pile them into the bowl with the oil. Season to taste with salt and pepper. Cover and keep chilled until you are ready to serve the salad.

4 To serve, toss the leaves in the o in the base of the bowl, then sprinkle with the lemon juice and toss again. Scatter the crostini and the leaves and flowers over the to and serve immediately.

1 Cut the slices of bread into ½-inch cubes. Heat half the olive oil in a heavy frying pan and fry the bread cubes over a medium-low heat, tossing and turning them until they are well coated and lightly browned. Remove and cool.

2 Rub the inside of a large salad bowl with the cut sides of the garlic clove, then discard the clove. Pour the remaining olive oil into the base of the bowl.

FRESH SPINACH AND AVOCADO SALAD

○ ○ ○

*oung spinach leaves make a
*hange from lettuce. They are
*elicious served with avocado,
*herry tomatoes and radishes in
n unusual tofu sauce.

INGREDIENTS

1 large avocado
juice of 1 lime
8 ounces baby spinach leaves
4 ounces cherry tomatoes
4 scallions, sliced
1/2 cucumber
2 ounces radishes, sliced

FOR THE DRESSING
4 ounces soft silken tofu
3 tablespoons milk
2 teaspoons mustard
1/2 tsp white wine vinegar
cayenne pepper
salt and freshly ground
black pepper
radish roses and fresh herb sprigs,
to garnish

SERVES 2–3

Cut the avocado in half, remove
he pit and peel. Cut the flesh into
lices. Transfer to a plate, and
rizzle over the lime juice.

2 Wash and dry the baby spinach
eaves. Put them in a mixing bowl.

3 Cut the larger cherry tomatoes
in half and add all the tomatoes to
the mixing bowl with the scallions.
Cut the cucumber into chunks
and add to the bowl with the
sliced radishes.

Cook's Tip
Use soft silken tofu rather
than the firm block variety.
It can be found in most
supermarkets in
small cartons.

4 To make the dressing, put the
tofu, milk, mustard, white wine
vinegar and a pinch of cayenne
pepper in a blender or food
processor. Season with salt and
pepper to taste. Process for
30 seconds, until smooth.

5 Scrape the dressing into a bowl
and add a little extra milk if you
like a thinner dressing. Sprinkle
with a little extra cayenne, garnish
with radish roses and herb sprigs
and serve separately. Place the
avocado slices with the spinach
salad on a serving dish and serve
with the tofu dressing.

RADISH, MANGO AND APPLE SALAD

Radish is a year-around vegetable, and this salad, with its clean, crisp tastes and mellow flavors, can be served at any time of year.

INGREDIENTS

10–15 radishes
1 apple, peeled, cored and
thinly sliced
2 celery sticks, thinly sliced
1 small ripe mango
fresh dill sprigs, to garnish

FOR THE DRESSING
4 fluid ounces/½ cup sour cream
2 teaspoons creamed horseradish
1 tablespoon chopped fresh dill
salt and freshly ground
black pepper

SERVES 4

1 To prepare the dressing, blend together the sour cream, creamed horseradish and dill in a small bowl and season to taste with a little salt and pepper.

2 Trim the radishes and slice them thinly. Put in a medium serving bowl together with the apple and celery slices.

3 Halve the mango lengthwise, cutting either side of the pit. Make even, criss-cross cuts through the flesh of each side section, without cutting through the skin, and bend it back to separate the cubes. Remove the cubes with a small knife and add to the bowl.

4 Pour the dressing over the vegetables and fruit and stir gently so that all the ingredients are well coated. Garnish with dill sprigs and serve immediately.

MANGO, TOMATO AND RED ONION SALAD

This salad makes a flavorsome appetizer or accompaniment.

INGREDIENTS

1 firm under-ripe mango
½ cucumber
2 large tomatoes, sliced
½ red onion, sliced into rings

FOR THE DRESSING
2 tablespoons sunflower oil
1 tablespoon lemon juice
1 garlic clove, crushed
½ teaspoon hot pepper sauce
salt and freshly ground
black pepper
chopped chives, to garnish

SERVES 4

1 Halve the mango lengthwise, cutting either side of the pit. Cut the flesh into slices and peel off the skin.

2 Peel and slice the cucumber very thinly with a sharp knife. Arrange the slices of mango, tomato, red onion and cucumber decoratively on a large serving plate.

3 Blend the sunflower oil, lemon juice, garlic and pepper sauce in a blender or food processor, or place in a small screw-top jar and shake vigorously. Season to taste with salt and pepper.

4 Pour the dressing over the salad and serve immediately garnished with chopped chives.

ORANGE AND WATER CHESTNUT SALAD

◦ ◦ ◦

Crunchy water chestnuts combine with radicchio and oranges in this unusual salad.

INGREDIENTS

1 red onion, thinly sliced into rings
2 oranges, peeled and cut into segments
1 can drained water chestnuts, peeled and cut into strips
2 radicchio heads, cored
3 tablespoons chopped fresh parsley
3 tablespoons chopped fresh basil
1 tablespoon white wine vinegar
2 fluid ounces/¼ cup walnut oil
salt and freshly ground black pepper
1 fresh basil sprig, to garnish

SERVES 4

1 Put the onion in a colander and sprinkle with 1 teaspoon salt. Leave to drain for 15 minutes.

2 In a large mixing bowl combine the oranges and water chestnuts.

3 Spread out the radicchio leaves in a large, shallow bowl or on a serving platter to make a bed for the salad.

4 Rinse the onion to remove excess salt and dry on paper towels. Add to the mixing bowl and toss it with the water chestnuts and oranges.

5 Arrange the water chestnut, orange and onion mixture on top of the radicchio leaves. Sprinkle with the chopped parsley and basil.

6 Put the white wine vinegar, walnut oil and salt and pepper to taste in a screw-top jar and shake vigorously to combine. Pour the dressing over the salad and serve immediately, garnished with a sprig of basil.

COLESLAW WITH PESTO MAYONNAISE

• • •

oth the pesto and the
ayonnaise can be made for
is dish, but if time is short,
uy them ready-prepared.

INGREDIENTS

1 small white cabbage
3–4 carrots, grated
4 scallions, sliced
1–1½ ounces/¼–⅓ cup
pine nuts
1 tablespoon chopped fresh mixed
herbs such as parsley, basil, chervil

FOR THE PESTO MAYONNAISE
1 egg yolk
about 2 teaspoons lemon juice
7 fluid ounces/scant 1 cup
sunflower oil
2 teaspoons pesto
4 tablespoons plain yogurt
salt and freshly ground
black pepper

SERVES 4–6

1 To make the mayonnaise, place
the egg yolk in a blender or food
processor and process with the
lemon juice. With the machine
running, gradually add the oil. As
the mayonnaise emulsifies, add it
more quickly in a steady stream.

2 Season to taste with salt and
pepper and a little more lemon
juice if necessary. Alternatively,
make the mayonnaise by hand
using a balloon whisk and adding
the oil drop by drop.

3 Spoon 5 tablespoons of the
mayonnaise into a bowl and stir in
the pesto and yogurt, beating well
until thoroughly combined into
a fairly thin dressing.

4 Remove the outer leaves of the
cabbage and discard. Using a food
processor or a sharp knife, thinly
slice the cabbage and place in a
large salad bowl.

5 Add the carrots and scallions,
together with the pine nuts and
herbs, mixing thoroughly with
your hands. Stir the pesto dressing
into the salad or serve separately in
a small dish.

Variation

You can also make the dressing
with sun-dried tomato pesto.

PEPPER AND CUCUMBER SALAD

• • •

Generous quantities of herbs transform ordinary ingredients.

INGREDIENTS

1 yellow or red bell pepper
1 large cucumber
4–5 tomatoes
1 bunch scallions
2 tablespoons fresh parsley
2 tablespoons fresh mint
2 tablespoons fresh cilantro
2 pitta breads, to serve

FOR THE DRESSING
2 garlic cloves, crushed
5 tablespoons olive oil
juice of 2 lemons
salt and ground black pepper

SERVES 4

1 Slice the pepper and discard the seeds and core. Coarsely chop the cucumber and tomatoes. Place in a large salad bowl.

2 Trim and slice the scallions. Add to the cucumber, tomatoes and pepper. Finely chop the parsley, mint and cilantro and add to the bowl. If you have plenty of herbs, you can add as much as you like.

3 To make the dressing, blend the garlic with the olive oil and lemon juice in a pitcher, then season to taste with salt and pepper. Pour the dressing over the salad and toss lightly to mix.

4 Toast the pitta breads in a toaster or under a hot broiler until crisp and serve them with the pepper and cucumber salad.

Variation

If you like, make this Eastern salad in the traditional way. After toasting the pitta breads, crush them in your hand and then sprinkle over the salad before serving.

294

GUACAMOLE SALSA IN RED LEAVES

This is a lovely, light, summery and attractive appetizer.

INGREDIENTS

2 tomatoes
1 tablespoon grated onion
1 garlic clove, crushed
1 fresh green chile, halved, seeded and chopped
2 ripe avocados
2 tablespoons olive oil
½ teaspoon ground cumin
2 tablespoons chopped fresh cilantro or parsley
juice of 1 lime
radicchio leaves
salt and freshly ground black pepper
fresh cilantro sprigs, to garnish
garlic bread and lime wedges, to serve

SERVES 4

2 Put the tomato flesh into a bowl together with the onion, garlic and chile. Halve the avocados, remove the pits, then scoop the flesh into the bowl, mashing it coarsely with a fork.

3 Add the oil, cumin, cilantro or parsley and lime juice. Mix well and season to taste.

4 Lay the radicchio leaves on a platter and spoon in the salsa. Serve garnished with cilantro sprigs and accompanied by garlic bread and lime wedges.

1 Using a sharp knife, slash a small cross on the top of the tomatoes, then place them in a bowl of boiling water for 30 seconds. The skins will slip off easily. Remove the core of each tomato and roughly chop the flesh.

THAI FRUIT AND VEGETABLE SALAD

° ° °

*A cooling, refreshing salad
served with a coconut dipping
sauce that has a slight kick.*

INGREDIENTS

1 small pineapple
1 small mango, peeled
and sliced
1 green apple, cored and sliced
6 lychees, peeled and pitted
4 ounces green beans, trimmed
and halved
1 medium red onion, sliced
1 small cucumber, cut into
short fingers
4 ounces/1/2 cup beansprouts
2 scallions, sliced
1 ripe tomato, quartered
8 ounces romaine or iceberg
lettuce leaves

FOR THE COCONUT DIPPING SAUCE
2 tablespoons coconut cream
2 tablespoons sugar
5 tablespoons/1/3 cup boiling water
1/4 tsp chili sauce
1 tablespoon Thai fish sauce
juice of 1 lime

SERVES 4–6

1 To make the coconut dipping
sauce, put the coconut cream,
sugar and boiling water in a screw-
top jar. Add the chili and fish
sauces and lime juice and shake.

2 Trim both ends of the pineapple
with a serrated knife, then cut
away the outer skin. Remove the

central core with an apple corer.
Alternatively, cut the pineapple
into quarters down the middle and
remove the core with a knife.
Roughly chop the pineapple and
set aside with the other fruits.

3 Bring a small pan of salted water
to the boil and cook the beans for
3–4 minutes. Refresh under cold
running water and set aside. To
serve, arrange the fruits and
vegetables in small heaps in a wide,
shallow bowl. Serve the coconut
sauce separately as a dip.

SWEET CUCUMBER COOLER

° ° °

*Sweet dipping sauces such as
this bring instant relief to the
hot chili flavors of Thai food.*

INGREDIENTS

5 tablespoons water
2 tablespoons sugar
1/2 teaspoon salt
1 tablespoons rice or
white wine vinegar
1/4 small cucumber
2 shallots, or 1 small red onion

MAKES 4 FLUID OUNCES/1/2 CUP

1 With a small sharp knife, thinly
slice the cucumber and cut into
quarters. Thinly slice the shallots
or red onion.

2 Measure the water, sugar, salt
and vinegar into a stainless steel or
enamel pan, bring to the boil and
simmer, stirring constantly, until
the sugar has dissolved, for less
than 1 minute.

3 Remove the pan from the heat
and set aside to cool. Add the
cucumber and shallots or onion
and serve at room temperature.

TRICOLOR SALAD

This can be a simple appetizer if served on individual salad plates, or part of a light buffet meal laid out on a platter.

INGREDIENTS

1 small red onion, thinly sliced
6 large full-flavored tomatoes
extra virgin olive oil, to sprinkle
2 ounces arugula or
  watercress leaves,
  coarsely chopped
6 ounces mozzarella cheese, thinly
  sliced or grated
2 tablespoons pine nuts (optional)
salt and freshly ground
  black pepper

SERVES 4–6

1 Soak the onion slices in a bowl of cold water for 30 minutes, then drain well and pat thoroughly dry with paper towels.

2 Peel the tomatoes by cutting a cross in the skin and plunging into boiling water for 30 seconds: the skins can then be easily slipped off.

3 Slice the tomatoes and arrange half on a large platter, or divide them among small plates.

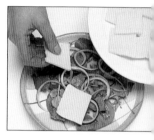

4 Sprinkle liberally with olive oil, then layer with the chopped arugula or watercress, onion slices and cheese, sprinkling over more olive oil and seasoning well with salt and pepper between the layers.

5 Season well with more salt and pepper to finish and complete with a drizzle of oil and a good sprinkling of pine nuts, if you like. Cover the salad with plastic wrap and chill in the refrigerator for at least 2 hours before serving.

TUSCAN TUNA AND BEAN SALAD

. . .

*A great pantry dish that can be
put together in very little time.
Served with fresh bread, it is a
meal in itself.*

INGREDIENTS

1 red onion
2 tablespoons French mustard
½ pint/1¼ cups olive oil
4 tablespoons white wine vinegar
2 tablespoons chopped fresh parsley
2 tablespoons chopped fresh chives
2 tablespoons chopped fresh
tarragon or chervil
14-ounce can navy beans
14-ounce can kidney beans
8 ounces canned tuna in oil,
drained and lightly flaked
fresh chives and tarragon sprigs,
to garnish

SERVES 4

Chop the red onion finely, using
sharp knife.

To make the dressing, whisk
together the mustard, olive oil,
wine vinegar, parsley, chives and
tarragon or chervil.

3 Drain the canned navy and
kidney beans through a colander,
then rinse well under cold running
water and drain again.

4 Mix the chopped onion, beans
and dressing together thoroughly,
then carefully fold in the flaked
tuna. Garnish with chives and
tarragon and serve immediately.

ARUGULA, PEAR AND PARMESAN SALAD

∘ ∘ ∘

For a sophisticated start to an elaborate meal, try this simple, but delicious salad.

INGREDIENTS

3 ripe pears
2 teaspoons lemon juice
3 tablespoons hazelnut or walnut oil
4 ounces arugula leaves
3-ounce piece Parmesan cheese
freshly ground black pepper

SERVES 4

2 Combine the hazelnut or walnut oil with the pears in a large bowl. Add the arugula leaves and toss lightly to mix.

3 Turn the salad out onto four individual plates and top with shavings of Parmesan cheese. Season to taste with black pepper and serve immediately.

1 Peel and core the pears and slice thickly. Brush all over with lemon juice to keep the flesh white.

Cook's Tip

Parmesan cheese is a delicious main ingredient in a salad. Buy a chunk of fresh Parmesan and shave strips off the side, using a vegetable peeler. The distinctive flavor is quite strong. Store the rest of the Parmesan uncovered in the refrigerator.

TOMATO AND FETA CHEESE SALAD
. . .

Sweet, sun-ripened tomatoes are rarely more delicious than when served with feta cheese.

INGREDIENTS
2 pounds tomatoes
7 ounces feta cheese
4 fluid ounces/¹/₂ cup olive oil
12 black olives
4 fresh basil sprigs
freshly ground black pepper

SERVES 4

2 Slice the tomatoes thickly and arrange them attractively in a shallow serving dish.

3 Crumble the feta over the tomatoes, sprinkle with oil, then strew with the olives and basil sprigs. Season to taste with pepper and serve at room temperature.

Carefully remove the tough cores from the tomatoes, using a small, sharp knife.

Cook's Tip
Feta cheese has a strong flavor and can be salty. The least salty variety is imported from Greece and Turkey, and is available from specialist delicatessens.

Using cooked ingredients, such as roasted peppers, grilled
cheese, hard-boiled eggs or crispy bacon vastly increases your
repertoire of side salads. This chapter is packed with delicious
accompaniments to serve at dinner parties, barbecues, picnics
and family suppers.

COOKED SIDE
SALADS

SIMPLE COOKED SALAD

∘ ∘ ∘

This is a version of a popular Mediterranean recipe.

INGREDIENTS

2 tomatoes, quartered
2 onions, chopped
½ cucumber, halved lengthwise, seeded and sliced
1 green bell pepper, halved, seeded and chopped

FOR THE DRESSING
2 tablespoons lemon juice
3 tablespoons olive oil
2 garlic cloves, crushed
2 tablespoons chopped fresh cilantro
salt and freshly ground black pepper

SERVES 4

1 Put the tomato quarters, onions, cucumber and green bell pepper into a large pan, add 4 tablespoons of water and bring to the boil. Lower the heat and simmer for 5 minutes. Remove the pan from the heat and leave to cool.

2 For the dressing, mix together the lemon juice, olive oil and garlic.

3 Strain the cooled vegetables, the transfer them to a serving bowl. Pour over the dressing, season to taste with salt and pepper and stir in the chopped cilantro. Serve the salad immediately, garnished with cilantro sprigs.

SWEET-AND-SOUR ARTICHOKE SALAD

∘ ∘ ∘

sweet-and-sour sauce is
oured over lightly cooked
mmer vegetables.

INGREDIENTS

6 small globe artichokes
juice of 1 lemon
2 tablespoons olive oil
2 medium onions, chopped
ounces/1¹/2 cups fresh or frozen
fava beans (shelled weight)
ounces/1¹/2 cups fresh or frozen
peas (shelled weight)
salt and freshly ground
black pepper
fresh mint leaves, to garnish

FOR THE SWEET-AND-SOUR SAUCE
4 fluid ounces/¹/2 cup white
wine vinegar
1 tablespoon sugar
a handful of fresh mint leaves,
roughly torn

SERVES 4

Cut off the outer leaves of the
tichokes. Cut the artichokes into
arters and place them in a bowl
water with the lemon juice.

Heat the olive oil in a large,
avy pan and add the onions.
ook, stirring occasionally, for
minutes until the onions are
lden. Add the beans and stir,
en drain the artichokes and add
the pan. Pour in 1¹/4 cups water
d cook, covered, for a further
–15 minutes.

3 Add the peas, season to taste
with salt and pepper and cook,
stirring occasionally, for a further
5 minutes, until the vegetables are
tender. Strain through a strainer
or colander and place all the
vegetables in a bowl. Leave to
cool, then cover with plastic wrap
and chill.

4 To make the sweet-and-sour
sauce, mix all the ingredients in
a small pan. Heat gently for about
2–3 minutes, until the sugar has
dissolved. Simmer gently for about
5 minutes, stirring occasionally.
Leave to cool. To serve, drizzle the
sauce over the vegetables and
garnish with mint leaves.

TOMATO, SAVORY AND GREEN BEAN SALAD

Savory and beans could have
been invented for each other.
This salad mixes them with ripe
tomatoes, making a superb
accompaniment for cold meats.

INGREDIENTS

1 pound green beans
2¼ pounds ripe tomatoes
3 scallions, sliced
1 tablespoon pine nuts
4 fresh savory sprigs

FOR THE DRESSING
2 tablespoons extra virgin olive oil
juice of 1 lime
3 ounces Dolcelatte cheese
1 garlic clove, crushed
salt and freshly ground
black pepper

SERVES 4

1 Prepare the dressing first so that
it can stand for a while before use.
Place all the dressing ingredients in
the bowl of a food processor,
season to taste and blend until the
cheese is finely chopped and you
have a smooth dressing. Pour it
into a pitcher.

2 Trim the beans, and cook in
lightly salted boiling water until
they are just cooked.

3 Drain the beans and refresh
under cold running water until th
have completely cooled. Slice the
tomatoes, or, if they are fairly
small, quarter them.

4 Place the beans, tomatoes and
scallions in a large bowl and
toss well to mix. Pour on the
dressing, sprinkle the pine nuts
and savory sprigs over the top an
serve immediately.

SQUASH À LA GRECQUE

. . .

This recipe, usually made with small mushrooms, also works exceptionally well with patty-pan squash.

INGREDIENTS

6 ounces patty-pan squash
8 fluid ounces/1 cup white wine
juice of 2 lemons
1 fresh thyme sprig
1 bay leaf
small bunch of fresh chervil,
coarsely chopped
¼ teaspoon crushed
coriander seeds
¼ teaspoon crushed
black peppercorns
5 tablespoons olive oil
bay leaves, to garnish

SERVES 4

1 Blanch the patty-pan squash in boiling water for 3 minutes, then refresh them in cold water.

Variation

Try using other summer squash, such as yellow zucchini, in this recipe.

2 Place the wine, lemon juice, thyme, bay leaf, chervil, coriander and peppercorns in a pan, add ⅔ cup water and simmer for 10 minutes, covered. Add the squash and cook for 10 minutes, until they are tender. Remove with a slotted spoon.

3 Reduce the liquid in the pan by boiling hard for 10 minutes. Strain and pour it over the squash. Leave until cool for the flavors to be absorbed. Serve cold, garnished with bay leaves.

WARM FAVA BEAN AND FETA SALAD

This medley of fresh-tasting salad ingredients is lovely warm or cold as an appetizer or as an accompaniment to a main course fish dish.

INGREDIENTS

2 pounds fava beans, shelled
4 tablespoons olive oil
6 ounces fresh plum tomatoes, halved, or quartered if large
4 garlic cloves, crushed
4 ounces firm feta cheese, cut into chunks
3 tablespoons chopped fresh dill
12 black olives
salt and freshly ground black pepper
chopped fresh dill, to garnish

SERVES 4–6

1 Cook the fava beans in salted boiling water until just tender. Drain and set aside.

2 Meanwhile, heat the olive oil in a large, heavy frying pan and add the tomatoes and garlic. Cook over a low heat, gently shaking the pan and turning occasionally, until the tomatoes are just beginning to change color.

3 Add the chunks of feta to the pan and toss the ingredients together for 1 minute. Mix with the drained beans, dill and olives and season to taste with salt and pepper. Serve warm or cold, garnished with chopped dill.

Cook's Tip

Plum tomatoes are now widely available in supermarkets fresh as well as canned. Their deep red, oval shape is very attractive in salads, and they have a sweet, rich flavor.

HALLOUMI AND GRAPE SALAD

In this recipe, firm, salty halloumi cheese is fried and tossed with sweet, juicy grapes that really complement its distinctive flavor.

INGREDIENTS

5 ounces mixed green salad leaves
3 ounces seedless green grapes
3 ounces seedless black grapes
9 ounces halloumi cheese
3 tablespoons olive oil
fresh young thyme leaves or fresh dill, to garnish

FOR THE DRESSING
4 tablespoons olive oil
1 tablespoon lemon juice
1/2 teaspoon superfine sugar
1 tablespoon chopped fresh thyme
salt and freshly ground black pepper

SERVES 4

1 To make the dressing, mix together the olive oil, lemon juice and sugar. Season to taste with salt and pepper. Stir in the chopped thyme and set aside.

2 Lightly toss together the salad leaves and the green and black grapes in a large bowl, then transfer to a large serving plate.

3 Thinly slice the cheese. Heat the oil in a large, heavy frying pan. Add the cheese and fry briefly until golden on the underside. Turn the cheese with a metal spatula and cook the other side.

4 Arrange the cheese over the salad. Pour over the dressing and garnish with sprigs of fresh thyme or dill. Serve while the cheese is still warm, as it becomes inedibly rubbery when cold.

ARUGULA AND GRILLED GOAT CHEESE SALAD
. . .

For this recipe, use a cylinder-shaped cheese or small rolls that can be cut into halves, weighing about 2 ounces.

INGREDIENTS
1 tablespoon olive oil
1 tablespoon vegetable oil
4 slices French bread

FOR THE DRESSING
3 tablespoons walnut oil
1 tablespoon lemon juice
8 ounces cylinder-shaped
goat cheese
generous handfuls of
arugula leaves
4 ounces frisée lettuce leaves
salt and freshly ground
black pepper

FOR THE SAUCE
3 tablespoons apricot jam
4 tablespoons white wine
1 teaspoon Dijon mustard

SERVES 4

1 Heat the oils in a frying pan and fry the bread on one side only, until lightly golden. Transfer to a plate lined with paper towels.

2 To make the sauce, heat the jam in a small pan until it is warm and runny, but not boiling. Push it through a strainer into a clean pan, to remove the pieces of fruit, then stir in the white wine and mustard. Heat gently and keep warm until ready to serve.

3 Blend the walnut oil and lemon juice and season to taste with a little salt and pepper.

4 Preheat the broiler a few minutes before serving the salad. Cut the goat cheese in 2-ounce rounds and place each piece on a piece of French bread, untoasted-side up. Place them under the hot grill and cook for 3–4 minutes, until the cheese melts.

5 Toss the arugula and frisée lettuce leaves in the walnut oil dressing and arrange attractively on four individual serving plates. When the cheese croûtons are ready, arrange one each plate, pour over a little of the apricot sauce and serve.

RUSSIAN SALAD

. . .

Russian salad became fashionable in the hotel dining rooms of the 1920s and 1930s. Originally it consisted of lightly cooked vegetables, egg, shellfish and mayonnaise. Today we find it diced in plastic pots in supermarkets. This version recalls better days and plays on the theme of the Fabergé egg.

INGREDIENTS

4 ounces large white mushrooms
4 fluid ounces/½ cup mayonnaise
1 tablespoon lemon juice
12 ounces peeled
cooked shrimp
1 large gherkin, chopped, or
2 tablespoons capers
4 ounces fava beans
(shelled weight)
4 ounces small new potatoes,
scrubbed or scraped
4 ounces young carrots, trimmed
and peeled
4 ounces baby corn cobs
4 ounces baby
turnips, trimmed
1 tablespoon olive oil
4 eggs, hard-boiled
and shelled
1 ounce canned anchovy
fillets, drained and cut into
fine strips
ground paprika
salt and freshly ground
black pepper

SERVES 4

1 Slice the mushrooms thinly, then cut into matchsticks and place in a large bowl. Combine the mayonnaise and lemon juice. Fold the mayonnaise into the mushrooms, then add the prawns and gherkin or capers and season to taste with salt and pepper.

2 Bring a large pan of lightly salted water to the boil, add the fava beans and cook for 3 minutes. Drain and refresh under cold running water, then pinch the beans between your thumb and forefinger to release them from their tough skins.

3 Boil the potatoes for about 15 minutes, and the remaining vegetables for 6 minutes. Drain and cool under running water. Moisten the vegetables with oil and divide among four shallow bowls.

4 Spoon on the shrimp mixture and place a hard-boiled egg in the center. Decorate the egg with strips of anchovy, sprinkle with paprika and serve.

311

POACHED EGG SALAD WITH CROÛTONS
∘ ∘ ∘

Soft poached eggs, hot croûtons and cool, crisp salad leaves make a great combination.

INGREDIENTS
½ small loaf white bread
5 tablespoons/⅓ cup olive oil
2 eggs
4 ounces mixed salad leaves
2 garlic cloves, crushed
½ tablespoons white wine vinegar
1-ounce piece Parmesan cheese
freshly ground black pepper

SERVES 2

1 Remove the crust from the loaf of bread. Cut the bread into 1-inch cubes.

2 Heat 2 tablespoons of the oil in a large, heavy frying pan. Cook the bread for about 5 minutes, tossing the cubes occasionally, until they are golden brown.

3 Meanwhile, bring a pan of water to the boil. Carefully slide in the eggs, one at a time. Gently poach the eggs for 4 minutes, until lightly cooked and the white is just set.

4 Divide the salad leaves among two individual plates. Remove the croûtons from the frying pan and arrange them over the leaves. Wipe out the frying pan clean with paper towels.

5 Heat the remaining oil in the pan, add the garlic and vinegar and cook over a high heat for 1 minute. Divide the warm dressing among the two salads.

Variation
To make garlic croûtons, heat the oil as in step 2, then add one chopped large garlic clove and fry for 2 minutes, without browning. Remove and discard the garlic and cook the bread cubes in the flavored oil.

6 Place a poached egg on each plate of salad. Sprinkle with thin shavings of Parmesan and a little black pepper.

Cook's Tip
Add a dash of vinegar to the water before poaching the eggs. This helps to keep the whites together.

To make sure that a poached egg has a good shape, swirl the water with a spoon, whirlpool-fashion, before sliding in the egg.

Before serving, trim the edges of the egg for a neat finish.

PEPPERS WITH TOMATOES AND ANCHOVIES

* * *

This is a Sicilian-style salad full of warm Mediterranean flavors. The salad improves if it is made and dressed an hour or two before serving.

INGREDIENTS

1 red bell pepper
1 yellow bell pepper
4 ripe plum tomatoes, sliced
2 canned anchovies, drained
and chopped
4 sun-dried tomatoes in oil,
drained and sliced
1 tablespoon capers, drained
1 tablespoon pine nuts
1 garlic clove, very finely sliced

FOR THE DRESSING
5 tablespoons extra virgin olive oil
1 tablespoon balsamic vinegar
1 teaspoon lemon juice
chopped fresh mixed herbs
salt and freshly ground
black pepper

SERVES 4

1 Preheat the broiler. Cut the peppers in half and remove the seeds and stalks. Cut into quarters and broil, skin-side up, until the skin chars. Transfer to a bowl, cover with paper towels and leave to cool. Peel the peppers and cut into strips.

2 Arrange the peppers and fresh tomatoes on a serving dish. Sprinkle over the anchovies, sun-dried tomatoes, capers, pine nuts and garlic.

3 To make the dressing, mix together the olive oil, vinegar, lemon juice and chopped fresh herbs and season with plenty of salt and pepper. Pour the dressing over the salad before serving.

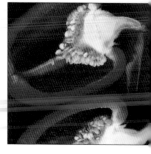

SWEET AND SOUR ONION SALAD

This recipe for tangy, glazed onions in the Provençal style makes an unusual and flavorful accompaniment to steaks cooked on the barbecue.

INGREDIENTS

1 pound pearl onions
uid ounces/¼ cup wine vinegar
3 tablespoons olive oil
3 tablespoons superfine sugar
3 tablespoons tomato paste
1 bay leaf
2 fresh parsley sprigs
2½ ounces/½ cup raisins
salt and freshly ground
black pepper

SERVES 6

1 Put all the ingredients in a pan with 1¼ cups water. Bring to the boil and simmer gently, uncovered, for 45 minutes, or until the onions are tender and the liquid has evaporated.

2 Remove the bay leaf and parsley, from the pan and check the seasoning. Transfer the contents of the pan to a large serving dish. Serve the salad at room temperature.

SPICED EGGPLANT SALAD

· · ·

Serve this Middle-Eastern influenced salad with warm pitta bread as an appetizer, or as an accompaniment to any number of main course dishes.

INGREDIENTS

2 small eggplant, sliced
5 tablespoons olive oil
2 fluid ounces/¼ cup red
wine vinegar
2 garlic cloves, crushed
1 t ablespoon lemon juice
½ teaspoon ground cumin
½ teaspoon ground coriander
½ cucumber, thinly sliced
2 tomatoes, thinly sliced
2 tablespoons plain yogurt
salt and freshly ground
black pepper
chopped flat leaf parsley, to garnish

SERVES 4

1 Preheat the broiler. Brush the eggplant slices lightly with some of the olive oil and broil or cook over a hot barbecue until golden and tender, turning once to cook evenly. Allow the slices to cool slightly, then cut them into quarters.

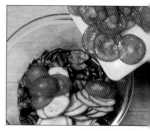

2 Mix the remaining olive oil with vinegar, crushed garlic, lemon juice cumin and ground coriander. Seas with plenty of salt and pepper and thoroughly. Add the warm eggplan stir well and chill for at least 2 hot Add the cucumber and tomatoes. Transfer the salad to a serving dish and spoon the yogurt on top. Gar with chopped parsley to serve.

BABY EGGPLANT WITH RAISINS AND PINE NUTS

This is a recipe with an Italian influence, in a style that would have been familiar in Renaissance times. If possible, make it a day in advance, to allow the sweet and sour flavors to develop.

INGREDIENTS

12 baby eggplant, halved
8 fluid ounces/1 cup olive oil
juice of 1 lemon
tablespoons balsamic vinegar
3 cloves
1 ounce/⅓ cup pine nuts
1 ounce/2 tbsp raisins
1 tablespoon sugar
1 bay leaf
arge pinch of dried chili flakes
salt and freshly ground
black pepper

SERVES 4

1 Preheat the broiler. Brush the eggplant with olive oil and broil, turning once, for 10 minutes.

2 To make the dressing, combine the remaining olive oil with the lemon juice, vinegar, cloves, pine nuts, raisins, sugar and bay leaf. Add the chili flakes and salt and pepper and mix well.

3 Place the hot eggplant in an earthenware or glass bowl, and pour over the dressing. Leave to cool, turning the eggplant once or twice. Serve the salad cold.

ROASTED BELL PEPPER AND TOMATO SALAD

° ° °

A lovely, colorful recipe that perfectly combines several red ingredients. Eat this dish at room temperature.

INGREDIENTS

3 red bell peppers
6 large plum tomatoes
½ teaspoon dried red chili flakes
1 red onion, thinly sliced
3 garlic cloves, finely chopped
grated rind and juice of 1 lemon
3 tablespoons chopped fresh
flat leaf parsley
2 tablespoons extra virgin olive oil
salt and freshly ground
black pepper
black and green olives and extra
chopped flat leaf parsley, to garnish

SERVES 4

1 Preheat the oven to 425°F. Place the peppers on a baking sheet and roast, turning occasionally, for 10 minutes or until the skins are charred and almost blackened. Add the plum tomatoes to the baking sheet and bake for 5 minutes more.

2 Place the peppers in a strong plastic bag, close the top loosely, trapping in the steam. Set aside, with the tomatoes, until cool enough to handle.

3 Carefully pull the skin off the peppers. Remove the core and seeds, then chop the peppers and tomatoes coarsely and place in a mixing bowl.

4 Add the chili flakes, onion, garlic, lemon rind and juice. Sprinkle over the parsley. Mix we then transfer to a serving dish. Season with salt and pepper, drizz over the olive oil and sprinkle the olives and extra parsley over the top. Serve at room temperature.

MARINATED ZUCCHINI

° ° °

This is a simple vegetable dish that uses the best of the season's zucchini. It can be eaten either hot or cold.

INGREDIENTS

4 zucchini
4 tablespoons extra virgin olive oil
2 tablespoons chopped fresh mint
2 tablespoons white wine vinegar
salt and freshly ground
black pepper
fresh mint leaves, to garnish
whole-wheat Italian bread and
green olives, to serve

SERVES 4

1 Cut the zucchini into thin slices. Heat 2 tablespoons of the olive oil in a wide, heavy pan. Add the zucchini slices in batches, and cook, stirring and turning occasionally, for 4–6 minutes, until tender and brown around the edges. Transfer the zucchini to a bowl. Season to taste with salt and black pepper.

2 Heat the remaining oil in the pan, then add the chopped mint and vinegar and let it bubble for a few seconds.

3 Pour the mint dressing over the zucchini. Cover and marinate for 1 hour, then serve garnished with mint leaves and accompanied by bread and olives.

GREEN BEAN AND SWEET RED PEPPER SALAD

° ° °

INGREDIENTS

*12 ounces cooked green
beans, quartered
2 red bell peppers, seeded
and chopped
2 scallions, both white and green
parts chopped
1 or more drained pickled serrano
chiles, well rinsed, seeded
and chopped
1 iceberg lettuce, shredded, or
mixed salad leaves
green olives, to garnish*

FOR THE DRESSING
*3 tablespoons red wine vinegar
9 tablespoons olive oil
salt and freshly ground
black pepper*

SERVES 4

1 Place the cooked green beans, peppers, scallions and pickled chiles in a salad bowl and toss lightly to mix.

2 To make the dressing, pour the vinegar into a bowl or pitcher. Add salt and pepper to taste, then gradually whisk in the olive oil until well combined.

3 Pour the dressing over the prepared vegetables and toss lightly together to mix well and coat them all thoroughly.

4 Line a large serving platter with the shredded lettuce or mixed salad leaves and arrange the vegetable mixture attractively on top. Garnish with the olives and serve.

GREEN GREEN SALAD

. . .

...ven with frozen vegetables you ...ould still get a pretty salad.

INGREDIENTS

6 ounces shelled fava beans
4 ounces green beans, quartered
4 ounces snow peas
8–10 small fresh mint leaves
3 scallions, chopped

FOR THE DRESSING

4 tablespoons green olive oil
1 tablespoon cider vinegar
1 tablespoon chopped fresh mint
1 garlic clove, crushed
salt and freshly ground
black pepper

SERVES 4

Plunge the fava beans into a pan ...f boiling water and bring back to ...e boil. Remove from the heat ...mmediately and plunge into cold ...ater. Drain. Repeat with the ...reen beans.

Cook's Tip

Frozen fava beans are a good stand-by, but for this salad it is worth shelling fresh beans for the extra flavor.

2 In a large bowl, combine the blanched fava beans and green beans with the raw snow peas, mint leaves and scallions.

3 In another bowl, mix together the olive oil, cider vinegar, chopped or dried mint, garlic and seasoning. Pour over the salad and toss well. Cover with plastic wrap and chill until ready to serve.

LEEK AND EGG SALAD

· · ·

*Smooth-textured leeks are
especially delicious warm when
partnered with an earthy sauce
of parsley, olive oil and walnuts.*

INGREDIENTS

*1¹/₂ pounds young leeks
1 egg
fresh parsley sprigs, to garnish*

FOR THE DRESSING
*1 ounce/1 cup fresh parsley
2 tablespoons olive oil
juice of ¹/₂ lemon
2 ounces/¹/₂ cup broken
walnuts, toasted
1 teaspoon superfine sugar
salt and freshly ground
black pepper*

SERVES 4

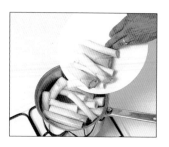

1 Bring a pan of salted water to the
boil. Cut the leeks into 4-inch
lengths and rinse well to flush out
any grit or soil. Cook the leeks for
8 minutes. Drain and partially cool
under cold running water.

2 Lower the egg into boiling water
and cook for 12 minutes. Cool
under cold running water, shell and
set aside.

3 Meanwhile, to make the salad
dressing, finely chop the parsley in
a food processor. Alternatively, use
a sharp knife or mezzaluna.

4 If you have chopped the parsley
by hand, transfer it to a food
processor. Add the olive oil, lemon
juice and toasted walnuts to the
food processor. Process for about
1–2 minutes, until smooth.

5 Adjust the consistency with
about 6 tablespoons of water. Add
the sugar and season to taste with
salt and pepper.

6 Place the leeks on an attractive
plate, then spoon on the sauce.
Finely grate the hard-boiled egg
and sprinkle it over the sauce.
Garnish with the reserved parsley
sprigs and serve immediately.

Cook's Tip

While raw and lightly cooked eggs
increase the risk of salmonella and
may be inadvisable for vulnerable
people, such as the young, the
elderly, pregnant women and
the unwell, to eat, hard-boiled
eggs are quite safe.

WINTER VEGETABLE SALAD

∘ ∘ ∘

*Mixed vegetables are flavored
with white wine and herbs.*

INGREDIENTS

*6 fluid ounces/³/4 cup white wine
1 teaspoon olive oil
2 tablespoons lemon juice
2 bay leaves
1 fresh thyme sprig
4 juniper berries
1 pound leeks, trimmed and cut
into 1-inch lengths
1 small cauliflower, broken
into florets
4 celery sticks, sliced diagonally
2 tablespoons chopped fresh parsley
salt and freshly ground
black pepper*

SERVES 4

1 Put the white wine, olive oil,
lemon juice, bay leaves, thyme and
juniper berries into a large, heavy
pan and bring to the boil. Lower
the heat, cover and simmer for
20 minutes.

2 Add the leeks, cauliflower and
celery. Simmer very gently for
5–6 minutes, or until just tender.

3 Remove the vegetables with a
slotted spoon and transfer them to
a serving dish. Briskly boil the
cooking liquid for 15–20 minutes,
or until reduced by half. Put in
a strainer.

4 Stir the parsley into the liquid
and season to taste with salt and
pepper. Pour over the vegetables
and leave to cool. Chill in the
refrigerator for at least 1 hour
before serving.

Cook's Tip
Vary the vegetables
for this salad according to
the season.

AVOCADO AND SMOKED FISH SALAD

Avocado and smoked fish make a good combination.

INGREDIENTS

2 avocados
1/2 cucumber
1 tablespoon lemon juice
2 firm tomatoes
1 fresh green chile
salt and freshly ground black pepper

FOR THE FISH
1/2 ounce/1 tablespoon butter
1/2 onion, thinly sliced
1 teaspoon mustard seeds
8 ounces smoked mackerel, flaked
2 tablespoons fresh chopped cilantro leaves
2 firm tomatoes, peeled and chopped
1 tablespoon lemon juice

SERVES 4

1 For the fish, melt the butter in a frying pan, add the onion and mustard seeds and cook for about 5 minutes, until the onion is soft.

2 Add the mackerel, chopped cilantro, tomatoes and lemon juice and cook over a low heat for 2–3 minutes. Remove from the heat and leave to cool.

3 To make the salad, cut the avocados in half and remove the pits. Peel and slice the flesh thinly. Peel the cucumber thinly. Place together in a bowl and sprinkle with the lemon juice. Slice the tomatoes and seed them. Finely chop the chile.

4 Place the fish mixture in the center of a serving plate.

5 Arrange the avocados, cucumber and tomatoes decoratively around the outside. Alternatively, spoon a quarter of the fish mixture onto each of four serving plates and divide the avocados, cucumber and tomatoes equally among them. Sprinkle with the chopped chile, season to taste with a little salt and pepper and serve.

Variation
Smoked haddock or cod can also be used in this salad, or a mixture of smoked mackerel and haddock.

TOMATO AND BREAD SALAD

◦ ◦ ◦

This salad, which conveniently uses up stale bread, is best made with sun-ripened tomatoes.

INGREDIENTS
14 ounces stale white bread
4 large tomatoes
1 large red onion or
6 scallions
a few fresh basil leaves, to garnish

FOR THE DRESSING
4 tablespoons extra virgin olive oil
2 tablespoons white wine vinegar
salt and freshly ground `
black pepper

SERVES 4

1 Thickly slice the bread. Place in a shallow bowl, cover with cold water and set aside for 30 minutes.

2 Cut the tomatoes into chunks and place in a serving bowl. Thinly slice the onion or scallions and add them to the tomatoes. Squeeze as much water out of the bread as possible and add it to the bowl of vegetables.

3 To make the dressing, mix the oil and vinegar. Season to taste with salt and pepper, pour over the salad and mix well. Garnish with the basil leaves. Leave to stand in a cool place for at least 2 hours before serving.

GRILLED BELL PEPPER SALAD

◦ ◦ ◦

Ideally, this salad should be made with a combination of red and yellow peppers for the most jewel-like, colorful effect and the sweetest flavor.

INGREDIENTS
4 large bell peppers, red or yellow or a combination of both
2 tablespoons capers, rinsed
18–20 black or green olives

FOR THE DRESSING
6 tablespoons extra virgin olive oil
2 garlic cloves, finely chopped
2 tablespoons balsamic or red wine vinegar
salt and freshly ground black pepper

SERVES 6

1 Place the peppers under a hot broiler and turn occasionally until they are black and blistered on all sides. Remove from the heat, place in a strong plastic bag and close the top loosely. Set aside until they are cool enough to handle. Carefully peel the peppers, then cut them into quarters. Remove and discard the stems and seeds.

2 Cut the peppers into strips, and arrange them on a serving dish. Distribute the capers and olives evenly over the peppers.

3 For the dressing, mix the oil and garlic in a small bowl, crushing the garlic with a spoon to release the flavor. Mix in the vinegar and season to taste with salt and pepper. Pour over the salad, mix well and leave to stand for at least 30 minutes before serving.

FRISÉE LETTUCE SALAD WITH BACON

. . .

INGREDIENTS

2 ounces white bread
8 ounces frisée lettuce or
    escarole leaves
5–6 tablespoons extra virgin
    olive oil
6-ounce piece smoked bacon,
diced, or 6 thick-cut smoked
bacon strips, cut crosswise
    into thin strips
1 small garlic clove,
    finely chopped
1 tablespoon red wine vinegar
2 teaspoons Dijon mustard
salt and freshly ground
    black pepper

SERVES 4

1 Remove and discard the crusts, then cut the bread into small cubes. Tear the frisée lettuce or escarole into bitesize pieces and put into a salad bowl.

2 Heat 1 tablespoon of the oil in a medium, non-stick frying pan over a medium-low heat and add the bacon. Fry gently until well browned, stirring occasionally. Remove the bacon with a slotted spoon and drain on paper towels.

3 Add another 2 tablespoons of the oil to the pan and fry the bread cubes over a medium-high heat, turning frequently, until evenly browned. Remove the bread cubes with a slotted spoon and drain well on paper towels. Discard any remaining fat.

4 Stir the garlic, vinegar and mustard into the pan with the remaining oil and heat until just warm, whisking to combine. Season to taste with salt and pepper, then pour the dressing over the salad and sprinkle with the fried bacon and croûtons. Serve immediately while still warm.

ASPARAGUS AND ORANGE SALAD

∘ ∘ ∘

*slightly unusual combination
f ingredients with a simple
live oil dressing.*

INGREDIENTS

8 ounces asparagus, trimmed and
cut into 2-inch lengths
2 large oranges
2 well-flavored tomatoes,
cut into eighths
2 ounces romaine
lettuce leaves
tablespoons extra virgin olive oil
1/2 teaspoon sherry vinegar
salt and freshly ground
black pepper

SERVES 4

Cook the asparagus in lightly
alted boiling water for about
-4 minutes, until just tender.
Drain and refresh under cold water,
en leave on one side to cool.

Grate the rind from half an
range and reserve. Working over
bowl to catch the juice, peel both
he oranges and cut them into
egments by slicing between the
nembranes with a small, sharp
nife. Squeeze the juice from the
nembrane and reserve.

Put the asparagus, orange
egments, tomatoes and lettuce into
salad bowl.

4 Mix together the olive oil and
sherry vinegar, and add 1 tablespoon
of the reserved orange juice.

5 Add 1 teaspoon of the grated
rind. Season to taste with salt and
pepper. Just before serving, pour
the dressing over the salad and mix
gently to coat all the ingredients.

Cook's Tip

The asparagus cooking time will
vary depending on the thickness
of the stems. Thick stems can
take as long as 10 minutes.

329

HARD-BOILED EGGS WITH TUNA SAUCE

. . .

*A tasty tuna mayonnaise
poured over hard-boiled eggs
makes a nourishing first course
that is quick to prepare.*

INGREDIENTS
*6 extra large eggs
7-ounce can tuna in olive oil
3 canned anchovy fillets
1 tablespoon capers, drained
2 tablespoons lemon juice
4 tablespoons olive oil
salt and freshly ground
black pepper
capers and anchovy fillets,
to garnish*

FOR THE MAYONNAISE
*1 egg yolk
1 teaspoon Dijon mustard
1 teaspoon white wine vinegar or
lemon juice
¼ pint/⅔ cup olive oil*

SERVES 6

1 Boil the eggs for 12–14 minutes.
Cool them under cold water. Shell
the eggs carefully and set aside.

2 Make the mayonnaise by
whisking the egg yolk, mustard and
vinegar or lemon juice together.

3 Whisk in the olive oil, a few
drops at a time to begin with, until
3–4 tablespoons have been fully
incorporated. Then pour in the
remaining oil in a slow, steady
stream, whisking constantly.

4 Place the tuna with the oil from
the can, the anchovies, capers,
lemon juice and olive oil in a
blender or food processor. Process
until the mixture is smooth.

5 Fold the tuna mixture carefully
into the mayonnaise. Season to
taste with black pepper, and salt if
necessary. Cover with plastic wrap
and chill in the refrigerator for at
least 1 hour.

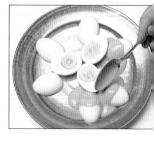

6 Cut the hard-boiled eggs in half
lengthwise. Arrange on a serving
platter. Spoon on the mayonnaise
and garnish with capers and
anchovy fillets. Serve chilled.

ARTICHOKE AND EGG SALAD

Artichoke hearts are best when cut from fresh artichokes, but can also be bought frozen.

INGREDIENTS

*4 large artichokes or 4 frozen
artichoke hearts, thawed
1/2 lemon
4 eggs, hard-boiled
fresh parsley sprigs, to garnish*

FOR THE MAYONNAISE
*1 egg yolk
2 teaspoons Dijon mustard
1 tablespoon white wine vinegar
8 fluid ounces/1 cup olive oil
2 tablespoons chopped fresh parsley
salt and freshly ground
black pepper*

SERVES 4

If using fresh artichokes, wash them. Squeeze the lemon and put the juice and the squeezed half in a bowl of cold water.

Prepare the artichokes one at a time. Cut off only the tip from the stem. Peel the stem with a small knife, pulling upward toward the leaves. Pull off the small leaves around the stem and continue snapping off the upper part of the dark outer leaves until you reach the taller inner leaves. Cut the tops of the leaves with a sharp knife. Place the artichoke in the acidulated water to prevent it from discoloring. Repeat the process with the other artichokes.

3 Boil or steam fresh artichokes until just tender (when a leaf comes away quite easily when pulled). Cook frozen artichoke hearts according to the packet instructions. Remove the pan from the heat and set aside to cool.

4 To make the mayonnaise, combine the egg yolk, mustard and vinegar in a mixing bowl. Season with salt and pepper to taste. Add the oil, a few drops at a time, beating constantly with a wire whisk. When 3–4 tablespoons have been fully incorporated, add the oil in a slow, steady stream, beating constantly. When the mixture is thick and smooth, stir in the chopped parsley. Blend well. Cover and chill until needed.

5 If using fresh artichokes, pull off the leaves. Cut the stems off level with the base. Scrape off the hairy "choke" with a knife or the side of a spoon.

6 Shell the eggs and cut them and the artichokes into wedges. Place on a serving plate, spoon the mayonnaise over the top, garnish with parsley sprigs and serve.

PANZANELLA

° ° °

Tomato juice, olive oil and wine vinegar dresses a colorful mixture of roasted peppers, anchovies and toasted ciabatta.

INGREDIENTS

8 ounces ciabatta (about 2/3 loaf)
1/4 pint/2/3 cup olive oil
3 red bell peppers
3 yellow bell peppers
2-ounce can anchovy fillets, drained
1 1/2 pounds ripe plum tomatoes
4 garlic cloves, crushed
4 tablespoons red wine vinegar
2 ounces capers
4 ounces/1 cup pitted black olives
salt and freshly ground black pepper
fresh basil leaves, to garnish

SERVES 4–6

1 Preheat the oven to 400°F. Cut the ciabatta into 3/4-inch chunks and drizzle with 1/4 cup of the oil. Broil lightly until just golden.

2 Place the peppers on a foil-lined baking sheet and bake for about 45 minutes, until the skins begin to char and blacken. Remove the peppers from the oven, place in a strong plastic bag, close the end and set aside to cool slightly.

3 Pull the skins off the peppers and cut the flesh into quarters, discarding the stalk ends and seeds. Coarsely chop the anchovies and set aside.

4 To make the tomato dressing, peel and halve the tomatoes. Scoop the seeds and pulp into a strainer set over a bowl. Using the back of a spoon, press the tomato pulp in the strainer to extract as much juice as possible. Discard the pulp and add the remaining oil, the garlic and vinegar to the juices.

5 Layer the toasted ciabatta, peppers, tomatoes, anchovies, capers and olives in a large salad bowl. Season the tomato dressing with salt and black pepper to taste and pour it over the salad. Leave to stand in a cool place for about 30 minutes. Serve garnished with plenty of fresh basil leaves.

RADICCHIO, ARTICHOKE AND WALNUT SALAD

° ° °

The distinctive, earthy taste of Jerusalem artichokes makes a lovely contrast to the sharp freshness of radicchio and lemon. Serve the salad warm or cold as an accompaniment to grilled steak or meats cooked on the barbecue.

INGREDIENTS

1 large radicchio or 5 ounces radicchio leaves
1 1/2 ounces/1/3 cup walnut pieces
3 tablespoons walnut oil
1 1/4 pounds Jerusalem artichokes
thinly pared rind and juice of 1 lemon
coarse sea salt and freshly ground black pepper
fresh flat leaf parsley, to garnish (optional)

SERVES 4

1 If using a whole radicchio, cut it into 8–10 wedges. Put the wedges or leaves in a flameproof dish. Sprinkle over the walnuts, then spoon over the oil and season to taste with salt and pepper. Broil for 2–3 minutes.

2 Peel the artichokes and cut up any large ones so that the pieces are all roughly the same size. Add the artichokes to a pan of boiling salted water with half the lemon juice and cook for 5–7 minutes, until tender. Drain well. Preheat the broiler to high.

3 Toss the artichokes into the salad with the remaining lemon juice and the pared lemon rind. Season with coarse sea salt and pepper. Broil until beginning to brown. Serve immediately garnished with torn pieces of parsley, if you like.

Cook's Tip
Look for Treviso radicchio, which has long, pointed leaves with thick white ribs. It is said to have the best flavor.

EGG, BACON AND AVOCADO SALAD

∘ ∘ ∘

INGREDIENTS

1 large romaine lettuce
8 bacon strips, fried
until crisp
2 large avocados, peeled and diced
6 hard-boiled eggs, shelled
and chopped
2 beefsteak tomatoes, peeled,
seeded and chopped
6 ounces blue cheese, crumbled

FOR THE DRESSING

1 garlic clove, crushed
1 teaspoon sugar
1½ teaspoons lemon juice
1½ tablespoons red wine vinegar
4 fluid ounces/½ cup peanut oil
salt and freshly ground
black pepper

SERVES 4

1 Slice the lettuce into thin strips across the leaves. Crumble the fried bacon strips.

2 To make the dressing, combine all the ingredients in a screw-top jar, season to taste and shake well. Spread out the strips of lettuce to make a bed on a large rectangular or oval platter.

3 Arrange the diced avocados, hard-boiled eggs, tomatoes and crumbled blue cheese neatly in rows on top of the lettuce. Sprinkle the bacon on top.

4 Pour the dressing carefully and evenly all over the salad just before serving.

SPICY CORN SALAD

∘ ∘ ∘

INGREDIENTS

2 tablespoons vegetable oil
1 pound drained canned
corn, or frozen corn, thawed
1 green bell pepper, seeded
and diced
1 small fresh red chile, seeded
and finely diced
4 scallions, sliced
3 tablespoons chopped fresh parsley
8 ounces cherry tomatoes, halved
salt and freshly ground
black pepper

FOR THE DRESSING

½ teaspoon sugar
2 tablespoons white wine vinegar
½ teaspoon Dijon mustard
1 tablespoon chopped
fresh basil
1 tablespoon mayonnaise
¼ teaspoon chili sauce

SERVES 4

1 Heat the oil in a large, heavy frying pan. Add the corn, green pepper, chili and scallions. Cook over a medium heat for about 5 minutes, until softened, stirring frequently.

2 Transfer the vegetables to a salad bowl. Stir in the parsley and the cherry tomatoes.

3 To make the dressing, combine all the ingredients in a small bowl and whisk together.

4 Pour the dressing over the corn mixture. Season to taste with salt and pepper. Toss well to combine, then serve immediately, while the salad is still warm.

CHORIZO IN OLIVE OIL

• • •

*Spanish chorizo sausage has a deliciously pungent taste. Frying chorizo with onions and olive oil
is one of the best ways of using it; you can also cook it on the barbecue, brushed with olive oil.*

INGREDIENTS

5 tablespoons extra virgin olive oil
12 ounces chorizo, sliced
1 large onion, thinly sliced
flat leaf parsley, coarsely chopped,
to garnish

SERVES 4

1 Heat the olive oil in a frying pan and
fry the chorizo over a high heat until
beginning to color. Remove from the
pan with a slotted spoon.

2 Add the onion slices to the pan and
cook until golden. Return the sausage
slices to the pan to heat through for
about 1 minute.

3 Tip the mixture into a shallow
serving dish and sprinkle with the
coarsely chopped flat leaf parsley.
Serve the chorizo on its own or as
a side dish, with warm crusty brea

Variation

Chorizo is usually available
in large supermarkets and
delicatessens, but any other
similar spicy sausage can be
used as a substitute.

FAVA BEAN, MUSHROOM AND CHORIZO SALAD

This salad can be served as a first course or as part of a buffet menu. Prepare it a day in advance and store it in the refrigerator until needed.

INGREDIENTS

8 ounces shelled fava beans
6 ounces chorizo
ablespoons extra virgin olive oil
8 ounces cremini
mushrooms, sliced
handful of fresh chives
salt and freshly ground
black pepper

SERVES 4

ok the fava beans in a large pan of
y salted boiling water until just
r. Drain and refresh under cold
ng water. If the beans are large,
way the tough outer skins.

move the skin from the chorizo
ut it into small chunks. Heat the
oil in a heavy frying pan, add the
zo and cook over a low heat for
nutes. Transfer to a bowl with
nushrooms, mix well and set aside
ol.

3 Chop half the chives and stir the
beans and chopped chives into the
mushroom mixture. Season to taste.
Serve the salad at room temperature,
garnished with the remaining chives.

LEEK AND BROILED RED BELL PEPPER SALAD
WITH GOAT CHEESE

The contrasting textures of silky, broiled peppers, soft cheese and slightly crisp leeks makes this salad extra-specially delicious. This would be a sophisticated first course served with plenty of fresh, rustic bread.

INGREDIENTS

*4 x ¹/₂-inch thick slices
chèvre cheese
2¹/₂ ounces/1 cup fine dry
white bread crumbs
1¹/₂ pounds young slender
leeks, trimmed
1 tablespoon olive oil
2 large red bell peppers
few fresh thyme sprigs, chopped
vegetable oil, for shallow frying
3 tablespoons chopped fresh flat
leaf parsley
salt and freshly ground
black pepper*

FOR THE DRESSING

*5 tablespoons extra virgin olive oil
1 small garlic clove, finely chopped
1 teaspoon Dijon mustard, plain or
flavored with herbes de Provence
1 tablespoon red wine vinegar*

SERVES 6

1 Remove any skin from the cheese. Spread out the bread crumbs on a plate and roll the cheese slices in them, pressing them in so that the cheese is well coated. Chill the coated cheese for 1 hour.

2 Cook the leeks in lightly salted boiling water for 3–4 minutes. Drain and cut into 3–4-inch lengths and toss in the olive oil and season to taste. Broil the leeks for 3–4 minutes on each side.

3 Halve and seed the peppers, then grill them, skin-side uppermost, until the skin is blackened and blistered. Place them in a bowl, cover and leave to stand for about 10 minutes, so that they soften in their own steam. Remove the skin and cut the flesh into strips, then mix with the leeks and thyme, adding pepper to taste.

4 Make the dressing by shaking all the ingredients together in a screw-top jar, adding seasoning to taste. Pour the dressing over the salad and chill it for several hours. Bring the salad back to room temperature before serving.

5 When ready to serve, heat a shallow layer of vegetable oil in a non-stick frying pan and fry the chèvre cheese slices quickly until golden brown on each side. Drain them on paper towels and cool slightly, then cut into bitesize pieces. Toss the cheese and parsley into the salad and serve immediately.

ROASTED CHERRY TOMATO AND ARUGULA SALAD

. . .

*ttle cherry tomatoes are sweet
d juicy, and roasting them in
e oven makes the flavor
onderfully rich and intense.
gether with the pungent, fresh
ste of arugula, they make an
citingly different salad.*

INGREDIENTS

8 ounces/2 cups dried chifferini
or pipe pasta
1 pound ripe baby Italian plum
tomatoes, halved lengthwise
tablespoons extra virgin olive oil
garlic cloves, cut into thin slivers
2 tablespoons balsamic vinegar
pieces sun-dried tomato in olive
oil, drained and chopped
large pinch of sugar
handful arugula, about 2½ ounces
salt and ground black pepper

SERVES 4

1 Preheat the oven to 375°F.
Meanwhile, cook the pasta in
lightly salted boiling water for
about 10 minutes, or according to
the instructions on the packet.

2 Arrange the halved tomatoes cut-
side up in a roasting pan, drizzle
2 tablespoons of the olive oil over
them and sprinkle with the slivers
of garlic. Season to taste with salt
and pepper. Roast in the oven for
20 minutes, turning once.

3 Put the remaining olive oil in a
large bowl with the vinegar, sun-
dried tomato pieces, sugar and a
little salt and pepper to taste. Stir
well to mix. Drain the pasta, add it
to the bowl of dressing and toss to
combine. Add the roasted tomatoes
and mix gently.

4 Before serving, add the arugula,
toss lightly and taste for seasoning.
Serve either at room temperature
or chilled.

SALAD OF ROASTED SHALLOTS AND BUTTERNUT SQUASH WITH FETA CHEESE

This is especially good served with a grain or starchy salad, made with rice or couscous, for example. Serve plenty of good bread to mop up the juices.

INGREDIENTS

5 tablespoons olive oil
1 tablespoon balsamic vinegar, plus
a little extra if you like
1 tablespoon sweet soy sauce
12 ounces shallots, peeled but
left whole
3 fresh red chiles
1 butternut squash, peeled, seeded
and cut into chunks
1 teaspoon finely chopped
fresh thyme
1/2 ounces flat leaf parsley
1 small garlic clove, finely chopped
3 ounces/3/4 cup chopped walnuts
5 ounces feta cheese
salt and freshly ground
black pepper

SERVES 4–6

1 Preheat the oven to 400°F. Beat the oil, vinegar and soy sauce together in a large bowl, then season with salt and pepper.

2 Toss the shallots and two of the chiles in the oil mixture and turn into a large roasting pan or an ovenproof dish. Roast, stirring once or twice, for 15 minutes.

3 Add the butternut squash and roast for a further 30–35 minutes, stirring once, until the squash is tender and browned. Remove from the oven, stir in the chopped thyme and set the vegetables aside to cool.

Cook's Tip

To peel shallots, place them in a bowl and cover with boiling water for 2 minutes. Drain and remove the skins with a knife.

4 Chop the flat leaf parsley and garlic together and mix with the walnuts. Seed and finely chop the remaining chile.

5 Stir the parsley, garlic and walnut mixture into the vegetables. Add chopped red chilli to taste and adjust the seasoning, adding a little extra balsamic vinegar if you like. Crumble the feta cheese and add to the salad. Transfer to a serving dish and serve immediately.

LENTIL AND SPINACH SALAD WITH ONION, CUMIN AND GARLIC

◦ ◦ ◦

This wonderful, earthy salad is great for a picnic or with food cooked on the barbecue. It improves with standing and is at its best served at room temperature rather than chilled.

INGREDIENTS
5 ounces/1 cup Puy lentils
1 fresh bay leaf
1 celery stick
fresh thyme sprig
2 tablespoons olive oil
1 onion or 3–4 shallots, finely chopped
2 teaspoons crushed toasted cumin seeds
14 ounces young spinach
salt and ground black pepper
2–3 tablespoons chopped fresh parsley, plus a few extra sprigs
toasted French bread, to serve

FOR THE DRESSING
5 tablespoons extra virgin olive oil
1 teaspoon Dijon mustard
3–5 teaspoons red wine vinegar
1 small garlic clove, finely chopped
½ teaspoon finely grated lemon rind

SERVES 6

1 Rinse the lentils, place them in a large pan and add water to cover. Tie the bay leaf, celery and thyme into a bundle and add to the pan. Bring to the boil, reduce the heat and cook for 30–45 minutes, until just tender.

2 Meanwhile, to make the dressing, mix the olive oil, mustard, 3 teaspoons of vinegar, the garlic and lemon rind, and season to taste with salt and pepper.

3 Drain the cooked lentils and turn them into a large bowl. Add most of the dressing and toss well so that they are well coated, then set the lentils aside, stirring occasionally. Be careful not to break up the lentils when stirring.

4 Heat the oil in a deep frying pan and cook the finely chopped onion or shallots over a low heat for 4–5 minutes, until they are beginning to soften but not brown. Add the toasted cumin seeds and cook for 1 minute.

5 Add the spinach, season to taste, cover and cook for 2 minutes. Stir, then cook again briefly until wilted.

6 Stir the spinach into the lentils and set aside to cool. Stir in the remaining dressing and chopped parsley. Adjust the seasoning, adding extra vinegar if necessary.

7 Put the salad on a serving platter and sprinkle over some parsley. Serve with toasted French bread.

341

TOFU AND CUCUMBER SALAD

· · ·

This refreshing salad has a hot, sweet-and-sour dressing.

INGREDIENTS
1 small cucumber
4 ounces square tofu
vegetable oil, for frying
4 ounces/½ cup beansprouts
salt
celery leaves, to garnish

FOR THE DRESSING
1 small onion, grated
2 garlic cloves, crushed
1–1½ teaspoons chili sauce
2–3 tablespoons dark soy sauce
1–2 tablespoons rice
wine vinegar
2 teaspoons dark brown sugar

SERVES 4–6

1 Cut the cucumber into neat cubes and place on a plate. Sprinkle with salt to extract the excess liquid. Set aside, while you are preparing the remaining ingredients.

2 Cut the tofu into cubes. Heat a little oil in a pan and cook on both sides until golden brown. Drain on paper towels.

3 To make the dressing, put the onion, garlic and chili sauce in a screw-top jar and shake well. Stir in the soy sauce, vinegar, sugar and salt to taste.

4 Just before serving, rinse the cucumber under cold running water. Drain and dry thoroughly. Toss the cucumber, tofu and beansprouts together in a serving bowl and pour over the dressing. Garnish with the celery leaves and serve the salad immediately.

PLANTAIN AND GREEN BANANA SALAD

Cook the plantains and bananas in their skins. Their soft texture will then absorb the dressing.

INGREDIENTS

2 firm yellow plantains
3 green bananas
1 garlic clove, crushed
1 red onion
1–2 tablespoons chopped
fresh cilantro
3 tablespoons sunflower oil
1½ tablespoons malt vinegar
salt and freshly ground
black pepper

SERVES 4

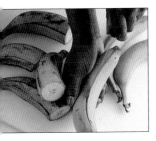

1 Slit the plantains and bananas lengthwise along their natural ridges, then cut in half and place in a large pan.

2 Cover the plantains and bananas with water, add a little salt and bring to the boil. Boil gently for 20 minutes, until tender, then remove from the water. When they are cool enough to handle, peel and cut into medium-size slices.

3 Put the plantain and banana slices into a large bowl and add the garlic, turning the mixture with a wooden spoon to distribute the garlic evenly.

4 Cut the onion in half and slice thinly. Add it to the bowl with the chopped cilantro, oil and vinegar. Season to taste with salt and pepper. Toss together to mix, then transfer to a serving bowl.

GREEN BEAN SALAD

Beans are great served with a simple vinaigrette, but this dish is a little more elaborate.

INGREDIENTS

1 pound green beans
1 tablespoon olive oil
1 ounce/2 tablespoons butter
1/2 garlic clove, crushed
2 ounces/1 cup fresh
white bread crumbs
1 tablespoon chopped fresh parsley
1 hard-boiled egg, shelled and
finely chopped

FOR THE DRESSING

2 tablespoons olive oil
2 tablespoons sunflower oil
2 teaspoons white wine vinegar
1/2 garlic clove, crushed
1/4 teaspoon Dijon mustard
pinch of sugar
pinch of salt

SERVES 4

1 Cook the beans in salted boiling water for 5–6 minutes, until tender. Drain, refresh under cold running water and place in a serving bowl.

2 To make the dressing, whisk the oils, vinegar garlic, mustard, sugar and salt in a pitcher. Pour the dressing over the beans and toss.

3 Heat the oil and butter in a frying pan and cook the garlic, stirring, for 1 minute. Stir in the bread crumbs and fry over a moderate heat, stirring frequently, for 3–4 minutes, until golden brown.

4 Remove the pan from the heat and stir in the chopped parsley and then the hard-boiled egg. Sprinkle the bread crumb mixture over the green beans. Serve warm or at room temperature.

CORONATION SALAD

. . .

The salad dressing in this dish was created for the coronation dinner of Queen Elizabeth II. It makes a wonderful accompaniment to hard-boiled eggs and vegetables.

INGREDIENTS

1 pound new potatoes
3 tablespoons French Dressing
3 scallions, chopped
6 eggs, hard-boiled, shelled
and halved
frisée lettuce leaves
1/4 cucumber, cut into thin strips
6 large radishes, sliced
1 carton salad cress
salt and freshly ground
black pepper

FOR THE CORONATION DRESSING
2 tablespoons olive oil
1 small onion, chopped
1 tablespoon mild curry powder
or korma spice mix
2 teaspoons tomato paste
2 tablespoons lemon juice
2 tablespoons sherry
1/2 pint/1 1/4 cups mayonnaise
1/4 pint/2/3 cup plain yogurt

SERVES 6

1 Boil the potatoes in salted water until tender. Drain and transfer them to a large bowl.

2 Toss the potatoes in the French Dressing, stir in the scallions, season to taste and leave to cool.

3 Meanwhile, make the coronation dressing. Heat the oil in a small pan and cook the chopped onion for 3 minutes, until soft. Stir in the curry powder or spice mix and cook for 1 minute more. Remove from the heat and mix in all the other dressing ingredients.

4 Stir the dressing into the cooled potatoes, add the eggs, then cover with plastic wrap and chill in the refrigerator. Line a serving platter with lettuce leaves and pile the salad in the center. Sprinkle over the cucumber strips, radishes and cress.

SWEET POTATO AND CARROT SALAD

This warm salad has a sweet-and-sour flavor.

INGREDIENTS

1 medium sweet potato
2 carrots, cut into thick
    diagonal slices
3 medium tomatoes
8–10 iceberg lettuce leaves
3 ounces/¹/₂ cup canned
    chickpeas, drained
    and rinsed

FOR THE DRESSING
1 tablespoon clear honey
6 tablespoons plain yogurt
¹/₂ teaspoon salt
1 teaspoon freshly ground
    black pepper

FOR THE GARNISH
1 tablespoon walnuts
1 tablespoon golden raisins
1 small onion, cut into rings

SERVES 4

1 Peel the sweet potato and cut roughly into cubes. Boil it until it is soft but not mushy, then cover the pan and set aside.

2 Boil the carrots for just a few minutes, making sure that they remain crunchy. Add the carrots to the sweet potato.

3 Drain the water from the sweet potato and carrots and place them together in a bowl.

4 Slice the tops off the tomatoes, then scoop out the seeds with a spoon and discard. Coarsely chop the flesh. Slice the lettuce into strips across the leaves.

5 Line a salad bowl with the shredded lettuce leaves. Mix together the sweet potato, carrots, chickpeas and tomatoes and place the mixture in the center.

6 To make the dressing, mix together all the ingredients and beat well, using a fork.

7 Garnish the salad with the walnuts, golden raisins and onion rings. Pour the dressing over the top just before serving, or serve it in a separate bowl with the salad.

Cook's Tip

This salad makes an excellent light lunch or an easy family supper. Serve it with a sweet mango chutney and warm naan bread.

Variation

You can substitute other canned peas or beans for the chickpeas, such as gunga peas, also known as pigeon peas, or ful medames.

POTATO SALADS

. . .

Here are two versions of a light, summery potato salad.

INGREDIENTS
2 pounds new potatoes
1 teaspoon salt

FOR THE DRESSING FOR THE
WARM SALAD
2 tablespoons hazelnut or walnut oil
4 tablespoons sunflower oil
juice of 1 lemon
15 pistachio nuts
salt and freshly ground black pepper
flat leaf parsley, to garnish

FOR THE DRESSING FOR THE
COLD SALAD
5 tablespoons olive oil
2 teaspoons white wine vinegar
1 garlic clove, crushed
6 tablespoons finely chopped fresh parsley
2 large scallions, finely chopped
salt and freshly ground black pepper

SERVES 4

1 Scrub the potatoes but don't peel them. Place them in a large pan, cover with cold water and bring to the boil over a medium heat. Add the salt, lower the heat and simmer for about 15 minutes, until tender. Drain the potatoes well and set aside to cool slightly.

2 For the warm salad, mix together the hazelnut or walnut oil with the sunflower oil and lemon juice and season well with salt and pepper.

3 Use a large, heavy knife to crush the pistachio nuts coarsely.

4 When the potatoes have cooled slightly, pour over the dressing and sprinkle with the chopped nuts. Serve immediately garnished with sprig of parsley.

5 For the cold salad, cook the potatoes as above, drain and leave to cool completely.

6 Whisk together the olive oil, white wine vinegar, garlic, parsley and scallions and season to taste with salt and pepper. Pour the dressing over the potatoes. Cover tightly and chill overnight. Allow to come to room temperature before serving.

POTATO SALAD WITH EGG AND LEMON DRESSING

. . .

*his recipe draws on the
ontrasting flavors of egg and
'mon. Chopped parsley
rovides a fresh green finish.*

INGREDIENTS

2 pounds new potatoes
1 medium onion, finely chopped
1 hard-boiled egg
1/2 pint/1 1/4 cups mayonnaise
1 garlic clove, crushed
finely grated rind and juice of
1 lemon
4 tablespoons chopped
fresh parsley
salt and freshly ground
black pepper
fresh parsley sprig, to garnish

SERVES 4

Scrub or scrape the potatoes,
lace in a large pan, cover with
old water and bring to the boil
ver a medium heat. Add a pinch
f salt, lower the heat and simmer
or 15 minutes, until tender. Drain
well and set aside to cool.

Cut the potatoes into large dice
nd season to taste with salt and
epper. Add the chopped onion.

3 Shell the hard-boiled egg and
grate into a mixing bowl, then add
the mayonnaise. Combine the
garlic and lemon rind and juice in a
small bowl and stir them carefully
into the mayonnaise.

4 Fold the mayonnaise mixture
gently, but thoroughly into the
potatoes, then fold in the chopped
parsley. Serve the potato salad
warm or cold, garnished with
sprigs of parsley.

Variation

Fresh chives make an excellent
alternative to parsley.

SPICY POTATO SALAD

· · ·

This tasty and versatile salad is quick to prepare.

INGREDIENTS

2 pounds potatoes
2 red bell peppers
2 celery sticks
1 shallot
2–3 scallions
1 fresh green chile
1 garlic clove, crushed
2 teaspoons finely chopped
fresh chives, plus extra to garnish
2 teaspoons finely chopped
fresh basil
1 tablespoon finely chopped
fresh parsley
1 tablespoon light cream
2 tablespoons sour cream
1 tablespoon mayonnaise
1 teaspoon prepared mild mustard
1½ teaspoons sugar
salt

SERVES 6

3 Blend the light cream, sour cream, mayonnaise, mustard and sugar in a small bowl, stirring until the mixture is well combined.

4 Pour the dressing over the salad and stir gently, but thoroughly to coat evenly. Serve, garnished with extra chopped chives.

1 Peel the potatoes. Boil in lightly salted water for 10–12 minutes, until tender. Drain and cool, then cut into cubes and place in a large mixing bowl.

2 Halve the red bell peppers, cut away and discard the core and seeds and cut the flesh into small pieces. Finely chop the celery, shallot and scallions and slice the chile very thinly, discarding the seeds. Add all the vegetables to the potatoes together with the garlic chives, basil and parsley.

POTATO SALAD WITH GARLIC SAUSAGE

*his tasty potato salad would
so make a light lunch dish.*

INGREDIENTS

1 pound small waxy potatoes
2–3 tablespoons dry white wine
2 shallots, finely chopped
tablespoon chopped fresh parsley
tablespoon chopped fresh tarragon
6 ounces cooked garlic sausage
fresh flat leaf parsley sprig,
to garnish

FOR THE VINAIGRETTE
2 teaspoons Dijon mustard
tablespoon tarragon vinegar or
white wine vinegar
tablespoons extra virgin olive oil
salt and freshly ground
black pepper

SERVES 4

Scrub the potatoes. Boil in salted
ater for 10–12 minutes, until
nder. Drain and refresh under
old running water.

Peel the potatoes if you like, or
ave in their skins, and cut into
4-inch slices. Sprinkle with the
ine and shallots.

Variation

The potatoes are also delicious
served on their own and
perhaps accompanied by
marinated herrings.

3 To make the vinaigrette, mix the
mustard and vinegar in a small
bowl, then whisk in the oil,
1 tablespoon at a time. Season and
pour over the potatoes.

4 Add the herbs to the potatoes
and toss until well mixed.

5 Slice the garlic sausage thinly and
toss with the potatoes. Season the
salad with salt and pepper to taste
and serve at room temperature,
garnished with a sprig of parsley.

PEPPERY BEAN SALAD

· · ·

This pretty salad uses canned beans for convenience.

INGREDIENTS

15-ounce can red kidney beans
15-ounce can black-eyed peas
425g/15oz can chickpeas
¼ red bell pepper
¼ green bell pepper
6 radishes
1 tablespoon chopped scallion

FOR THE DRESSING
1 teaspoon ground cumin
1 tablespoon tomato ketchup
2 tablespoons extra virgin olive oil
1 tablespoon white wine vinegar
1 garlic clove, crushed
½ teaspoon hot pepper sauce

SERVES 4–6

1 Drain the red kidney beans, black-eyed peas and chickpeas and rinse under cold running water. Shake off the excess water and tip them into a large bowl.

2 Core, seed and chop the red and green bell peppers. Trim the radishes and slice thinly. Add the peppers, radishes and scallion to the mixed beans.

3 Mix together the cumin, tomato ketchup, oil, vinegar and garlic in small bowl. Add a little salt and hot pepper sauce to taste and stir again thoroughly.

4 Pour the dressing over the salad and mix gently, but thoroughly. Cover the bowl with plastic wrap and chill the salad in the refrigerator for at least 1 hour before serving, garnished with the chopped scallion.

SMOKED HAM AND BEAN SALAD

This is a fairly substantial salad that should be served in small quantities if intended as an accompaniment.

INGREDIENTS

6 ounces dried black-eyed peas
1 onion
1 carrot
8 ounces smoked ham, diced
4 medium tomatoes, peeled, seeded and diced
salt and freshly ground black pepper

FOR THE DRESSING
2 garlic cloves, crushed
3 tablespoons olive oil
3 tablespoons red wine vinegar
2 tablespoons vegetable oil
1 tablespoon lemon juice
1 tablespoon chopped fresh basil

1 tablespoon whole-grain mustard
1 teaspoon soy sauce
1/2 teaspoon dried oregano
1/2 teaspoon superfine sugar
1/4 teaspoon Worcestershire sauce
1/2 teaspoon chili sauce

SERVES 8

1 Soak the beans in cold water to cover overnight. Drain.

2 Put the beans in a large pan and add the onion and carrot. Cover with fresh cold water and bring to the boil. Boil vigorously for 15 minutes, then lower the heat and simmer for about 1 hour, until the beans are tender.

3 Drain the beans, reserving the onion and carrot. Transfer the beans to a salad bowl.

4 Finely chop the onion and carrot. Toss with the beans. Stir in the smoked ham and tomatoes.

5 For the dressing, combine all the ingredients in a small bowl and whisk to mix.

6 Pour the dressing over the ham and beans. Season to taste with salt and pepper. Toss the salad to combine, then serve.

WHITE BEAN AND CELERY SALAD

o o o

This simple bean salad is a delicious alternative to the ubiquitous potato salad.

INGREDIENTS

1 pound dried white beans
(cannellini, navy or
lima beans)
1¾ pints/4 cups vegetable stock
3 celery sticks, cut into
½-inch strips
4 fluid ounces/½ cup
French Dressing
3 tablespoons chopped
fresh parsley
salt and freshly ground
black pepper

SERVES 4

1 Put the beans in a bowl, cover with cold water and soak for at least 4 hours. Discard the soaking water, then place the beans in a heavy pan. Cover with water.

2 Bring to the boil and simmer without a lid for 1½ hours, or until the skins are broken. Cooked beans will squash readily between a thumb and forefinger. Drain well.

Variation

If you are short of time, you can substitute three 14-ounce cans of white beans for the dried beans. Drain, rinse and follow the recipe from step 3.

3 Place the cooked beans in a large pan. Add the vegetable stock and celery, bring to the boil, cover and simmer for 15 minutes. Drain thoroughly. Moisten the beans with the French Dressing and leave to cool completely.

4 Add the chopped parsley to the beans and mix well. Season to tast with salt and pepper, transfer to a salad bowl and serve.

LENTIL AND CABBAGE SALAD

. . .

This is quite a filling salad with lovely crunchy texture.

INGREDIENTS

8 ounces/1 cup Puy lentils
3 garlic cloves
1 bay leaf
small onion, peeled and studded with 2 cloves
1 tablespoon olive oil
1 red onion, thinly sliced
1 tablespoon fresh thyme leaves
12 ounces cabbage, shredded
grated rind and juice of 1 lemon
1 tablespoon raspberry vinegar
salt and freshly ground black pepper

SERVES 4–6

Rinse the lentils in cold water and place in a large pan with 2¼ cups cold water, one of the garlic cloves, the bay leaf and clove-studded onion. Bring to the boil and cook for 10 minutes. Reduce the heat, cover the pan and simmer gently for 15–20 minutes. Drain and discard the onion, garlic and bay leaf.

Crush the remaining garlic cloves. Heat the oil in a large pan. Add the red onion, crushed garlic and thyme and cook, stirring occasionally, for 5 minutes, until the onion has softened.

3 Add the cabbage and cook for 3–5 minutes, until just cooked, but still crunchy.

4 Stir in the cooked lentils, lemon rind and juice and the raspberry vinegar. Season to taste with salt and pepper, transfer to a serving dish and serve warm.

BROWN BEAN SALAD

. . .

Brown beans are available from
health-food stores.

INGREDIENTS

12 ounces/1½ cups dried
brown beans
3 fresh thyme sprigs
2 bay leaves
1 onion, halved
4 garlic cloves, crushed
1½ teaspoons crushed cumin seeds
3 scallions, chopped
6 tablespoons chopped fresh parsley
4 teaspoons lemon juice
6 tablespoons olive oil
3 hard-boiled eggs, shelled and
coarsely chopped
1 pickled cucumber,
coarsely chopped
salt and freshly ground
black pepper

SERVES 6

1 Put the beans in a bowl, cover
with plenty of cold water and leave
to soak overnight. Drain, transfer
to a pan and cover with fresh
water. Bring to the boil.

2 Reduce the heat and add the
thyme, bay leaves and onion.
Simmer very gently for about
1 hour, until tender. Drain and
discard the herbs and onion.

Cook's Tip

The cooking time for dried
beans can vary considerably.
They may need only
45 minutes, or much longer.

3 Place the beans in a large bowl.
Mix together the garlic, cumin
seeds, scallions, parsley, lemon jui[ce]
and olive oil in a small bowl, and
add a little salt and pepper. Pour
over the beans and toss the
ingredients lightly together.

4 Gently stir in the hard-boiled
eggs and chopped pickled
cucumber. Transfer the salad to a
serving dish and serve immediate[ly]

CRACKED WHEAT SALAD

. . .

Flavorsome, fresh herbs are essential for this salad.

INGREDIENTS

8 ounces/1⅓ cups cracked wheat
12 fluid ounces/1½ cups
vegetable stock
1 cinnamon stick
generous pinch of ground cumin
pinch of cayenne pepper
pinch of ground cloves
1 teaspoon salt
5 black olives
10 snow peas
1 red and 1 yellow bell pepper,
roasted, peeled, seeded and diced
2 plum tomatoes, peeled, seeded
and diced
2 shallots, thinly sliced
2 tablespoons each shredded fresh
basil, mint and parsley
2 tablespoons coarsely
chopped walnuts
2 tablespoons balsamic vinegar
4 fluid ounces/½ cup extra virgin
olive oil
freshly ground black pepper
onion rings, to garnish

SERVES 4

Place the cracked wheat in a large bowl. Pour the stock into a pan and bring to the boil with the cinnamon stick, cumin, cayenne, cloves and salt.

Cook for 1 minute, then pour the stock, with the cinnamon stick, over the cracked wheat. Leave to stand for 30 minutes.

3 In a separate bowl, mix together the snow peas, red and yellow bell peppers, tomatoes, shallots, olives, basil, mint parsley and walnuts. Add the balsamic vinegar, olive oil and a little black pepper and stir thoroughly to mix.

4 Strain the cracked wheat of any liquid and discard the cinnamon stick. Place the cracked wheat in a serving bowl, stir in the fresh vegetable and herb mixture and serve the salad, garnished with onion rings.

FRUITY BROWN RICE SALAD

° ° °

INGREDIENTS

4 ounces/²/₃ cup brown rice
1 small red bell pepper, seeded
and diced
7-ounce can corn
kernels, drained
3 tablespoons golden raisins
8-ounce can pineapple pieces
in fruit juice
1 tablespoon light soy sauce
1 tablespoon sunflower oil
1 tablespoon hazelnut oil
1 garlic clove, crushed
1 teaspoon finely chopped fresh
root ginger
salt and freshly ground
black pepper
4 scallions, sliced,
to garnish

SERVES 4–6

1 Cook the brown rice in a large pan of lightly salted boiling water for about 30 minutes, or until it is tender. Drain thoroughly and set aside to cool. Meanwhile, prepare the garnish. Slice the scallions at an angle, as shown, then set aside until required.

2 Tip the rice into a large serving bowl and add the red bell pepper, corn and golden raisins. Drain the pineapple pieces, reserving the juice, then add them to the rice mixture and toss lightly to mix.

3 Pour the reserved pineapple juice into a clean screw-top jar. Add the soy sauce, sunflower and hazelnut oils, garlic and root ginger. Season to taste with salt and black pepper. Close the jar tightly and shake well to combine.

4 Pour the dressing over the salad and toss well. Sprinkle the scallions over the top and serve.

Cook's Tip
Hazelnut oil gives a wonderfully distinctive flavor to any salad dressing. Like olive oil, it contains mainly monounsaturated fats.

COUSCOUS SALAD

∘ ∘ ∘

This salad has a delicate flavor and is excellent with kebabs.

INGREDIENTS

10 ounces/1²/₃ cups couscous
18 fluid ounces/2¹/₄ cups boiling vegetable stock
16–20 black olives
2 small zucchini
1 ounce/¹/₄ cup sliced almonds, toasted
4 tablespoons olive oil
1 tablespoon lemon juice
1 tablespoon chopped fresh cilantro
1 tablespoon chopped fresh parsley
good pinch of ground cumin
good pinch of cayenne pepper
salt

SERVES 4

3 Carefully mix the zucchini strips, olives and toasted almonds into the couscous.

4 Mix together the olive oil, lemon juice, herbs, spices and a pinch of salt in a small pitcher or bowl. Stir into the salad.

1 Place the couscous in a bowl and pour over the boiling stock. Stir with a fork and then set aside for 10 minutes for the stock to be absorbed. Fluff up with a fork.

2 Halve the olives, discarding the pits. Trim the zucchini and cut them into small julienne strips.

Variation

You can add a variety of other vegetables to this salad. Try peeled and chopped tomatoes or seeded red bell pepper cut into small julienne strips.

ORANGE AND CRACKED WHEAT SALAD

. . .

Cracked wheat makes an excellent alternative to rice or pasta as a filling side salad with a delightful texture.

INGREDIENTS

1 small green bell pepper
5 ounces/scant 1 cup cracked wheat
¹/₄ cucumber, diced
¹/₂ ounce/¹/₂ cup chopped fresh mint
1¹/₂ ounces/¹/₃ cup sliced almonds, toasted
grated rind and juice of 1 lemon
2 seedless oranges, peeled
salt and freshly ground black pepper
fresh mint sprigs, to garnish

SERVES 4

1 Using a sharp vegetable knife, carefully halve and seed the green bell pepper. Cut into small cubes and set aside.

2 Place the cracked wheat in a large pan and add 2¹/₂ cups water. Bring to the boil, lower the heat, cover and simmer for 10–15 minutes, until tender. Alternatively, place the cracked wheat in a heatproof bowl, pour over boiling water and leave to soak for 30 minutes. Most, if not all, of the water should be absorbed; drain off any excess.

3 Toss the cracked wheat with the cucumber, green bell pepper, mint and toasted almonds in a serving bowl. Add the grated lemon rind and the lemon juice.

4 Working over the salad bowl to catch the juice, cut the oranges into neat segments, leaving the membrane behind. Add the segments to the cracked wheat mixture, then season to taste with salt and pepper and toss lightly. Garnish with mint sprigs and serve.

Cook's Tip

Cracked wheat is known by a number of names, the best known being bulghur wheat. It is also called burghul and pourgouri in the Middle East.

VARIATION
Cracked Wheat Salad with Fennel and Pomegranate

This version uses the added crunchiness of fennel and the sweetness of pomegranate seeds. It is a perfect choice for a summer lunch.

INGREDIENTS

8 ounces/1¹/₃ cups cracked wheat
2 fennel bulbs
1 small red chile, seeded and finely chopped
1 celery stick, thinly sliced
2 tablespoons olive oil
finely grated rind and juice of 2 lemons
6–8 scallions, chopped
6 tablespoons chopped fresh mint
6 tablespoons chopped fresh parsley
the seeds from 1 pomegranate
salt and freshly ground black pepper
lettuce leaves, to serve

SERVES 6

1 Place the cracked wheat in a bowl and pour over enough boiling water to cover. Leave to stand for 30 minutes. Drain through a strainer, pressing out excess water.

2 Halve the fennel bulbs and cut into very thin slices.

3 Mix all the remaining ingredients together, then stir in the cracked wheat and fennel. Season to taste with salt and pepper, cover and set aside for 30 minutes before serving with lettuce leaves.

Not just for summer, main course salads are so versatile they are
welcome all year around. This chapter includes a wonderful
range of dishes made with fish and shellfish, chicken and cheese,
nuts, noodles and, of course, salad vegetables.

MAIN COURSE
SALADS

SALADE NIÇOISE

Served with good French bread, this regional classic makes a wonderful summer lunch or light supper dish.

INGREDIENTS

8 ounces green beans
1 pound new potatoes, peeled and cut into 1-inch pieces
white wine vinegar and olive oil, for sprinkling
1 small romaine or round lettuce, torn into bitesize pieces
4 ripe plum tomatoes, quartered
1 small cucumber, peeled, seeded and diced
1 green or red bell pepper, seeded and thinly sliced
4 hard-boiled eggs, shelled and quartered
24 black olives
8-ounce can tuna in brine, drained
2-ounce can anchovy fillets in olive oil, drained
basil leaves, to garnish
garlic croûtons, to serve

FOR THE ANCHOVY VINAIGRETTE
4 teaspoons Dijon mustard
2-ounce can anchovy fillets in olive oil, drained
1 garlic clove, crushed
4 tablespoons lemon juice or white wine vinegar
4 fluid ounces/¹/₂ cup sunflower oil
4 fluid ounces/¹/₂ cup extra virgin olive oil
freshly ground black pepper

SERVES 4–6

1 First, make the anchovy vinaigrette. Place the mustard, anchovies and garlic in a bowl and mix together by pressing the garlic and anchovies against the sides of the bowl. Season generously with pepper. Using a small whisk, blend in the lemon juice or vinegar. Slowly whisk in the sunflower oil in a thin stream, followed by the olive oil, whisking until the dressing is smooth and creamy.

2 Alternatively, put all the ingredients except the oils in a food processor fitted with the metal blade and process to combine. With the machine running, slowly add the oils in a thin stream until the vinaigrette is thick and creamy.

3 Drop the green beans into a large pan of boiling water and boil for 3 minutes, until tender, but crisp. Transfer the beans to a colander with a slotted spoon, then rinse under cold running water to refresh. Drain well again and set aside until required.

4 Add the potatoes to the same boiling water, reduce the heat and simmer for 10–15 minutes, until just tender, then drain. Sprinkle with a little vinegar and olive oil and a spoonful of the vinaigrette.

5 Arrange the lettuce on a serving platter to make a bed, top with the tomatoes, cucumber and red or green bell pepper, then add the green beans and potatoes.

6 Arrange the eggs around the edge. Place the olives, tuna and anchovies on top and garnish with the basil leaves. Drizzle with the remaining vinaigrette and serve with garlic croûtons.

Cook's Tip

To make garlic croûtons, thinly slice a French loaf or cut a larger loaf, such as rustic bread, into 1-inch cubes. Place the bread in a single layer on a baking sheet and cook in the oven, preheated to 350°F, for 7–10 minutes, or until golden, turning once. Rub the toast with a garlic clove and serve hot, or leave to cool and store in an airtight container until needed.

MOROCCAN TUNA SALAD

• • •

This salad is similar to the classic salade Niçoise but uses tuna or swordfish steaks and fresh fava beans along with the familiar green beans.

INGREDIENTS

about 2 pounds fresh tuna or
swordfish, sliced into
3/4-inch steaks
olive oil, for brushing

FOR THE SALAD
1 pound green beans
1 pound fava beans
1 romaine lettuce
1 pound cherry tomatoes, halved,
unless very tiny
2 tbsp coarsely chopped
fresh cilantro
3 hard-boiled eggs
3 tablespoons olive oil
2–3 teaspoons lime or
lemon juice
1/2 garlic clove, crushed
6–8 ounces /11/2–2 cups pitted
black olives

FOR THE MARINADE
1 onion
2 garlic cloves
1/2 bunch fresh parsley
1/2 bunch fresh cilantro
2 teaspoons paprika
3 tablespoons olive oil
2 tablespoons white wine vinegar
1 tablespoon lime or lemon juice

SERVES 6

1 To make the marinade, place all the ingredients in a food processor, add 3 tablespoons of water and process for 30–40 seconds.

2 Prick the fish steaks all over with a fork, place in a shallow dish and pour over the marinade, turning the fish to coat. Cover with plastic wrap and leave in a cool place for 2–4 hours.

3 To prepare the salad, cook the green beans and fava beans in boiling salted water until tender. Drain and refresh under cold water. Discard the outer shells from the fava beans and place in a large serving bowl with the green beans.

4 Discard the outer lettuce leaves and tear the inner leaves into pieces. Add to the beans with the tomatoes and cilantro. Shell the eggs and cut into eighths.

5 Mix the olive oil, lime or lemon juice and garlic to make a dressing.

6 Preheat the broiler to high and arrange the tuna or swordfish steaks in a broiler pan. Brush with the marinade together with a little extra olive oil and broil for 5–6 minutes on each side, until the fish is tender and flakes easily. Brush again with marinade and more olive oil when you turn the fish over.

7 Allow the fish to cool a little, then break the steaks into large pieces. Toss into the salad with the olives and the dressing. Decorate with the eggs and serve.

WARM FISH SALAD WITH MANGO DRESSING
• • •

*his spicy salad is best served
uring the summer months,
referably out of doors.*

INGREDIENTS
1 French loaf
4 redfish, black bream or porgy,
each about 10 ounces
1 tablespoon vegetable oil
1 mango
/2-inch piece of fresh root ginger
1 fresh red chile, seeded and
finely chopped
2 tablespoons lime juice
2 tablespoons chopped
fresh cilantro
6 ounces young spinach leaves
5 ounces bok choy
5 ounces cherry tomatoes, halved

SERVES 4

Preheat the oven to 350°F.
ut the French loaf into 8-inch
ngths. Slice lengthwise, then
ut into thick fingers. Place the
read on a baking sheet and
ace in the oven for 15 minutes
 dry.

Preheat the broiler or light the
arbecue and allow the embers to
ttle. Slash the fish deeply on both
des and brush them all over with
e vegetable oil. Broil or cook the
sh on the barbecue for 6 minutes,
rning once.

3 Peel the mango and cut in half,
discarding the pit. Thinly slice one
half of the mango flesh and set it
aside. Place the other half in a food
processor. Peel the ginger, grate it
finely, then add it to the mango
with the red chile, lime juice and
chopped cilantro. Process until
smooth. Adjust to a pouring
consistency by adding
2–3 tablespoons water.

4 Wash the spinach and bok choy
leaves in cold water and spin dry
or pat them dry with paper towels,
then distribute them among four
serving plates. Place the fish on top
of the leaves. Spoon the mango
dressing over them and finish with
the reserved slices of mango and
the tomato halves. Serve
immediately with the fingers of
crispy French bread.

BROILED SALMON AND SPRING VEGETABLE SALAD

*Spring is the time to enjoy
sweet, young vegetables. Serve
with grilled salmon topped with
sorrel and quail eggs.*

INGREDIENTS

*12 ounces small new potatoes,
scrubbed or scraped
4 quail eggs
4 ounces young carrots, peeled
4 ounces baby corn cobs
4 ounces sugar snap peas
4 ounces fine green beans
4 ounces young zucchini
4 ounces patty-pan
squash (optional)
4 fluid ounces/¹/₂ cup
French Dressing
4 salmon fillets, each about
5 ounces, skinned
4 ounces sorrel,
stems removed
salt and freshly ground
black pepper*

SERVES 4

1 Bring the potatoes to the boil in
lightly salted water, lower the heat
and simmer for about 15 minutes,
until tender. Drain well, cover and
keep warm.

2 Cover the quail eggs with boiling
water and cook for 8 minutes.
Refresh under cold water, shell and
cut in half.

3 Bring a pan of lightly salted
water to the boil, add the carrots,
corn, sugar snap peas, beans,
zucchini and squash, if using, and
cook for 2–3 minutes, until tender-
crisp. Drain well. Place the hot
vegetables and potatoes in a bowl,
moisten with a little of the French
Dressing and set aside to cool.

4 Brush the salmon fillets
with some of the French
Dressing and broil for 6 minutes,
turning once.

5 Place the sorrel in a stainless-steel
or enamel pan with 2 tablespoons
French Dressing. Cover and soften
over a gentle heat for 2 minutes.
Put in a small strainer and cool to
room temperature.

6 Divide the potato and vegetable
mixture among four large serving
plates, then position a piece of
salmon to one side of each plate.
Place a spoonful of sorrel on each
piece of salmon and top with two
pieces of quail egg. Season to taste
with salt and pepper and serve at
room temperature.

Cook's Tip

If sorrel is unavailable, use
young spinach leaves instead.
Cook it gently in the same way
as the sorrel.

NOODLES WITH PINEAPPLE, GINGER AND CHILES

o o o

A coconut, lime and fish sauce dressing is the perfect partner to this fruity and spicy salad.

INGREDIENTS

*10 ounces dried udon noodles
1/2 pineapple, peeled, cored and sliced into 1 1/2-inch rings
3 tablespoons light brown sugar
4 tablespoons lime juice
4 tablespoons coconut milk
2 tablespoons Thai fish sauce
2 tablespoons grated fresh root ginger
2 garlic cloves, finely chopped
1 ripe mango or 2 peaches, finely diced
freshly ground black pepper
2 scallions, thinly sliced, 2 red chiles, seeded and finely shredded, and fresh mint leaves, to garnish*

SERVES 4

1 Cook the noodles in a large pan of boiling water until tender, following the directions on the packet. Drain, refresh under cold water and drain again.

2 Place the pineapple rings in a flameproof dish, sprinkle with 2 tablespoons of the sugar and broil for about 5 minutes, or until golden. Cool slightly and cut into small dice.

3 Mix the lime juice, coconut milk and fish sauce in a salad bowl. Add the remaining brown sugar with the ginger, garlic and black pepper and whisk well. Add the noodles and pineapple.

4 Add the diced mango or peaches and toss lightly to mix. Sprinkle over the sliced scallions, shredded chiles and mint leaves before serving.

BUCKWHEAT NOODLES WITH SMOKED SALMON

o o o

Young pea sprouts are available for only a short time. You can substitute watercress, salad cress, young leeks or your favorite green vegetable or herb in this dish.

INGREDIENTS

*8 ounces buckwheat or soba noodles
1 tablespoon oyster sauce
juice of 1/2 lemon
2–3 tablespoons light olive oil
4 ounces smoked salmon, cut into fine strips
4 ounces young pea sprouts
2 ripe tomatoes, peeled, seeded and cut into strips
1 tablespoon chopped chives
freshly ground black pepper*

SERVES 4

1 Cook the noodles in a large pan of boiling water until tender, following the directions on the packet. Drain, then rinse under cold running water and drain well.

Cook's Tip

Soba noodles, popular in Japan, are made from a mixture of buckwheat and wheat flour.

2 Tip the noodles into a large bowl. Add the oyster sauce and lemon juice and season with pepper to taste. Moisten the noodles with the olive oil.

3 Add the smoked salmon, pea sprouts, tomatoes and chives. Mix well and serve immediately.

SMOKED TROUT AND NOODLE SALAD

• • •

It is important to use ripe, juicy tomatoes for this fresh-tasting salad. For a special occasion, you could use smoked salmon.

INGREDIENTS

8 ounces somen noodles
2 smoked trout, skinned and boned
2 hard-boiled eggs, shelled and coarsely chopped
2 tablespoons chopped fresh chives
lime halves, to serve (optional)

FOR THE DRESSING
6 ripe plum tomatoes
2 shallots, finely chopped
2 tablespoons tiny capers, rinsed
2 tablespoons chopped fresh tarragon
finely grated rind and juice of ½ orange
4 tablespoons extra virgin olive oil
salt and freshly ground black pepper

SERVES 4

1 To make the dressing, halve the tomatoes, remove the cores and cut the flesh into chunks. Place in a bowl with the shallots, capers, tarragon, orange rind and juice and olive oil. Season to taste and mix well. Leave to marinate at room temperature for 1–2 hours.

2 Cook the noodles in a pan of boiling water, according to the packet instructions. Drain, rinse in cold water and drain again.

3 Toss the noodles with the dressing, then adjust the seasoning to taste. Arrange the noodles on a large serving platter or divide among four individual plates.

4 Flake the smoked trout over the noodles, then sprinkle the eggs and chives over the top. Serve, with lime halves on the side of the plate if you like.

SMOKED TROUT AND HORSERADISH SALAD

artner crisp lettuce leaves with
noked fish, warm potatoes
nd a creamy dressing.

INGREDIENTS

1½ pounds new potatoes
4 smoked trout fillets
4 ounces mixed lettuce leaves
4 slices dark rye bread, cut
into fingers
salt and freshly ground
black pepper

FOR THE DRESSING
tablespoons creamed horseradish
4 tablespoons peanut oil
1 tablespoon white wine vinegar
2 teaspoons caraway seeds

SERVES 4

Scrub the potatoes. Bring to the
oil in a pan of lightly salted water
nd simmer for about 15 minutes,
ntil tender. Drain well.

Meanwhile, remove the skin
rom the trout fillets and lift the
esh from the bone.

Cook's Tip

In some cases, it is better to
season the leaves themselves
rather than the dressing when
making a salad.

3 To make the dressing, place all
the ingredients in a screw-top jar
and shake vigorously. Season the
lettuce leaves and moisten them
with the dressing. Distribute
among four serving plates.

4 Flake the trout fillets and cut the
potatoes in half. Distribute them,
together with the rye bread fingers,
over the salad leaves and toss to
mix. Season the salad to taste with
salt and pepper and serve.

SHRIMP AND ARTICHOKE SALAD

○ ○ ○

INGREDIENTS

1 garlic clove
2 teaspoons Dijon mustard
4 tablespoons red wine vinegar
¼ pint/⅔ cup extra virgin olive oil
3 tablespoons shredded fresh basil leaves or 2 tbsp finely chopped fresh parsley
1 red onion, very thinly sliced
12 ounces peeled cooked prawns (shrimp)
14-ounce can artichoke hearts
½ iceberg lettuce
salt and freshly ground black pepper

SERVES 4

1 Chop the garlic, then crush it to a pulp with 1 teaspoon salt, using the flat edge of a heavy knife blade. Mix the garlic and mustard to a paste in a small bowl.

2 Beat in the vinegar and, finally, add the olive oil, beating hard to make a thick, creamy dressing. Season with black pepper and, if necessary, additional salt.

3 Stir the basil or parsley into the dressing, followed by the sliced onion. Leave the mixture to stand for 30 minutes at room temperature, then stir in the shrimp and chill for 1 hour, or until ready to serve.

4 Drain the artichoke hearts well and halve each one. Shred the lettuce finely.

5 Make a bed of lettuce on a large serving platter or four individual salad plates and spread the halved artichoke hearts over it.

6 Just before serving, pour the shrimp and their marinade over the top of the salad.

GHANAIAN SHRIMP SALAD

· · ·

The addition of plantain brings an unusual flavour to this salad.

INGREDIENTS

4 ounces peeled cooked shrimp
1 garlic clove, crushed
1½ teaspoons vegetable oil
2 eggs
1 yellow plantain, halved
4 lettuce leaves
2 tomatoes
1 red bell pepper, seeded
1 avocado
juice of 1 lemon
1 carrot
7-ounce can tuna or sardines, drained
1 fresh green chile, seeded and finely chopped
2 tablespoons chopped scallion
salt and freshly ground black pepper

SERVES 4

1 Put the shrimp and garlic in a small bowl. Add a little seasoning.

2 Heat the oil in a small pan, add the shrimp and cook over a low heat for a few minutes. Transfer to a plate to cool.

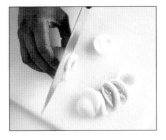

3 Hard-boil the eggs, place in cold water to cool, then shell and cut into slices.

4 Boil the unpeeled plantain in a large pan of water for 15 minutes. Drain, cool, then peel and cut into thick slices.

5 Shred the lettuce and arrange on a large serving plate. Slice the tomatoes and red bell pepper and peel and slice the avocado, sprinkling it with a little lemon juice.

6 Cut the carrot into matchsticks and arrange on top of the lettuce with the other vegetables.

7 Add the plantain, eggs, shrimp and tuna or sardines. Sprinkle with the remaining lemon juice, then sprinkle the chile and scallion on top. Season to taste with salt and pepper and serve.

Variation

To vary this salad, use other types of canned fish and a mixture of interesting and colourful lettuce leaves.

SHRIMP SALAD WITH CURRY DRESSING

. . .

Curry spices add an unexpected twist to this salad. The warm flavors combine especially well with the sweet shrimp and grated apple. Curry paste is needed here rather than curry powder, since there is no cooking involved.

INGREDIENTS

1 ripe tomato
1/2 iceberg lettuce
1 small onion
1 small bunch fresh cilantro
1 tablespoon lemon juice
1 pound peeled cooked shrimp
1 apple
8 whole shrimp, 8 lemon wedges
and 4 fresh cilantro sprigs,
to garnish
salt

FOR THE CURRY DRESSING
5 tablespoons mayonnaise
1 teaspoon mild curry paste
1 tablespoon tomato ketchup

SERVES 4

1 To peel the tomato, cut a cross in the skin with a sharp knife and immerse in boiling water for about 30 seconds. Remove from the bowl with a slotted spoon and cool under cold running water. Peel off the skin. Halve the tomato, push the seeds out with your thumb and discard them. Cut the flesh into large dice.

2 Finely shred the lettuce and put in a large bowl, then finely chop the onion and cilantro. Add to the bowl together with the tomato, moisten with lemon juice and season with salt.

3 To make the dressing, put the mayonnaise, curry paste and tomato ketchup in a small bowl and mix well. Add 2 tablespoons of water to thin the dressing and season to taste with salt.

Cook's Tip

Fresh cilantro is inclined to wilt if it is kept out of water. Put it in a jar of water, cover with a plastic bag and place in the refrigerator. It will stay fresh for several days.

4 Add the shrimp to the bowl and stir gently, but thoroughly so that all the shrimp are evenly coated with the dressing.

5 Quarter and core the apple and grate coarsely directly into the shrimp and dressing mixture.

6 Distribute the shredded lettuce mixture among four serving plates or bowls. Pile the shrimp mixture in the center of each and decorate each with two whole shrimp, two lemon wedges and a sprig of fresh cilantro. Serve immediately.

SHRIMP AND MINT SALAD

. . .

*Cooking raw shrimp in butter
adds to the flavor, making all
the difference to this salad.
Garnish with shaved fresh
coconut for a tropical touch.*

INGREDIENTS

*12 large raw shrimp
1 tablespoon sweet butter
1 tablespoon Thai fish sauce
juice of 1 lime
3 tablespoons thin coconut milk
1 teaspoon superfine sugar
1 garlic clove, crushed
1-inch piece of fresh root ginger,
peeled and grated
2 fresh red chiles, seeded and
finely chopped
2 tablespoons fresh mint leaves
8 ounces light green lettuce leaves
freshly ground black pepper*

SERVES 4

1 Carefully peel the shrimp,
removing and discarding the heads
and outer shells, but leaving the
tails intact.

2 Using a sharp knife, carefully
remove and discard the dark-
colored vein that runs along the
back of each peeled shrimp.

3 Melt the butter in a large frying
pan. When the melted butter is
foaming add the shrimp and toss
over a high heat until they have
just turned pink. Remove from the
heat; it is important not to cook
them for too long so that their
tenderness is retained.

4 In a small bowl mix the fish
sauce, lime juice, coconut milk,
sugar, garlic, ginger and chiles.
Season to taste with freshly ground
black pepper.

5 Toss the warm shrimp into the
sauce with the mint leaves. Arrange
the lettuce leaves on a serving plate
and place the shrimp and mint
mixture in the center.

Variation

Instead of shrimp, this dish also
works very well with lobster
tails if you are feeling
very extravagant.

Cook's Tip

If you can't find any fresh, raw
shrimp, you could use frozen
ones. To make the most of their
flavor, toss very quickly in the
hot butter when they are
completely thawed.

MIXED SHELLFISH SALAD

° ° °

Use fresh shellfish in season or a mixture of fresh and frozen.

INGREDIENTS

12 ounces small squid
1 small onion, cut into quarters
1 bay leaf
7 ounces raw shrimp,
in their shells
1½ pounds fresh mussels,
in their shells
1 pound fresh small clams
6 fluid ounces/¾ cup white wine
1 fennel bulb

FOR THE DRESSING
5 tablespoons extra virgin olive oil
3 tablespoons lemon juice
1 garlic clove, finely chopped
salt and freshly ground
black pepper

SERVES 6–8

1 Clean the squid by first peeling off the thin skin from the body section. Rinse well.

2 Using your fingers, pull the head and tentacles away from the sac section. Remove and discard the translucent quill and any remaining insides from the sac. Sever the tentacles and head.

3 Discard the head and intestines. Remove the small, hard beak from the base of the tentacles. Rinse the tentacles and sac under cold running water. Drain.

4 Bring a large pan of water to the boil. Add the onion and bay leaf. Drop in the squid tentacles and sacs and cook for 10 minutes, or until tender. Remove with a slotted spoon and leave to cool before slicing the sacs into rings ½-inch wide. Cut each tentacle section into two pieces. Set aside.

5 Drop the shrimp into the same boiling water and cook for about 2 minutes, until they turn pink. Remove the shrimp with a slotted spoon. Peel and devein. (The cooking liquid may be strained and kept for soup.)

6 Cut the "beards" from the mussels. Scrub and rinse the mussels and clams well in several changes of cold water. Any that are open should close if given a sharp tap; if they fail to do so, discard. Place in a large pan with the wine. Cover and steam until all the shells have opened. (Discard any that do not open.) Lift the clams and mussels out of the pan.

7 Remove all the clams from their shells with a small spoon. Place in a large serving bowl. Remove all but eight of the mussels from their shells and add them to the clams in the bowl. Leave the remaining mussels in their half-shells, and set aside for the garnish.

8 Cut the green, ferny part of the fennel away from the bulb. Chop finely and set aside. Chop the bulb into bitesize pieces and add it to the serving bowl together with the squid and shrimp.

9 To make the dressing, combine the oil, lemon juice and garlic in a bowl. Add the reserved chopped fennel green and season to taste with salt and pepper. Pour the dressing over the salad, and toss well to mix. Garnish with the remaining mussels in their half-shells. Serve at room temperature or chill very briefly before serving.

AVOCADO, CRAB AND CILANTRO SALAD

This sophisticated salad is full of complementary flavors.

INGREDIENTS

SERVES 4

1 1/2 pounds small new potatoes
1 fresh mint sprig
2 pounds boiled crabs
1 frisée or Boston lettuce
6 ounces mâche
1 avocado, peeled and sliced
6 ounces cherry tomatoes
salt, freshly ground black pepper
and freshly grated nutmeg

FOR THE DRESSING

75ml/5 tablespoons olive oil
1 tablespoon lime juice
3 tablespoons chopped
fresh cilantro
1/2 teaspoon superfine sugar

SERVES 4

1 Scrape or peel the potatoes and place in a large pan. Cover with water, add a good pinch of salt and a sprig of mint. Bring to the boil and simmer for about 15 minutes, until tender. Drain the potatoes, cover and keep warm until needed.

Variation

Frozen crab meat is a good alternative to fresh and retains much of its original sweetness. You will require 10 ounces.

2 Remove the legs and claws from each crab. Crack these open with the back of a chopping knife and remove the white meat.

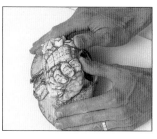

3 Turn the crab on its back and push the rear leg section away with the thumb and forefinger of each hand. Remove the flesh from inside the shell.

4 Discard the "dead men's fingers," the soft gills that the crab uses to filter impurities in its diet. These lie close together along either side of the body. Apart from these and the shell, everything else is edible, both white and dark, or brown, meat.

5 Split the central body section open with a knife and remove the white and dark flesh with a pick or a metal skewer.

6 To make the dressing, combine all the ingredients in a screw-top jar and shake well. Put the salad leaves in a large bowl, pour the dressing over them and toss well.

7 Distribute the leaves among four serving plates. Top with the avocado, crab, tomatoes and warm new potatoes. Season to taste with salt, pepper and freshly grated nutmeg and serve.

Cook's Tip

Young crabs offer the sweetest meat, but they are are more awkward to prepare than older, larger ones. The hen crab carries more flesh than the cock, which is considered to have a better overall flavor. The cock crab, shown here, is identified by his narrow apron flap at the rear. The hen has a broader flap, under which she carries her eggs.

THAI NOODLE SALAD

· · ·

The addition of coconut milk and sesame oil gives an unusual nutty flavor to this salad.

INGREDIENTS

12 ounces somen noodles
1 large carrot, cut into thin strips
1 bunch asparagus, trimmed and
cut into 1¹/₂-inch lengths
1 red bell pepper, seeded and cut
into fine strips
4 ounces snow peas, trimmed
and halved
4 ounces baby corn cobs,
halved lengthwise
4 ounces beansprouts
4-ounce can water chestnuts,
drained and thinly sliced
1 lime, cut into wedges,
2 ounces/¹/₂ cup roasted peanuts,
coarsely chopped, and fresh
cilantro leaves, to garnish

FOR THE DRESSING

3 tablespoons torn fresh basil
5 tablespoons chopped fresh mint
8 fluid ounces/1 cup coconut milk
2 tablespoons dark sesame oil
1 tablespoon grated fresh
root ginger
2 garlic cloves, finely chopped
juice of 1 lime
2 scallions, chopped
salt and cayenne pepper

SERVES 4–6

1 To make the dressing, combine all the ingredients in a bowl and mix well. Season to taste with salt and cayenne pepper.

2 Cook the noodles in a pan of boiling water, following the directions on the packet, until just tender. Drain, rinse under cold running water and drain again, then set aside until required.

3 Cook all the vegetables, except the water chestnuts, in separate pans of lightly salted boiling water until they are tender, but still crisp. Drain, plunge them immediately into cold water and drain again.

4 Toss the noodles, vegetables, water chestnuts and dressing together. Arrange on individual serving plates and garnish with the lime wedges, chopped peanuts and cilantro leaves.

SHRIMP NOODLE SALAD WITH FRAGRANT HERBS

• • •

A light, refreshing salad with all the tangy flavor of the sea.

INGREDIENTS

4 ounces cellophane noodles,
soaked in hot water until soft
1 small green bell pepper, seeded
and cut into strips
1/2 cucumber, cut into strips
1 tomato, cut into strips
2 shallots, thinly sliced
16 peeled cooked shrimp
salt and freshly ground
black pepper
fresh cilantro leaves,
to garnish

FOR THE DRESSING

1 tablespoon rice-wine vinegar
2 tablespoons Thai fish sauce
2 tablespoons lime juice
1/2 teaspoon grated fresh
root ginger
1 lemon grass stalk, finely chopped
1 red chile, seeded and thinly sliced
2 tablespoons coarsely chopped
fresh mint
few sprigs of tarragon, chopped
1 tablespoon chopped fresh chives

SERVES 4

1 To make the dressing, combine all the ingredients in a small bowl or pitcher and whisk well.

2 Drain the noodles, then plunge them into a pan of boiling water for 1 minute. Drain, rinse under cold running water to refresh and drain again well.

3 In a large bowl, combine the noodles with the green bell pepper strips, cucumber, tomato and shallots. Lightly season with salt and black pepper, then toss with the dressing.

> ### Cook's Tip
> Shrimp are available ready-cooked and often shelled.
> To cook shrimp, boil them for 5 minutes. Leave them to cool in the cooking liquid, then gently pull off the tail shell and twist off the head.

4 Spoon the cellophane noodles onto four individual serving plates and arrange the shrimp on top of them. Garnish with a few cilantro leaves and serve immediately.

Egg Noodle Salad with Sesame Chicken

∘ ∘ ∘

INGREDIENTS

14 ounces fresh thin egg noodles
1 carrot, cut into long fine strips
2 ounces snow peas, trimmed,
cut into fine strips
and blanched
4 ounces/½ cup beansprouts,
blanched
2 tablespoons olive oil
8 ounces skinless, boneless
chicken breast portions,
thinly sliced
2 tablespoons sesame seeds, toasted
2 scallions, thinly sliced
diagonally, and fresh cilantro
leaves, to garnish

FOR THE DRESSING
3 tablespoons sherry vinegar
5 tablespoons soy sauce
4 tablespoons sesame oil
6 tablespoons light olive oil
1 garlic clove, finely chopped
1 teaspoon grated fresh root ginger
salt and freshly ground
black pepper

SERVES 4–6

1 To make the dressing, whisk together all the ingredients in a small bowl. Season to taste.

2 Cook the noodles in a large pan of boiling water. Stir them occasionally to separate. They will take only a few minutes to cook; be careful not to overcook them. Drain the noodles, rinse under cold running water and drain well. Tip into a bowl.

3 Add the carrot, snow peas and beansprouts to the noodles. Pour in about half the dressing, then toss the mixture well and adjust the seasoning according to taste.

4 Heat the oil in a large frying pan. Add the chicken and stir-fry for 3 minutes, or until cooked and golden. Remove from the heat. Add the sesame seeds and drizzle in some of the remaining dressing.

5 Arrange the noodle mixture on individual serving plates, making a nest on each plate. Spoon the chicken on top, dividing it equally. Sprinkle with the scallions and cilantro leaves and serve any remaining dressing separately.

CHICKEN AND PASTA SALAD

This is a delicious way to use up left-over cooked chicken.

INGREDIENTS

8 ounces tricolor pasta twists
2 tablespoons bottled pesto sauce
1 tablespoon olive oil
1 beefsteak tomato
12 pitted black olives
8 ounces green beans, cooked
12 ounces cooked chicken, cubed
salt and freshly ground
black pepper
fresh basil, to garnish

SERVES 4

3 Peel the beefsteak tomato by cutting a cross in the skin at the top with a sharp knife and then plunging it in boiling water for about 30 seconds. The skin will now pull off easily. Cut the tomato flesh into small cubes.

4 Add the tomato and olives to the pasta. Cut the green beans into 1½-inch lengths. Add the beans and chicken and season to taste with salt and pepper. Toss gently, transfer to a serving platter, garnish with basil and serve.

Cook the pasta in plenty of lightly salted boiling water for 10–12 minutes, until *al dente*, or as directed on the packet.

Drain the pasta and rinse in plenty of cold running water. Put into a bowl and stir in the pesto sauce and olive oil.

HOT AND SOUR CHICKEN SALAD

。。。

This chicken salad from Vietnam is equally delicious made with shrimp.
Allow 1 pound fresh shrimp tails to serve four people.

INGREDIENTS

2 skinless, boneless chicken
breast portions
4 ounces beansprouts
1 head Chinese cabbage, shredded
2 medium carrots, cut into batons
1 red onion, thinly sliced
2 large gherkins, sliced

FOR THE MARINADE

1 small fresh red chile, seeded and
finely chopped
1/2-inch piece of fresh root
ginger, chopped
1 garlic clove, crushed
1 tablespoon crunchy
peanut butter
2 tablespoons chopped
fresh cilantro
1 teaspoon sugar
1/2 teaspoon salt
1 tablespoon rice or white
wine vinegar
4 tablespoon vegetable oil
2 teaspoons Thai fish sauce

SERVES 4–6

1 Slice the chicken breast portions
thinly and place in a shallow bowl.
Grind the chile, ginger and garlic in a
food processor or with a mortar and
pestle, then add the peanut butter,
chopped fresh cilantro, sugar and salt.

2 Add the rice or white wine vinegar,
2 tablespoons of the oil and the fish
sauce to the ingredients in the food
processor. Combine well. Cover the
chicken with the spice mixture and
marinate for at least 2–3 hours.

3 Cook the chicken in a frying pan
the stovetop or on a medium-hot
barbecue for about 5 minutes, bas
often and turning once. Arrange th
salad ingredients on a serving dish
top with the cooked chicken.

CHICKEN SALAD WITH CILANTRO DRESSING

Serve this salad warm to make the most of the wonderful flavor of chicken basted with a marinade of cilantro, sesame and mustard.

INGREDIENTS

*4 medium skinless, boneless
chicken breast portions
8 ounces snow peas
heads decorative lettuce such as
lollo rosso or oak leaf
3 carrots, cut into batons
ounces white mushrooms, sliced
ounces bacon, fried and chopped*

FOR THE CILANTRO DRESSING
*fluid ounces/¹/₂ cup lemon juice
ablespoons whole-grain mustard
8 fluid ounces/1 cup olive oil
/₂ fluid ounces/¹/₃ cup sesame oil
1 teaspoon coriander
seeds, crushed
1 tablespoon chopped fresh
cilantro, to garnish*

SERVES 6

x all the dressing ingredients in a
. Place the chicken in a dish and
over half the dressing. Cover and
nate overnight in the refrigerator.
the remaining dressing.

ok the snow peas for 2 minutes
iling water, then refresh in cold
r. Tear the lettuces into small
s and mix all the other salad
dients and the bacon together.
nge the salad on individual dishes.

3 Cook the chicken breast portions
under the broiler or on a medium
barbecue for 10–15 minutes, basting
with the marinade and turning once,
until cooked through. Thinly slice them
on the diagonal. Divide between the
bowls of salad and add some of the
dressing. Combine and sprinkle some
fresh cilantro over each bowl.

CHICKEN SALAD WITH GARLIC BREAD

° ° °

This salad also makes a light first course for eight people.

INGREDIENTS

4–4½ pounds chicken
½ pint/1¼ cups white wine and water, mixed
24 slices French bread, ¼-inch thick
1 garlic clove, peeled
8 ounces green beans
4 ounces young spinach leaves
2 celery sticks, thinly sliced
2 sun-dried tomatoes, chopped
2 scallions, sliced
fresh chives and parsley, to garnish

FOR THE VINAIGRETTE
2 tablespoons red wine vinegar
6 tablespoons olive oil
1 tablespoon whole-grain mustard
1 tablespoon clear honey
2 tablespoons chopped fresh mixed thyme, parsley and chives
2 teaspoons finely chopped capers
salt and freshly ground black pepper

SERVES 4

1 Preheat the oven to 375°F. Put the chicken into a casserole with the wine and water. Cook in the oven for about 1½ hours, until tender. Remove the casserole form the oven and leave the chicken to cool in the liquid. Remove the chicken and place on a chopping board. Discard the skin and bones and cut the flesh into small pieces.

2 To make the vinaigrette, put all the ingredients into a screw-top jar and shake vigorously to combine. Season to taste with a little salt and ground black pepper.

3 Toast the French bread under the broiler or in the oven until dry and golden brown, then lightly rub with the peeled garlic clove.

4 Trim the green beans, cut into 2-inch lengths and cook in boiling water until just tender. Drain and rinse under cold running water to refresh.

5 Wash the spinach, discarding the stalks, and tear into small pieces. Arrange on individual serving plates with the celery, green beans, sun-dried tomatoes, chicken and scallions.

6 Spoon over the vinaigrette dressing. Arrange the toasted slices of French bread on top, garnish with fresh chives and parsley and serve immediately.

WARM CHICKEN SALAD

· · ·

INGREDIENTS

2 ounces mixed salad leaves
2 ounces baby spinach leaves
2 ounces watercress
2 tablespoons chili sauce
2 tablespoons dry sherry
1 tablespoon light soy sauce
1 tablespoon tomato ketchup
2 teaspoons olive oil
8 shallots, finely chopped
1 garlic clove, crushed
12 ounces skinless, boneless
chicken breast portions,
cut into thin strips
1 red bell pepper, seeded
and sliced
6 ounces snow peas, trimmed
14-ounce can baby corn cobs,
drained and halved
10 ounces/scant 1½ cups brown
rice, cooked
salt and freshly ground
black pepper
fresh parsley sprig,
to garnish

SERVES 6

1 If any of the salad leaves are large, tear them into smaller pieces and arrange with the spinach leaves on a serving dish. Add the watercress and toss together.

2 In a small bowl, mix together the chili sauce, sherry, soy sauce and tomato ketchup. Set the sauce mixture aside.

3 Heat the oil in a large, non-stick frying pan or wok. Add the shallots and garlic and stir-fry over a medium heat for 1 minute.

4 Add the chicken to the pan and stir-fry for a further 3–4 minutes.

5 Add the pepper, snow peas, baby corn cobs and rice and stir-fry for a further 2–3 minutes.

6 Pour in the chili sauce mixture and stir-fry for 2–3 minutes, until hot and bubbling. Season to taste with salt and pepper.

7 Spoon the chicken mixture over the salad leaves, toss together to mix and serve immediately, while still warm, garnished with a sprig of fresh parsley.

Variation

Use other lean meat, such as turkey breast, beef or pork in place of the chicken.

Cook's Tip

Chili sauce varies in strength, depending on the brand. Be careful if you are using an unfamiliar one.

SPICY CHICKEN SALAD

∘ ∘ ∘

INGREDIENTS

1 teaspoon ground cumin seeds
1 teaspoon paprika
1 teaspoon ground turmeric
1–2 garlic cloves, crushed
2 tablespoons lime juice
4 skinless, boneless chicken
breast portions
8 ounces dried rigatoni
1 red bell pepper, seeded
and chopped
2 celery sticks, thinly sliced
1 shallot or small onion,
finely chopped
1 ounce/¼ cup stuffed green
olives, halved
2 tablespoons clear honey
1 tablespoon whole-grain mustard
1–2 tablespoons lime juice
salt and freshly ground
black pepper
mixed salad leaves,
to serve

SERVES 6

1 Combine the cumin, paprika, turmeric, garlic and lime juice in a bowl. Season to taste with salt and pepper. Rub this mixture over the chicken portions. Lay these in a shallow dish, cover with plastic wrap and leave in a cool place for 3 hours or overnight.

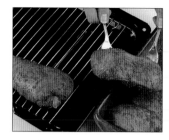

2 Preheat the oven to 400°F. Put the chicken on a rack in a single layer and bake for 20 minutes. Alternatively, broil for 8–10 minutes each side.

3 Cook the pasta in a large pan of lightly salted boiling water for 8–10 minutes, until *al dente*. Drain and rinse under cold water. Leave to drain thoroughly.

4 Put the red bell pepper, celery, shallot or small onion and stuffed olives into a large bowl with the pasta. Mix together.

5 Mix the honey, mustard and lime juice together in a small bowl and pour over the pasta mixture. Toss well to coat.

6 Cut the chicken portions into bitesize pieces. Arrange the mixed salad leaves on a serving dish, spoon the pasta mixture into the center and top with the spicy chicken pieces.

CHICKEN MARYLAND SALAD

∘ ∘ ∘

Grilled chicken, corn, bacon, banana and watercress combine in a sensational salad.

INGREDIENTS

*4 boneless chicken
breast portions
oil, for brushing
8 ounces rindless unsmoked bacon
4 corn cobs
3 tablespoons soft butter (optional)
4 ripe bananas, peeled and halved
4 firm tomatoes, halved
1 escarole or Boston lettuce
1 bunch watercress
salt and freshly ground
black pepper*

FOR THE DRESSING

*5 tablespoons peanut oil
1 tablespoon white wine vinegar
2 teaspoons maple syrup
2 teaspoons prepared mild mustard*

SERVES 4

1 Season the chicken breast portions with salt and pepper, brush with oil and broil or cook on a medium-hot barbecue for 15 minutes, turning once. Broil the bacon or cook on the barbecue for 8–10 minutes, or until crisp.

2 Bring a large pan of salted water to the boil. Shuck and trim the corn cobs or leave the husks on if you like. Boil the corn cobs for 20 minutes.

3 For extra flavor, brush the corn cobs with butter and brown under the broiler or on the barbecue. Broil the bananas and tomatoes or cook on the barbecue for 6–8 minutes; you can brush these with butter too if you like.

4 To make the dressing, combine the oil, wine vinegar, maple syrup and mustard with 1 tablespoon water in a screw-top jar and shake well to mix.

Cook's Tip

The most commonly used mustard in salad dressings is Dijon, but you can use other varieties. Bavarian mustard is mild and fairly sweet, while American mustard is very mild.

5 Wash the lettuce and watercress leaves and spin or pat dry. Place them in a large bowl, pour over the dressing and toss well.

6 Distribute the salad leaves among four large serving plates. Slice the chicken and arrange it on top of the salad leaves together with the bacon, banana, corn cobs and tomatoes.

CHICKEN, TONGUE AND GRUYÈRE CHEESE SALAD

o o o

The rich, sweet flavors of this salad marry well with the tart, peppery watercress. A minted lemon dressing freshens the overall effect.

INGREDIENTS

2 skinless, boneless chicken
breast portions
½ chicken bouillon cube
8 ounces ox tongue or cured ham,
sliced ¼-inch thick
8 ounces Gruyère cheese
1 lollo rosso lettuce
1 Boston or frisée lettuce
1 bunch watercress
2 green-skinned apples, cored
and sliced
3 celery sticks, sliced
4 tablespoons sesame seeds, toasted
salt, freshly ground black pepper
and freshly grated nutmeg

FOR THE DRESSING
5 tablespoons sunflower oil
1 teaspoon sesame oil
3 tablespoons lemon juice
2 teaspoons chopped fresh mint
3 drops Tabasco sauce

SERVES 4

2 To make the dressing, place the sunflower and sesame oils, lemon juice, chopped mint and Tabasco sauce into a screw-top jar and shake vigorously. Cut the chicken, tongue or cured ham and cheese into fine strips. Moisten with a little of the dressing and set aside until required.

3 Combine the lettuce and watercress leaves with the apple and celery. Add the dressing and toss well. Distribute among four large serving plates. Pile the chicken, tongue or ham and cheese in the center, sprinkle with sesame seeds, season with salt, pepper and freshly grated nutmeg and serve.

1 Place the chicken breast portions in a shallow pan, add 1¼ cups water and the bouillon cube and bring to the boil. Cover the pan and simmer for 15 minutes. Drain, reserving the stock for another occasion, then cool the chicken under cold running water.

CURRIED CHICKEN SALAD

INGREDIENTS

2 cooked, skinless, boneless
chicken breast portions
6 ounces green beans
12 ounces tricolor dried penne
¹/₄ pint/²/₃ cup plain yogurt
1 teaspoon mild curry powder
1 garlic clove, crushed
1 fresh green chile, seeded and
finely chopped
2 tablespoons chopped
fresh cilantro
4 firm ripe tomatoes,
peeled, seeded and
cut into strips
salt and freshly ground
black pepper
fresh cilantro leaves,
to garnish

SERVES 4

Cut the chicken into strips. Cut
the green beans into 1-inch lengths
and cook in boiling water for
minutes. Drain and rinse under
cold water.

Cook the pasta in a pan of salted
boiling water for 8–10 minutes,
until *al dente*. Drain and rinse.

3 To make the sauce, mix the
yogurt, curry powder, garlic, chile
and chopped cilantro together in a
bowl. Stir in the chicken pieces,
cover with plastic wrap and leave
to stand for 30 minutes.

4 Transfer the pasta to a large
serving bowl and toss with the
beans and tomatoes. Spoon over
the chicken and sauce mixture.
Garnish with the cilantro leaves
and serve immediately.

CHICKEN AND MANGO SALAD WITH ORANGE RICE

∘ ∘ ∘

This succulent, fruity salad is inspired by the exotic flavors of Indian cooking. Serve with poppadums for an authentic extra touch to a summer meal.

INGREDIENTS

1 tablespoon sunflower oil
1 onion, chopped
1 garlic clove, crushed
2 tablespoons red curry paste
2 teaspoons apricot jam
2 tablespoons chicken stock
1 pound cooked chicken, cut into small pieces
¼ pint/⅔ cup plain yogurt
4–5 tablespoons mayonnaise
1 large mango, cut into
½-inch dice
fresh flat leaf parsley sprigs, to garnish
poppadums, to serve

FOR THE ORANGE RICE
6 ounces/scant 1 cup white long grain rice
8 ounces/1½ cups grated carrots
1 large orange, cut into segments
1½ ounces/⅓ cup toasted sliced almonds

FOR THE DRESSING
3 tablespoons olive oil
4 tablespoons sunflower oil
3 tablespoons lemon juice
1 garlic clove, crushed
1 tablespoon chopped mixed fresh herbs, such as tarragon, parsley and chives
salt and ground black pepper

SERVES 4

1 Heat the oil in a frying pan. Add the onion and garlic and cook for 3–4 minutes, until soft.

2 Stir in the curry paste, cook for about 1 minute, then lower the heat and stir in the apricot jam and stock. Mix well, add the chopped chicken and stir until the chicken is thoroughly coated in the paste. Spoon the mixture into a large bowl and leave to cool.

3 Meanwhile, boil the rice in plenty of lightly salted water until just tender. Drain, rinse under cold water and drain again. When cool, stir into the grated carrots and add the orange segments and almonds.

4 Make the dressing by whisking all the ingredients together in a bowl.

5 When the chicken mixture is cool, stir in the yogurt and mayonnaise, then add the mango, stirring it in carefully so as not to break the flesh. Chill for about 30 minutes.

6 When ready to serve, pour the dressing into the rice salad and mix well. Spoon onto a platter and mound the cold curried chicken on top. Garnish with flat leaf parsley and serve with poppadums.

Cook's Tip

To toast almonds, place them on a baking sheet in a moderate oven for 3 minutes, or dry-fry in a small pan. Turn the nuts occasionally so that they brown evenly.

CRUNCHY SALAD WITH CHERRY TOMATOES

• • •

*ried until crisp, slices of blood
ausage are extremely good in
alad, particularly with crunchy
read croûtons and sweet cherry
omatoes. Serve this salad in
owls or shallow soup plates.*

INGREDIENTS
*9 ounces blood sausage, sliced
1 focaccia loaf, plain or flavoured
with sun-dried tomatoes
and herbs
3 tablespoons olive oil
1 romaine lettuce, torn into
bitesize pieces
9 ounces cherry tomatoes, halved*

FOR THE DRESSING
*juice of 1 lemon
6 tablespoons olive oil
2 teaspoons French mustard
1 tablespoon clear honey
2 tablespoons chopped fresh herbs,
such as cilantro, chives
and parsley
salt and freshly ground
black pepper*

SERVES 4

1 Dry-fry the blood sausage in a
large, non-stick frying pan for
5–10 minutes, or until browned
and crisp, turning occasionally.
Remove the blood sausage from the
pan with a slotted spoon and drain
on paper towels.

2 Cut the focaccia into chunks. Add
the oil to the juices in the frying
pan and cook the focaccia cubes in
two batches, turning frequently,
until golden on all sides. Drain on
kitchen paper.

3 Mix together the focaccia, blood
sausage, lettuce and cherry
tomatoes in a large bowl. Mix
together the dressing ingredients
and season to taste with salt and
pepper. Pour the dressing over the
salad. Mix well and serve.

PASTA SALAD WITH SALAMI AND OLIVES

Garlic and herb dressing gives a Mediterranean flavor to a few ingredients from the pantry and refrigerator, making this an excellent salad for winter.

INGREDIENTS

*8 ounces/2 cups dried gnocchi
or conchiglie
2 ounces/½ cup pitted black olives,
quartered lengthwise
3 ounces thinly sliced salami, any
skin removed, diced
½ small red onion, finely chopped
1 large handful fresh basil leaves*

FOR THE DRESSING

*4 tablespoons extra virgin
olive oil
good pinch of sugar, to taste
juice of ½ lemon
1 teaspoon Dijon mustard
2 teaspoons dried oregano
1 garlic clove, crushed
salt and ground black pepper*

SERVES 4

1 Cook the pasta in a pan of salted boiling water according to the packet instructions.

2 Meanwhile, make the herb dressing for the pasta. Put all the ingredients for the dressing in a large bowl with a little salt and ground black pepper to taste, and whisk well to mix.

3 Drain the pasta thoroughly, add it to the bowl of dressing and toss well to mix. Leave the dressed pasta to cool, stirring occasionally.

4 When the pasta is cold, add the remaining ingredients and toss well to mix again. Taste for seasoning, then serve immediately.

WALDORF HAM SALAD

○ ○ ○

*Waldorf salad first appeared at
the Waldorf-Astoria Hotel,
New York, in the 1890s. This
modern-day version is
something of a meal in itself.*

INGREDIENTS

*3 eating apples
1 tablespoon lemon juice
2 slices cooked cured ham, each
about 6 ounces
2 celery sticks
¼ pint/⅔ cup mayonnaise
1 escarole or frisée lettuce
1 small radicchio, finely shredded
½ bunch watercress
3 tablespoons walnut or olive oil
2 ounces/½ cup broken
walnuts, toasted
salt and freshly ground
black pepper*

SERVES 4

Peel, core, slice and finely shred
the apples. Moisten with lemon
juice to prevent them from turning
brown. Cut the ham into 2-inch
strips. Cut the celery sticks into
similar-size pieces. Combine the
apples, ham and celery in a bowl.

2 Add the mayonnaise and
mix thoroughly.

3 Shred all the salad leaves finely,
then moisten with oil. Distribute
the leaves among four serving
plates. Pile the mayonnaise mixture
in the center, sprinkle with toasted
walnuts, season and serve.

CHICKEN LIVER, BACON AND TOMATO SALAD
· · ·

Warm salads are especially welcome during the cooler months of the year.

INGREDIENTS

8 ounces young spinach, stems removed
1 frisée lettuce
7 tablespoons peanut or sunflower oil
6 ounces rindless unsmoked bacon, cut into strips
3 ounces day-old bread, crusts removed and cut into short fingers
1 pound chicken livers
4 ounces cherry tomatoes
salt and freshly ground black pepper

SERVES 4

1 Place the spinach and lettuce leaves in a salad bowl. Heat 4 tablespoons of the peanut or sunflower oil in a large, heavy frying pan, add the bacon strips and cook for 3–4 minutes, or until crisp and brown. Remove the bacon with a slotted spoon and drain on paper towels.

2 To make croûtons, fry the bread in the bacon-flavored oil, tossing until crisp and golden. Drain on paper towels.

3 Heat the remaining oil in the frying pan, add the chicken livers and fry briskly for 2–3 minutes. Turn the chicken livers out over the salad leaves and add the bacon, croûtons and tomatoes. Season to taste with salt and pepper, toss and serve warm.

Variation

If you can't find any baby spinach leaves you can use mâche. Watercress would make a deliciously peppery substitute, but you should use less of it and bulk the salad out with a milder leaf so that the watercress doesn't overwhelm the other flavors.

CURRY FRIED PORK AND RICE VERMICELLI SALAD

· · ·

INGREDIENTS

8 ounces lean pork
2 garlic cloves, finely chopped
2 slices fresh root ginger, peeled
and finely chopped
2–3 tablespoons rice wine
3 tablespoons vegetable oil
2 lemon grass stalks, finely chopped
2 teaspoons curry powder
6 ounces/³⁄4 cup beansprouts
8 ounces rice vermicelli, soaked
in warm water until soft,
then drained
¹⁄2 lettuce, finely shredded
2 tablespoons fresh mint leaves
lemon juice and Thai fish sauce,
to taste
salt and freshly ground
black pepper
2 scallions, chopped,
1 ounce/¹⁄2 cup toasted peanuts,
chopped, and pork crackling
(optional) to garnish

SERVES 4

1 Cut the pork into thin strips. Place in a shallow dish with half the garlic and ginger. Season to taste with salt and pepper, pour over 2 tablespoons rice wine and marinate for at least 1 hour.

2 Heat the vegetable oil in a frying pan or wok. Add the remaining garlic and ginger and stir-fry over a medium heat for a few seconds until fragrant and golden. Stir in the strips of pork, with the marinade, and add the lemon grass and curry powder.

3 Stir-fry over a high heat until the pork is golden and cooked through, adding more rice wine if the mixture seems too dry.

4 Place the beansprouts in a strainer. Blanch them by lowering the strainer into a pan of boiling water for 1 minute, then drain and refresh under cold running water. Drain again. Using the same water, cook the rice vermicelli for 3–5 minutes, until tender. Drain and rinse under cold running water.

5 Drain the vermicelli well and tip into a large bowl. Add the beansprouts, shredded lettuce and mint leaves. Season with lemon juice and fish sauce to taste. Toss lightly to combine the flavors.

6 Divide the vermicelli mixture among individual serving plates, making a nest on each plate. Arrange the pork mixture on top. Garnish with scallions, toasted peanuts and pork crackling, if using. Serve.

SWEET POTATO, EGG, PORK AND BEET SALAD

This is a good way to use up leftover pork. Sweet flavors balance the bitter endive.

INGREDIENTS

2 pounds sweet potatoes
4 Belgian endive heads
5 eggs, hard-boiled
1 pound pickled young beets
6 ounces cold roast pork
salt

FOR THE DRESSING

5 tablespoons sunflower oil
2 tablespoons white wine vinegar
2 teaspoons Dijon mustard
1 teaspoon fennel seeds, crushed

SERVES 4

1 Peel the sweet potatoes and dice into equal-size pieces.

2 Add the diced sweet potatoes to a pan of salted boiling water. Bring back to the boil, then simmer for 10–15 minutes, or until the potatoes are soft. Drain and set aside to cool.

3 To make the dressing, combine the sunflower oil, vinegar, mustard and fennel seeds in a screw-top jar and shake well.

4 Separate the Belgian endive leaves and arrange them around the edges of four serving plates.

5 Pour two-thirds of the dressing over the sweet potatoes, then stir so that all the pieces of potato are coated in the dressing. Spoon the sweet potatoes on top of the endive leaves.

6 Shell the hard-boiled eggs. Slice the eggs and beets and arrange to make an attractive pattern around the sweet potato.

7 Slice the pork, then cut into strips about 1½ inches wide. Place in a bowl and moisten with the rest of the dressing.

8 Pile the strips of pork into the center of each salad. Season with salt to taste and serve.

Cook's Tip

To crush the fennel seeds, grind using a mortar and pestle. If you don't have these, use two spoons instead. For extra flavor try toasting the fennel seeds before crushing.

FRANKFURTER SALAD WITH MUSTARD DRESSING

This is a last-minute salad, which you can make quickly.

INGREDIENTS

1½ pounds small new potatoes, scrubbed or scraped
2 eggs
12 ounces frankfurters
1 Boston or frisée lettuce
8 ounces young spinach leaves, stems removed
salt and freshly ground black pepper

FOR THE DRESSING

3 tablespoons safflower oil
2 tablespoons olive oil
1 tablespoon white wine vinegar
2 teaspoons mustard
1 teaspoon caraway seeds, crushed

SERVES 4

1 Bring the potatoes to the boil in lightly salted water and simmer for about 15 minutes, or until tender. Drain, cover and keep warm. Hard-boil the eggs for 12 minutes. Refresh in cold water, shell and cut into quarters.

2 Score the frankfurter skins corkscrew fashion with a small knife, then cover with boiling water and simmer for about 5 minutes to heat through. Drain well, cover and keep warm.

3 To make the dressing, place all the ingredients in a screw-top jar and shake well.

4 Moisten the salad leaves with half of the dressing and distribute among four large serving plates.

5 Moisten the warm potatoes and frankfurters with the remainder of the dressing and arrange them over the salad.

6 Finish off the salad by topping with sections of hard-boiled egg, season to taste with salt and black pepper and serve warm.

Cook's Tip

This salad has a German slant to it and calls for a sweet-and-sour German-style mustard. American mustards have a similar quality.

SMOKED BACON AND GREEN BEAN PASTA SALAD

. . .

INGREDIENTS
12 ounces/3 cups dried
whole-wheat pasta twists
8 ounces green beans
8 strips smoked bacon
12 ounces cherry tomatoes, halved
2 bunches scallions, chopped
14-ounce can chickpeas, drained
and rinsed

FOR THE DRESSING
6 tablespoons tomato juice
2 tablespoons balsamic vinegar
1 teaspoon ground cumin
1 teaspoon ground coriander
2 tablespoons chopped
fresh cilantro
salt and freshly ground
black pepper

SERVES 4

2 Preheat the broiler and cook the bacon for 2–3 minutes on each side, until tender. Dice the bacon and add to the beans.

3 Put the tomatoes, scallions and chickpeas in a large bowl.

4 In smaller bowl, mix together the tomato juice, vinegar, spices, fresh cilantro and seasoning.

5 Pour the dressing into a large bowl. Drain the cooked pasta thoroughly and add to the tomato mixture with the green beans and bacon. Toss all the ingredients together to mix thoroughly. Adjust the seasoning, if necessary. Serve warm or cold.

1 Cook the pasta in a large pan of lightly salted boiling water for about 8–10 minutes, until *al dente*. Meanwhile, trim and halve the green beans and cook them in boiling water for about 5 minutes, until tender. Drain thoroughly, set aside and keep warm.

Cook's Tip

Always rinse canned beans and pulses well before using, to remove as much of the salt solution as possible. Drain again before use.

WARM PASTA SALAD WITH ASPARAGUS
. . .

Warm pasta, ham, eggs and Parmesan – a heavenly match.

INGREDIENTS

1 pound asparagus
1 pound dried tagliatelle
8 ounces cooked cured ham, sliced ¼-inch thick, and cut into fingers
2 eggs, hard-boiled, shelled and sliced
2-ounce piece Parmesan cheese

FOR THE DRESSING
2 ounces cooked potato
5 tablespoons olive oil
1 tablespoon lemon juice
2 teaspoons Dijon mustard
4 fluid ounces/½ cup vegetable stock
salt and freshly ground black pepper

SERVES 4

1 Bring a pan of lightly salted water to the boil. Trim and discard the tough, woody part of the asparagus stalks. Cut the asparagus in half and boil the thicker halves for 12 minutes, adding the asparagus tips after 6 minutes. Refresh under cold water until warm, then drain.

Cook's Tip
You can use either thin, green asparagus or the thicker blanched type with yellow or purple tips.

2 Finely chop 5 ounces of the thicker asparagus pieces. Place in a food processor together with the dressing ingredients and process until smooth. Season the dressing to taste with salt and pepper.

3 Boil the pasta in a pan of salted water for 8–10 minutes, until *al dente*. Refresh under cold water.

4 Tip the pasta into a bowl and toss with the asparagus sauce. Turn out into four serving bowls. Top each pile of pasta with some of the ham, eggs and asparagus tips. Finish with shavings of Parmesan cheese and serve warm.

DEVILED HAM AND PINEAPPLE SALAD

° ° °

INGREDIENTS

8 ounces/2 cups dried
whole-wheat penne
1/4 pint/²/₃ cup plain yogurt
1 tablespoon cider vinegar
1 teaspoon whole-grain mustard
large pinch of superfine sugar
2 tablespoons hot mango chutney
4 ounces cooked lean
ham, cubed
7-ounce can pineapple
chunks, drained
2 celery sticks, chopped
1/2 green bell pepper, seeded
and diced
1 tablespoon toasted sliced
almonds, coarsely chopped
salt and freshly ground
black pepper
rustic bread, to serve

SERVES 4

1 Cook the pasta in a large pan of lightly salted boiling water for 8–10 minutes, until *al dente*. Drain well and rinse thoroughly. Leave to cool.

2 To make the dressing, mix the yogurt, vinegar, mustard, sugar and mango chutney together in a large bowl. Season to taste with salt and pepper. Add the pasta and toss lightly together.

3 Transfer the pasta to a serving dish. Add the ham, pineapple, celery and green bell pepper.

4 Sprinkle toasted almonds over the top of the salad. Serve with rustic bread.

PEAR AND PECAN NUT SALAD

• • •

Toasted pecan nuts have an affinity with crisp white pears.

INGREDIENTS

*3 ounces/³⁄4 cup shelled pecan
nuts, halved
3 crisp pears
6 ounces young spinach,
stems removed
1 escarole or Boston lettuce
1 radicchio
2 tablespoons Blue Cheese and
Chive Dressing
salt and freshly ground
black pepper
rustic bread,
to serve*

SERVES 4

1 Toast the pecan nuts under a moderate broiler to bring out their flavour.

Cook's Tip

The pecan nuts will burn very quickly under the broiler, so keep constant watch over them and remove them as soon as they change color.

2 Cut the pears into even slices, leaving the skins intact but discarding the cores.

3 Place the spinach, lettuce and radicchio leaves into a large bowl. Add the pears and toasted pecans, pour over the Blue Cheese and Chive Dressing and toss well.

4 Distribute equally among four large serving plates and season to taste with salt and pepper. Serve the salad with warm rustic bread.

GOAT CHEESE AND FIG SALAD

° ° °

Fresh figs and walnuts are perfect partners for goat cheese and toasted buckwheat. The olive and nut oil dressing contains no vinegar, depending instead on the acidity of the goat cheese.

INGREDIENTS

6 ounces/1 cup couscous
2 tablespoons toasted buckwheat
1 egg, hard-boiled
2 tablespoons chopped fresh parsley
4 tablespoons olive oil
3 tablespoons walnut oil
4 ounces arugula leaves
½ frisée lettuce
6 ounces crumbly white goat cheese
2 ounces/½ cup broken walnuts, toasted
4 ripe figs, trimmed and almost cut into four (leave the pieces joined at the base)

SERVES 4

Variation

If you find the flavor of goat cheese a little too strong, try making this salad with a milder, crumbly cheese, such as feta or Caerphilly.

Cook's Tip

Goat cheeses vary in strength from the youngest, which are soft and mild, to strongly-flavored, sharp cheeses, which have a firm and crumbly texture. The crumbly varieties are particularly well suited to salads.

1 Place the couscous and toasted buckwheat in a bowl, cover with boiling water and leave to soak for 15 minutes. Place in a strainer to drain off any remaining water, then spread out on a baking tray and allow to cool.

2 Shell the hard-boiled egg and grate finely.

3 Toss the grated egg, parsley, couscous and buckwheat together in a bowl. Combine the olive and walnut oils, using half to moisten the couscous mixture.

4 Toss the salad leaves in the remaining oil and distribute among four large serving plates.

5 Pile the couscous mixture in the center of each plate and crumble the goat cheese over the top. Sprinkle with toasted walnuts, place a fig in the center of each plate and serve immediately.

AVOCADO, TOMATO AND MOZZARELLA SALAD

· · ·

This popular salad is made from ingredients representing the colors of the Italian flag – a sunny, cheerful dish!

INGREDIENTS
6 ounces/1½ cups dried pasta bows
6 tomatoes
8 ounces mozzarella cheese
1 large avocado
2 tablespoons chopped fresh basil
2 tablespoons pine nuts, toasted fresh basil sprig, to garnish

FOR THE DRESSING
6 tablespoons olive oil
2 tablespoons wine vinegar
1 teaspoon balsamic vinegar
1 teaspoon whole-grain mustard
pinch of sugar
salt and freshly ground black pepper

SERVES 4

1 Cook the pasta bows in a large pan of lightly salted boiling water for 8–10 minutes, until *al dente*. Drain well, rinse in cold water and set aside.

2 Using a sharp knife, slice the tomatoes and mozzarella cheese into thin rounds.

3 Halve the avocado, remove the pit and peel off the skin. Slice the flesh lengthwise.

4 To make the dressing, put the olive oil, wine and balsamic vinegars, mustard and sugar into a small bowl and whisk until combined. Season to taste with salt and black pepper.

5 Arrange the tomato, mozzarella and avocado slices in overlapping slices around the edge of a flat serving plate.

6 Toss the pasta with half of the dressing and the chopped basil. Pile into the center of the plate. Pour over the remaining dressing, sprinkle over the pine nuts and garnish with a sprig of fresh basil. Serve immediately.

Cook's Tip
The pale green flesh of the avocado quickly discolors once it is cut. Prepare it at the last minute and place immediately in dressing. If you do have to prepare it ahead, squeeze lemon juice over the cut side and cover with plastic wrap.

ROQUEFORT AND WALNUT PASTA SALAD

This is a simple, earthy salad, relying totally on the quality of the ingredients. There is no real substitute for the Roquefort – a blue-veined ewe's-milk cheese.

INGREDIENTS

8 ounces/2 cups dried pasta shapes
selection of salad leaves such as
arugula, frisée, mâche, baby
spinach, radicchio
2 tablespoons walnut oil
4 tablespoons sunflower oil
2 tablespoons red wine vinegar
or sherry vinegar
8 ounces Roquefort
cheese, crumbled
4 ounces/1 cup walnut halves
salt and freshly ground
black pepper

SERVES 4

3 Pile the pasta in the center of the salad leaves, sprinkle the crumbled Roquefort over them and pour over the dressing.

4 Sprinkle the walnuts over the top. Gently toss the salad just before serving.

1 Cook the pasta in a large pan of lightly salted, boiling water for 8–10 minutes, until *al dente*. Drain well and cool. Place the salad leaves in a bowl.

2 Whisk together the walnut oil, sunflower oil and vinegar. Season to taste with salt and pepper.

> #### Cook's Tip
> Toast the walnuts under a preheated broiler to add extra flavor.

PASTA, ASPARAGUS AND POTATO SALAD

. . .

*Made with whole-wheat pasta,
this delicious salad is a real
treat, especially when made
with fresh asparagus that has
just come into season.*

INGREDIENTS

8 ounces/2 cups dried whole-wheat
pasta shapes
4 tablespoons extra virgin olive oil
12 ounces baby new potatoes
8 ounces asparagus
4-inch piece Parmesan cheese
salt and freshly ground
black pepper

SERVES 4

1 Cook the pasta in a large pan of
lightly salted boiling water for
8–10 minutes, until *al dente*. Drain
well and toss with the olive oil
while it is still warm. Season to
taste with salt and pepper.

2 Scrub the potatoes and cook in
boiling salted water for about
15 minutes, or until tender. Drain
and toss with the pasta.

3 Trim any woody ends off the
asparagus and halve the stalks if
very long. Blanch in lightly salted
boiling water for 6 minutes, until
bright green and still crunchy.
Drain well. Plunge into cold water
to stop the asparagus from further
cooking and leave to cool. Drain
and dry on paper towels.

4 Gently toss the asparagus with
the potatoes and pasta, adjust the
seasoning to taste, if necessary, and
transfer to a shallow serving bowl.
Using a vegetable peeler, shave the
Parmesan over the salad and serve.

ZUCCHINI, CARROT AND PECAN SALAD

• • •

INGREDIENTS

2 carrots
1 ounce/¼ cup pecan nuts
4 scallions, sliced
2 fluid ounces/¼ cup strained
plain yogurt
7 teaspoons olive oil
1 teaspoon lemon juice
1 tablespoon chopped
fresh mint
2 zucchini
1 ounce/¼ cup all-purpose flour
2 pitta breads
salt and freshly ground
black pepper
shredded lettuce, to serve

SERVES 2

3 To make the dressing, put the yogurt, 1½ teaspoons of the olive oil, the lemon juice and the mint into a bowl and whisk well. Stir into the carrot mixture and mix well. Cover with plastic wrap and chill until required.

5 Heat the remaining oil in a large, heavy frying pan. Add the coated zucchini slices and cook for about 3–4 minutes, turning once, until browned. Drain the zucchini on paper towels.

1 Trim the carrots. Grate them coarsely into a bowl.

4 Trim the zucchini and cut them diagonally into slices. Season the flour with salt and pepper. Spread it out on a plate and turn the zucchini slices in it until they are well coated.

6 Make a slit in each pitta bread to form a pocket. Fill the pittas with the carrot mixture and the zucchini slices. Serve immediately on a bed of shredded lettuce.

2 Stir in the pecans and scallions and toss well.

Cook's Tip

Warm the pitta breads in the oven or under a medium broiler. Do not fill the pitta breads too soon or the carrot mixture will make the bread soggy and liable to collapse.

PASTA, OLIVE AND AVOCADO SALAD

· · ·

The ingredients of this salad are united by a wonderful sun-dried tomato and fresh basil dressing.

INGREDIENTS

8 ounces/2 cups dried pasta spirals
or other small pasta shapes
4 ounces can corn, drained, or
frozen corn, thawed
1/2 red bell pepper, seeded
and diced
8 black olives, pitted and sliced
3 scallions, chopped
2 medium avocados

FOR THE DRESSING
2 sun-dried tomato halves, loose-
packed (not preserved in oil)
1 1/2 tablespoons balsamic vinegar
1 1/2 tablespoons red wine vinegar
1/2 garlic clove, crushed
1/2 teaspoon salt
5 tablespoons olive oil
1 tablespoon chopped fresh basil

SERVES 6

1 To make the dressing, drop the sun-dried tomatoes into a pan containing 1 inch of boiling water and simmer for about 3 minutes, until tender. Drain thoroughly and chop finely.

2 Combine the sun-dried tomatoes, both types of vinegar, the garlic and salt in a food processor. With the motor running, add the olive oil in a steady stream. Transfer to a bowl and stir in the basil.

3 Cook the pasta in a large pan of lightly salted boiling water for 8–10 minutes, until *al dente*. Drain well. In a large bowl, combine the pasta, corn, red bell pepper, olives and scallions. Pour in the dressing and toss well.

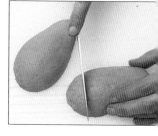

4 Just before serving, peel and pit the avocados and cut the flesh into cubes. Mix gently into the pasta, being careful not to break up the cubes, then transfer the salad to a serving dish. Serve at room temperature.

ROAST BELL PEPPER AND MUSHROOM PASTA SALAD

° ° °

Mixed peppers are combined with two kinds of mushrooms.

INGREDIENTS

1 red bell pepper, halved
1 yellow bell pepper, halved
1 green bell pepper, halved
12 ounces/3 cups dried
whole-wheat pasta shells
or twists
2 tablespoons olive oil
3 tablespoons balsamic vinegar
5 tablespoons tomato juice
2 tablespoons chopped fresh basil
1 tablespoon chopped fresh thyme
6 ounces/2¼ cups shiitake
mushrooms, diced
6 ounces/2¼ cups oyster
mushrooms, sliced
14-ounce can black-eyed peas,
drained and rinsed
4 ounces/¾ cup golden raisins
2 bunches scallions,
finely chopped
salt and freshly ground
black pepper

SERVES 6

1 Preheat the broiler to hot. Put the peppers, cut-side down, on a broiler pan rack and place under the broiler for 10–15 minutes, until the skins are charred. Transfer to a bowl, cover with a clean, damp dish towel and set aside to cool.

2 Meanwhile, cook the pasta shells or twists in lightly salted, boiling water for 8–10 minutes, until *al dente*, then drain thoroughly.

3 Mix together the oil, vinegar, tomato juice, basil and thyme, add to the warm pasta and toss.

4 Remove and discard the skins from the peppers. Seed and slice and add to the pasta.

5 Add the mushrooms, beans, golden raisins and scallions and season to taste with salt and pepper. Toss the ingredients to mix and serve warm. Alternatively, cover and chill in the refrigerator before serving.

MEDITERRANEAN PASTA SALAD

* * *

This is a type of salade Niçoise made with pasta.

INGREDIENTS

8 ounces/2 cups dried chunky
pasta shapes
6 ounces fine green beans
2 large ripe tomatoes
2 ounces fresh basil leaves
7-ounce can tuna in oil, drained
2 hard-boiled eggs, shelled and
sliced or quartered
2-ounce can anchovy
fillets, drained
capers and black olives, to taste

FOR THE DRESSING

6 tablespoons extra virgin olive oil
2 tablespoons white wine vinegar
2 garlic cloves, crushed
½ teaspoon Dijon mustard
2 tablespoons chopped fresh basil
salt and freshly ground
black pepper

SERVES 4

1 To make the dressing, whisk all the ingredients together in a small bowl. Season to taste with salt and pepper and set aside for the flavors to mingle while you prepare the salad.

Cook's Tip

Don't be tempted to chill this salad – the flavor will be dulled.

2 Cook the pasta in salted, boiling water for 8–10 minutes, until *al dente*. Drain well and cool.

3 Trim the green beans and blanch in lightly salted, boiling water for 3 minutes. Drain and refresh in cold water.

4 Slice the tomatoes and arrange on the base of a serving bowl. Moisten with a little dressing and cover with a quarter of the basil leaves. Then cover with the beans. Moisten with a little more dressing and cover with a third of the remaining basil.

5 Cover the vegetables with the pasta tossed in a little more dressing, half the remaining basil and the coarsely flaked tuna.

6 Arrange the eggs on top, then finally sprinkle over the anchovy fillets, capers and olives. Spoon over the remaining dressing and garnish with the remaining basil. Serve immediately.

The recipes in this chapter feature luxurious ingredients, exotic

combinations, spectacular presentations and sophisticated

flavors, for truly stylish dining. There is a special salad to suit

every occasion, from an *al fresco* dinner to a buffet party.

SPECIAL OCCASION
SALADS

GADO GADO

This classic Indonesian vegetable salad is served with a delicious hot peanut sauce.

INGREDIENTS

2 medium potatoes
6 ounces green beans, trimmed
6 ounces Chinese cabbage, shredded
1 iceberg lettuce
6 ounces beansprouts
½ cucumber, cut into fingers
5 ounces daikon, shredded
3 scallions
8 ounces tofu, cut into large slices
3 hard-boiled eggs, shelled and quartered
1 small bunch fresh cilantro
shrimp crackers, to serve

FOR THE PEANUT SAUCE
5 ounces/1¼ cups raw peanuts
1 tablespoon vegetable oil
2 shallots or 1 small onion, finely chopped
1 garlic clove, crushed
1–2 small fresh chiles, seeded and finely chopped
½-inch square shrimp paste or 1 tablespoon Thai fish sauce (optional)
2 tablespoons tamarind sauce
4 fluid ounces/½ cup canned coconut milk
1 tablespoon clear honey

SERVES 4–6

1 Peel the potatoes. Bring to the boil in salted water and simmer for about 15 minutes, or until tender. Cook the green beans for about 3–4 minutes. Drain the potatoes and beans and refresh under cold running water.

2 To make the peanut sauce, dry-fry the peanuts in a wok, or place under a moderate broiler, tossing them all the time to prevent them from burning.

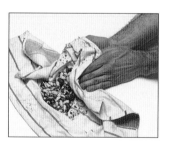

3 Turn the peanuts onto a clean cloth and rub them vigorously with your hands to remove the papery skins. Place the peanuts in a food processor and process for about 2 minutes until finely crushed.

4 Heat the vegetable oil in a wok and soften the shallots or onion, garlic and chiles without letting them color. Add the shrimp paste or fish sauce, if using, together with the tamarind sauce, coconut milk and honey.

5 Simmer briefly, add to the blended peanuts and process to form a thick sauce. Transfer to a small serving bowl and keep hot.

6 Arrange the potatoes, green beans and all the other salad ingredients on a large serving platter. Serve with the bowl of peanut sauce and shrimp crackers.

Cook's Tip

Shrimp paste, also known as terasi and blachan, is widely used throughout Southeast Asia. It is made from fermented shrimp, pounded to a paste with salt.

COMPOSED SALADS

. . .

A composed salad makes a perfect appetizer or light main course for a special occasion. They are light and colorful and lend themselves to endless variation – and the components can often be prepared ahead for quick assembly.

Almost any combination of ingredients can be used – let your imagination and your palate guide you. Arranged attractively on a plate or in a bowl, this type of salad offers contrasting flavors, textures and colors. Raw or cooked vegetables, fresh fruits, hard-boiled hen or quail eggs, smoked or cooked poultry, meat, fish or shellfish can all be used, but it is important that the dressing or other kind of seasoning unites all the elements harmoniously.

Unlike a more basic tossed salad in which the leaves or vegetables are tossed together with a simple vinaigrette, the components of a composed salad are kept more separate and distinctive. The ingredients might be arranged in groups, sometimes on a bed of lettuce or other salad leaves, or simply arranged in circles or rows on the serving plates.

Shrimp, Avocado and Citrus Salad

INGREDIENTS

1 tablespoon lemon juice
1 tablespoon lime juice
1 tablespoon clear honey
3 tablespoons olive oil
2–3 tablespoons walnut oil
2 tablespoons chopped fresh chives
1 pound large cooked shrimp, peeled and deveined
1 avocado, peeled, pitted and cut into small dice
1 pink grapefruit, peeled and segmented
1 large navel orange, peeled and segmented
2 tablespoons pine nuts, toasted
salt and freshly ground black pepper

SERVES 6

1 Blend the lemon and lime juices, salt and pepper and honey in a bowl. Gradually whisk in the olive oil, then the walnut oil, to make a creamy dressing. Stir in the chives.

2 Arrange the shrimp with the avocado and grapefruit and orange segments on individual serving plates. Drizzle over the dressing, sprinkle with the toasted pine nuts, and serve.

Smoked Salmon Salad with Dill

INGREDIENTS

8 ounces smoked salmon, thinly sliced
1 fennel bulb, thinly sliced
1 medium cucumber, seeded and cut into julienne strips
2 tablespoons lemon juice
4 fluid ounces/½ cup olive oil
2 tablespoons chopped fresh dill, plus a few sprigs to garnish
freshly ground black pepper
caviar, to garnish (optional)

SERVES 4

1 Arrange the salmon slices on four serving plates and arrange the slices of fennel alongside, together with the cucumber strips.

2 Combine the lemon juice and pepper in a small bowl. Gradually whisk in the olive oil to make a creamy vinaigrette. Stir in the dill.

3 Spoon a little vinaigrette over the fennel and cucumber. Drizzle the remaining vinaigrette over the smoked salmon and garnish with sprigs of dill. Top each salad with a spoonful of caviar, if you like, before serving.

Belgian Endive Salad with Roquefort

INGREDIENTS

2 tablespoons red wine vinegar
1 teaspoon Dijon mustard
2 ounces/¼ cup walnut oil
1–2 tablespoons sunflower oil
2 Belgian endive heads
1 celery heart or 4 celery sticks, cut into julienne strips
3 ounces/¾ cup walnut halves, lightly toasted
4 ounces Roquefort cheese
salt and freshly ground black pepper
fresh parsley sprigs, to garnish

SERVES 4

1 Whisk together the vinegar, mustard and salt and pepper to taste in a small bowl. Slowly whisk in the oils, to make a vinaigrette.

2 Arrange the endive on serving plates. Sprinkle over the celery and walnuts. Crumble the Roquefort on top of each salad, drizzle over a little vinaigrette, garnish and serve.

Clockwise from far right: Shrimp, Avocado and Citrus Salad; Smoked Salmon Salad with Dill; and Belgian Endive Salad with Roquefort.

WARM MONKFISH SALAD

. . .

Monkfish has a matchless flavor and benefits from being cooked simply. Teaming it with wilted baby spinach and toasted pine nuts is inspirational.

INGREDIENTS

2 monkfish fillets, about
12 ounces each
1 ounce/¹⁄₃ cup pine nuts
1 tablespoon olive oil
¹⁄₂ ounce/1 tablespoon butter
8 ounces baby spinach leaves,
washed and stalks removed
salt and freshly ground
black pepper

FOR THE DRESSING
1 teaspoon Dijon mustard
1 teaspoon sherry vinegar
4 tablespoons olive oil
1 garlic clove, crushed

SERVES 4

1 Holding the knife at a slight angle, cut each monkfish fillet into 12 diagonal slices. Season lightly with salt and pepper and set aside.

2 Dry-fry the pine nuts in a heavy frying pan, shaking it occasionally, until golden brown. Do not burn. Transfer to a plate; set aside.

Variation
Substitute a variety of salad leaves for the spinach.

3 Make the dressing by whisking all the ingredients together until smooth and creamy. Pour it into a small pan, season to taste with salt and pepper and heat gently.

4 Heat the oil and butter in a ridged griddle pan or frying pan until sizzling. Add the fish; sauté for 20–30 seconds on each side.

5 Put the spinach leaves in a bowl and pour over the warm dressing. Sprinkle with the toasted pine nuts, reserving a few, and toss together well. Divide the spinach leaves among four plates and arrange the monkfish slices on top. Sprinkle the reserved pine nuts on top and serve.

ASPARAGUS AND LANGOUSTINE SALAD

For a really extravagant treat, you could make this attractive salad with medallions of lobster. For a more economic version, use jumbo shrimp, allowing six per serving.

INGREDIENTS

16 langoustines
16 fresh asparagus spears, trimmed
2 carrots
2 tablespoons olive oil
1 garlic clove, peeled
4 fresh tarragon sprigs and some chopped, to garnish

FOR THE DRESSING
2 tablespoons tarragon vinegar
4 fluid ounces/½ cup olive oil
salt and freshly ground
black pepper

SERVES 4

1 Peel the langoustines and keep the shells for stock. Set aside.

2 Steam the asparagus over boiling salted water until just tender, but still a little crisp. Refresh under cold water, drain and place in a shallow dish.

3 Peel the carrots and cut into fine julienne shreds. Cook in a pan of lightly salted boiling water for about 3 minutes, until tender but still crunchy. Drain, refresh under cold water, then drain again. Place in the dish with the asparagus.

4 Make the dressing. Whisk the tarragon vinegar with the oil. Season to taste with salt and pepper. Pour over the vegetables and leave to marinate.

5 Heat the oil with the garlic in a frying pan until very hot. Add the langoustines and sauté until just heated through. Discard the garlic.

6 Cut the asparagus spears in half and arrange on four individual plates with the carrots. Drizzle over the dressing left in the dish and top each portion with four langoustine tails. Top with the tarragon sprigs and sprinkle the chopped tarragon on top. Serve immediately.

THAI SCENTED FISH SALAD

. . .

INGREDIENTS

12 ounces fillet of red mullet,
porgy or snapper
1 romaine lettuce
1/2 lollo biondo lettuce
1 papaya or mango, peeled
and sliced
1 pitahaya, peeled and sliced,
or 1 slice of melon, diced
1 large tomato, cut into wedges
1/2 cucumber, peeled and cut
into strips
3 scallions, sliced

FOR THE MARINADE

1 teaspoon coriander seeds
1 teaspoon fennel seeds
1/2 teaspoon cumin seeds
1 teaspoons superfine sugar
1/2 teaspoon hot chili sauce
2 tablespoons garlic oil
salt

FOR THE DRESSING

1 tablespoon coconut cream
4 tablespoons peanut or
safflower oil
finely grated rind and juice
of 1 lime
1 fresh red chili, seeded and
finely chopped
1 teaspoon sugar
3 tablespoons chopped
fresh cilantro
salt

SERVES 4

1 Cut the fish into even strips and place them on a plate or in a shallow bowl.

2 To make the marinade, crush the coriander, fennel and cumin seeds together with the superfine sugar. Add the chili sauce, garlic oil and salt and combine.

3 Spread the marinade over the fish, cover and leave to stand in a cool place for at least 20 minutes – longer if you have time.

4 To make the dressing, place the coconut cream and salt in a screw-top jar with 3 tablespoons boiling water and leave to dissolve. Add the oil, lime rind and juice, chili, sugar and chopped cilantro. Shake well and set aside.

5 Combine the lettuce leaves with the papaya or mango, pitahaya or melon, tomato, cucumber and scallions. Toss with the dressing, then distribute among four large serving plates.

6 Heat a large, heavy non-stick frying-pan, add the fish and cook for 5 minutes, turning once. Place the cooked fish on the salad and serve immediately.

Cook's Tip

If planning ahead, you can leave the fish in the marinade for up to 8 hours. The dressing can also be made in advance, without the fresh cilantro. Store at room temperature and add the cilantro just before assembling the salad.

SAN FRANCISCO SALAD

∘ ∘ ∘

California is a salad-maker's paradise and is renowned for the healthiness of its produce. San Francisco has become the salad capital of California.

INGREDIENTS

2 pounds langoustines or extra
large shrimp
2 ounces bulb fennel, sliced
2 medium tomatoes, quartered
4 small tomatoes
2 tablespoons olive oil,
plus extra for moistening the
salad leaves
4 tablespoons brandy
¼ pint/⅔ cup dry white wine
7-fluid-ounce can lobster or
crab bisque
2 tablespoons chopped
fresh tarragon
3 tablespoons heavy cream
8 ounces green beans, trimmed
2 oranges
6 ounces mâche
4 ounces arugula leaves
½ frisée lettuce
salt and cayenne pepper

SERVES 4

1 Bring a large pan of salted water to the boil, add the langoustines or shrimp and simmer for 10 minutes. Refresh under cold running water.

2 Preheat the oven to 425°F. Twist the tails from all but four of the langoustines or shrimp – reserve these to garnish the dish. Peel the outer shell from the tail meat. Put the tail peelings, carapace and claws in a heavy roasting pan with the fennel and medium tomatoes. Toss with the olive oil and roast near the top of the oven for 20 minutes to bring out the flavors.

3 Remove the roasting pan from the oven and place it over a moderate heat. Add the brandy and ignite to release the flavor of the alcohol. Add the white wine and simmer briefly.

4 Transfer the contents of the roasting pan to a food processor and reduce to a coarse purée: this will take only 10–15 seconds. Rub the purée through a fine nylon strainer into a bowl. Add the lobster or crab bisque, tarragon and cream. Season to taste with salt and a little cayenne pepper.

5 Bring a pan of salted water to the boil, add the beans and cook for 6 minutes. Drain and cool under cold running water. To segment the oranges, cut the peel from the top and bottom, and then from the sides, with a serrated knife. Loosen the segments by cutting between the membranes and the flesh with a small knife.

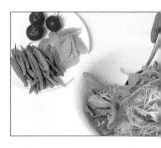

6 Moisten the salad leaves with olive oil and distribute among four serving plates. Fold the langoustine tails or shrimp into the dressing and distribute among the plates. Add the beans, orange segments and small tomatoes. Garnish each plate with a whole langoustine or shrimp and serve warm.

MILLIONAIRE'S LOBSTER SALAD

When money is no object and you're in a decadent mood, this salad is the perfect choice.

INGREDIENTS

1 medium lobster, live or cooked
1 bay leaf
1 fresh thyme sprig
1½ pounds new potatoes
2 ripe tomatoes
4 oranges
½ frisée lettuce
6 ounces mâche leaves
4 tablespoons extra virgin olive oil
7-ounce can young artichokes in brine, quartered
1 small bunch fresh tarragon, chervil or flat leaf parsley
salt

FOR THE DRESSING
2 tablespoons frozen concentrated orange juice, thawed
3 ounces/6 tablespoons sweet butter, diced
salt and cayenne pepper

SERVES 4

1 If the lobster needs cooking, add it whole to a large pan of cold salted water with the bay leaf and thyme. Bring to the boil and simmer for 15 minutes. Cool under running water.

2 Twist off the legs and claws, and separate the tail from the body. Break the claws with a hammer and remove the meat. Cut the tail piece open, slice the meat and set aside.

3 Bring the potatoes to the boil in salted water and simmer for about 15 minutes, until tender. Drain, cover and keep warm.

4 Cut a cross in the skin of the tomatoes, cover with boiling water and leave for 30 seconds. Cool under cold running water and slip off the skins. Halve the tomatoes, discard the seeds, then cut the flesh into large dice.

5 To segment the oranges, remove the peel from the top, bottom and sides with a serrated knife. With a small paring knife, loosen the orange segments by cutting carefully between the flesh and the membranes, holding the fruit over a small bowl.

Variation

This dish is also delicious prepared in exactly the same way with crayfish, which is also known as crawfish, langouste or rock lobster.

6 To make the dressing, pour the orange juice into a heatproof bowl and set it over a pan containing about 1 inch gently simmering water. Heat the juice for 1 minute, turn off the heat, then add the butter, a little at a time, whisking constantly, until the dressing reaches a coating consistency.

7 Season to taste with salt and a pinch of cayenne pepper, cover and keep warm.

8 Dress the salad leaves with olive oil, then divide among four large serving plates. Moisten the potatoes, artichokes and orange segments with olive oil and distribute among the leaves.

9 Lay the sliced lobster over the salad, spoon on the warm dressing, add the diced tomato and decorate with the fresh herbs. Serve the salad at room temperature.

GENOESE SQUID SALAD

INGREDIENTS

*1 pound prepared squid,
cut into rings*
4 garlic cloves, coarsely chopped
*½ pint/1¼ cups Italian
red wine*
*1 pound waxy new
potatoes, scrubbed*
*8 ounces green beans, trimmed and
cut into short lengths*
*2–3 sun-dried tomatoes in oil,
drained and thinly
sliced lengthwise*
4 tablespoons extra virgin olive oil
1 tablespoon red wine vinegar
*salt and freshly ground
black pepper*

SERVES 4–6

1 Preheat the oven to 350°F. Put
the squid rings in an earthenware
dish with half the garlic, the wine
and pepper to taste. Cover and
bake for 45 minutes, or until the
squid is tender.

2 Put the potatoes in a pan, cover
with cold water and add a good
pinch of salt. Bring to the boil,
cover and simmer over a low heat
for about 15 minutes, until tender.
Using a slotted spoon, lift out the
potatoes and set aside. Add the
beans to the boiling water and
cook for 3 minutes. Drain.

3 When the potatoes are cool
enough to handle, slice them
thickly on the diagonal and place
them in a bowl with the warm
beans and sun-dried tomatoes.
Whisk the oil, vinegar and the
remaining garlic in a pitcher and
add salt and pepper to taste. Pour
over the potato mixture.

4 Drain the squid and discard the
liquid. Add the squid to the potato
mixture and mix very gently.
Arrange on individual plates and
season liberally with pepper.

Cook's Tip

The French potato called
Charlotte is perfect for
this salad because it
retains its shape when
boiled. Prepared squid
can be bought from
supermarkets with fresh
fish counters.

TUNA CARPACCIO

Fillet of beef is most often used for carpaccio, but meaty fish, such as tuna and swordfish, make a change. The secret is to slice the fish extra thin.

INGREDIENTS

2 fresh tuna steaks, about 1 pound total weight
4 tablespoons extra virgin olive oil
1 tablespoon balsamic vinegar
1 teaspoon superfine sugar
2 tablespoons bottled green peppercorns or capers, drained
salt and freshly ground black pepper
lemon wedges and green salad, to serve

SERVES 4

1 Remove the skin from each tuna steak and place each steak between two sheets of plastic wrap or baking parchment. Pound with the side of a rolling pin or the flat side of a meat hammer until the steak is flattened slightly.

2 Roll up the tuna steaks as tightly as possible, then wrap tightly in plastic wrap. Place the tuna steaks in the freezer for about 4 hours, or until firm.

3 Unwrap the tuna and cut crosswise into the thinnest possible slices. Arrange the slices on four individual serving plates.

4 Whisk together the oil, vinegar, sugar and peppercorns or capers, season to taste with salt and pepper and pour over the tuna. Cover and allow to come to room temperature for 30 minutes before serving with lemon wedges and green salad.

Cook's Tip
Don't skimp the freezing, as this makes it possible to cut extra-thin slices of tuna.

Cook's Tip
Raw fish is safe to eat as long as it is very fresh, so check with your fish counter before purchase and make and serve the carpaccio the same day. Do not buy fish that has been frozen and thawed.

441

SALADE MOUCLADE

Mouclade is a famous dish from La Rochelle in southwestern France. It consists of mussels in a light curry cream sauce. Here the flavors appear in a salad of warm lentils and spinach. Serve at room temperature in summer.

INGREDIENTS

3 tablespoons olive oil
1 onion, finely chopped
12 ounces/1½ cups Puy or
green lentils
1½ pints/3¾ cups vegetable stock
4½ pounds fresh mussels
in their shells
5 tablespoons white wine
½ teaspoon curry paste
pinch of saffron
2 tablespoons heavy cream
2 large carrots, peeled
4 celery sticks
2 pounds young spinach,
stalks removed
1 tablespoon garlic oil
salt and cayenne pepper

SERVES 4

1 Heat the oil in a heavy pan and cook the onion for 6–8 minutes, until soft, but not colored. Add the lentils and vegetable stock, bring to the boil, lower the heat and simmer for 45 minutes, until tender. Remove from the heat and set aside to cool.

2 Clean the mussels thoroughly, discarding any that are damaged. Any that are open should close if given a sharp tap; if they fail to do so, discard these too.

3 Place the mussels in a large pan, add the wine, cover and steam over a high heat, shaking the pan occasionally, for 12 minutes. Strain the mussels in a colander, reserving the cooking liquid. Discard any that have not opened during the cooking. Take all but four of the mussels out of their shells.

4 Strain the mussel liquid through a fine strainer or cheesecloth into a wide, shallow pan to remove any grit or sand.

5 Add the curry paste and saffron to the pan, then reduce the liquid over a high heat until the pan is almost dry. Remove from the heat, stir in the cream, season to taste with salt and pepper and combine with the mussels.

6 Cut the carrot and celery into 2-inch matchsticks and cook in lightly salted boiling water for 3 minutes. Drain well, cool and moisten with olive oil.

7 Wash the spinach, put the wet leaves into a large pan, cover and steam for 30 seconds. Immerse in cold water, then press the leaves dry in a colander. Moisten with garlic oil and season.

8 Spoon the lentils into the center of four plates. Place heaps of spinach around the edge, with some carrot and celery on top. Spoon over the mussels and garnish with the reserved mussels in their shells.

HOT COCONUT, SHRIMP AND PAPAYA SALAD

∘ ∘ ∘

Transport yourself to the Far East with this wonderful dish that combines juicy papaya with succulent shrimp tails in a spicy coconut sauce.

INGREDIENTS

8 ounces raw or cooked shrimp
tails, peeled and deveined
2 ripe papayas
8 ounces romaine or iceberg lettuce
leaves, Chinese cabbage and
young spinach leaves
1 firm tomato, peeled, seeded and
coarsely chopped
3 scallions, shredded
1 small bunch fresh cilantro,
shredded, and 1 large chile,
sliced, to garnish

FOR THE DRESSING
3 tablespoons coconut cream
6 tablespoons vegetable oil
juice of 1 lime
1/2 teaspoon hot chili sauce
2 teaspoons Thai fish sauce
1 teaspoon sugar

SERVES 4–6

2 If using raw shrimp tails, cover with cold water in a pan, bring to the boil and simmer for no longer than 2 minutes. Drain thoroughly and set aside. If using cooked shrimp, pat dry with paper towels.

3 Cut the papayas in half from top to bottom and remove the black seeds. Peel off the skin and cut the flesh into equal-size pieces.

4 Place the salad leaves in a bowl. Add the shrimp tails, papayas, tomato and scallions. Pour over the dressing, garnish with the cilantro and chile, and serve.

1 To make the dressing, place the coconut cream, vegetable oil, lime juice, chili sauce, Thai fish sauce and sugar in a screw-top jar. Shake well to mix and set aside. Do not chill.

ROASTED CHICKEN AND WALNUT SALAD

• • •

The chickens may be cooked the day before eating and the salad finished on the day itself.

INGREDIENTS

4 fresh tarragon or rosemary sprigs
2 x 4–4½ pound chickens
2½ ounces/5 tbsp softened butter
¼ pint/⅔ cup chicken stock
¼ pint/⅔ cup white wine
4 ounces/1 cup walnut pieces
1 small cantaloupe melon
lettuce leaves
1 pound seedless grapes or
pitted cherries
salt and freshly ground
black pepper

FOR THE DRESSING
2 tablespoons tarragon vinegar
4 fluid ounces/½ cup light olive oil
2 tablespoons chopped fresh
mixed herbs such as parsley,
mint, tarragon

SERVES 8

1 Preheat the oven to 400°F. Put the herb sprigs inside the chickens and season with salt and pepper.

2 Spread the chickens with 4 tablespoons of the softened butter, place in a roasting pan and pour the stock around them. Cover loosely with foil and roast for about 1½ hours, basting twice, until browned, when the juices run clear. Remove from the roasting pan and leave to cool.

3 Add the wine to the roasting pan. Bring to the boil over a medium heat and cook until syrupy. Strain and leave to cool. Heat the remaining butter in a frying pan and gently fry the walnuts until lightly browned. Scoop the melon flesh into balls or cut into cubes.

4 To make the dressing, whisk the vinegar and olive oil together with a little salt and pepper to taste. Skim off the fat from the chicken juices and add the juices to the dressing with the herbs. Adjust the seasoning to taste.

5 Cut the chicken into serving portions and arrange them on a bed of lettuce leaves. Sprinkle over the grapes or cherries and melon balls or cubes and spoon over the dressing. Sprinkle with the toasted walnuts and serve.

CHICKEN LIVER SALAD

• • ◦

This delicious salad may be served as a main course for a summer lunch party, or as a tasty first course served on individual plates.

INGREDIENTS

mixed salad leaves, such as frisée, oak leaf lettuce, radicchio, arugula
1 avocado
2 tablespoons lemon or lime juice
2 pink grapefruit
12 ounces chicken livers
2 tablespoons olive oil
1 garlic clove, crushed
salt and freshly ground black pepper
whole fresh chives, to garnish

FOR THE DRESSING

2 tablespoons lemon juice
4 tablespoons olive oil
1/2 teaspoon whole-grain mustard
1/2 teaspoon clear honey
1 tablespoon chopped fresh chives
salt and freshly ground black pepper

SERVES 4

1 To make the dressing, put the lemon juice, olive oil, whole-grain mustard, honey and fresh chives into a screw-top jar, and shake vigorously. Season to taste with salt and freshly ground black pepper.

2 Arrange the mixed salad leaves attractively on a large serving plate.

3 Peel and pit the avocado, dice the flesh and mix with the lemon or lime juice to prevent it from browning. Add to the plate of mixed leaves.

4 Peel the grapefruit with a small serrated knife, removing as much of the white pith as possible. Split into segments and arrange with the salad leaves and avocado on the serving plate.

5 Pat dry the chicken livers on paper towels and remove any unwanted pieces.

6 Using a sharp knife, cut the larger chicken livers in half. Leave the smaller ones whole.

Cook's Tip

If using frozen chicken livers, thaw them thoroughly first.

7 Heat the oil in a large frying pan. Stir-fry the chicken livers and garlic briskly until the livers are brown all over (they should be slightly pink inside).

8 Season the chicken livers to taste with salt and black pepper, remove from the pan and drain well on paper towels.

9 Place the chicken livers, while still warm, on the salad leaves and spoon over the dressing. Garnish with the whole chives and serve the salad immediately.

BROILED CHICKEN SALAD WITH LAVENDER

Lavender may seem an odd ingredient, but its delightful scent has a natural affinity with garlic, orange and other herbs.

INGREDIENTS

4 boneless, skinless chicken breast portions
1 1/2 pints/3 3/4 cups light chicken stock
6 ounces/1 cup fine polenta or cornmeal
2 ounces/4 tablespoons butter
1 pound young spinach leaves
6 ounces mâche leaves
8 small tomatoes, halved
salt and ground black pepper
8 fresh lavender sprigs, to garnish

FOR THE LAVENDER MARINADE
6 fresh lavender flowers
2 teaspoons finely grated orange rind
2 garlic cloves, crushed
2 teaspoons clear honey
2 tablespoons olive oil
2 teaspoons chopped fresh thyme
2 teaspoons chopped fresh marjoram
salt

SERVES 4

1 To make the marinade, strip the lavender flowers from their stems and combine with the orange rind, garlic, honey and a pinch of salt. Add the olive oil, thyme and marjoram. Slash the chicken deeply, spread over the mixture and leave to marinate in a cool place for at least 20 minutes.

2 To prepare the polenta, bring the chicken stock to the boil in a large, heavy pan. Add the polenta or cornmeal in a slow, steady stream, stirring constantly, until thick: this will take 2–3 minutes. Turn the cooked polenta out onto a 1-inch deep buttered tray and leave to cool.

3 Heat the broiler to a moderate temperature. If using a barbecue, let the embers settle to a steady glow. Broil the chicken breast portions for about 15 minutes, turning them once.

Cook's Tip

This lavender marinade is a delicious flavoring for salt-water fish as well as chicken. Try it spread over grilled cod, haddock, halibut, sea bass or porgy.

4 Cut the cooled polenta into 1-inch cubes with a wet knife. Heat the remaining butter in a large frying pan and fry the polenta cubes until golden brown.

5 Divide the salad leaves and tomatoes among four large serving plates. Slice each chicken breast portion and lay over the salad. Place the polenta cubes among the salad and season to taste with salt and pepper. Garnish with the sprigs of lavender and serve.

DIJON CHICKEN SALAD

• • •

This attractive and classical dish is ideal to serve for a simple but tasty and elegant lunch.

INGREDIENTS
4 skinless, boneless chicken breast portions
mixed salad leaves such as frisée, oakleaf lettuce and radicchio

FOR THE MARINADE
2 tablespoons tarragon wine vinegar
1 teaspoon Dijon mustard
1 teaspoon clear honey
6 tablespoons olive oil
salt and freshly ground black pepper

FOR THE MUSTARD DRESSING
2 tablespoons Dijon mustard
3 garlic cloves, crushed
1 tablespoon grated onion
4 tablespoons white wine

SERVES 4

1 To make the marinade mix the vinegar, mustard, honey and olive oil, together in a shallow glass or earthenware dish that is large enough to hold the chicken breasts in a single layer. Season to taste with salt and pepper.

2 Add the chicken breast portions to the dish, making sure they do not overlap each other.

3 Turn the chicken over in the marinade to coat completely, cover with plastic wrap and chill in the refrigerator overnight.

4 Preheat the oven to 375°F. Transfer the chicken and the marinade into an ovenproof dish, cover with kitchen foil and bake for about 35 minutes, or until tender. Leave the chicken to cool in the liquid.

5 To make the mustard dressing, put all the ingredients into a screw-top jar and shake vigorously.

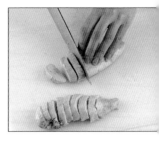

6 Thinly slice the chicken and fan out the slices.

7 Arrange the chicken slices on a serving dish with the salad leaves. Spoon over some of the mustard dressing and serve. Serve the rest of the dressing separately in a bowl or pitcher.

Cook's Tip
The dressing can be made several days in advance and stored in the refrigerator.

DUCK AND PASTA SALAD

° ° °

The acidity of fruit is a very good accompaniment to a rich meat, such as duck, since it adds a tartness that makes the meat more digestible. This luxurious salad includes apple, orange and, in the dressing, dried cherries. The rigatoni adds a welcome element of carbohydrate and makes the dish a complete meal.

INGREDIENTS

2 boneless duck breasts
1 teaspoon coriander
seeds, crushed
12 ounces dried rigatoni
1 apple, diced
2 oranges, segmented
salt and freshly ground
black pepper
fresh chopped cilantro and mint,
to garnish

FOR THE DRESSING
¼ pint/⅔ cup orange juice
1 tablespoon lemon juice
2 teaspoons clear honey
1 shallot, finely chopped
1 garlic clove, crushed
1 celery stick, chopped
3 ounces/¾ cup dried cherries
3 tablespoons port
1 tablespoon chopped fresh mint
2 tablespoons chopped
fresh cilantro

SERVES 6

1 Preheat the broiler. Remove the skin and fat from the duck breasts, season with salt and pepper and rub with the crushed coriander seeds.

2 Broil the duck breasts for 7–10 minutes (depending on the size). Wrap the duck breasts in foil and leave for 20 minutes.

3 Cook the pasta in a large pan of lightly salted, boiling water for 8–10 minutes, until *al dente*. Drain thoroughly and rinse under cold running water. Set the pasta aside to cool.

4 To make the dressing, put the orange juice, lemon juice, honey, shallot, garlic, celery, cherries, port, mint and fresh cilantro into a small bowl. Whisk together, cover with plastic wrap and leave to marinate for 30 minutes.

5 Unwrap the duck breasts from the foil and, using a very sharp carving knife, slice the duck very thinly. (It should still be slightly pink in the center.)

6 Put the pasta into a large mixing bowl, add the dressing, diced apple and segments of orange. Toss well to coat the pasta.

7 Transfer the salad to a serving plate with the duck slices and garnish with the chopped cilantro and mint.

DUCK SALAD WITH ORANGE SAUCE

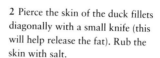

The rich flavor of duck provides the foundation for this delicious salad. Garlic croûtons add extra crunchy texture. Serve it late in summer or in the fall.

INGREDIENTS

1 small orange
2 boneless duck breast fillets
¼ pint/⅔ cup dry white wine
1 teaspoon ground coriander seeds
½ teaspoon ground cumin or fennel seeds
2 tablespoons superfine sugar
juice of ½ small lime or lemon
3 ounces day-old bread, thickly sliced
3 tablespoons garlic oil
½ escarole lettuce
½ frisée lettuce
2 tablespoons sunflower oil
salt and cayenne pepper
4 sprigs fresh cilantro, to garnish

SERVES 4

1 Halve the orange and slice thickly. Discard any seeds and place the slices in a small pan. Cover with water, bring to the boil and simmer for 5 minutes. Drain the orange slices and set aside.

2 Pierce the skin of the duck fillets diagonally with a small knife (this will help release the fat). Rub the skin with salt.

3 Place a steel or cast-iron frying pan over a steady heat and cook the fillets for 20 minutes, turning once, until they are medium-rare. Transfer to a warm plate, cover and keep warm.

4 Heat the sediment in the frying pan until it begins to darken and caramelize. Add the dry white wine and stir constantly to loosen the sediment. Add the ground coriander, cumin or fennel seeds, sugar and orange slices.

5 Boil quickly and reduce to a coating consistency. Sharpen with the lime or lemon juice and season to taste with salt and cayenne pepper. Transfer the orange sauce to a bowl, cover and keep warm.

6 Remove the crusts from the bread and cut the bread into short fingers. Heat the garlic oil in a heavy frying pan and brown the croûtons. Season with salt, then transfer to paper towels.

7 Moisten the salad leaves with a little sunflower oil and distribute them equally among four large serving plates.

8 Slice the duck diagonally with a carving knife. Divide the meat into four and lift onto each salad plate. Spoon on the orange sauce, sprinkle the salad with croûtons, decorate with a sprig of fresh cilantro and serve warm.

APRICOT DUCK WITH BEANSPROUT SALAD

*Duck is rich in fat, so it stays beautifully moist when cooked on a barbecue,
while any excess fat drains away.*

INGREDIENTS

4 duck breasts, with skin
1 small red onion, thinly sliced
4 ounces/³/4 cup ready-to-eat
dried apricots
1 tablespoon clear honey
1 teaspoon sesame oil
2 teaspoons ground star anise
salt and freshly ground
black pepper

FOR THE SALAD
2 scallions
1/2 head Chinese cabbage,
finely shredded
5 ounces/2 cups beansprouts
1 tablespoon light soy sauce
1 tablespoon peanut oil
1 teaspoon sesame oil
1 teaspoon clear honey

SERVES 4

1 Place the duck breasts, skin-side down, on a chopping board or clean work surface and cut a long slit down one side of each one with a sharp kitchen knife, cutting almost through, to form a large pocket.

2 Tuck the slices of onion and the apricots inside the pocket and press the breast firmly back into shape. Secure with metal skewers.

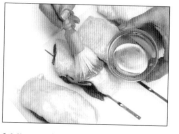

3 Mix together the clear honey and sesame oil and brush generously over the duck, particularly the skin. Sprinkle over the star anise and season with plenty of salt and fresh black pepper.

4 To make the salad, shred the scallions, then mix together with the shredded Chinese cabbage and beansprouts in a large bowl.

5 Shake together all the salad dressing ingredients in a screw-topped jar. Season to taste with salt and pepper. Toss into the salad.

6 Cook the duck under a medium-hot broiler or on a barbecue for 12–15 minutes, turning once, until golden brown on the outside.

Cook's Tip
If you prefer not to eat the beansprouts raw, they can be blanched by plunging them into boiling water for 1 minute. Drain and refresh in cold water.

SESAME DUCK AND NOODLE SALAD

· · ·

This salad is a complete meal in itself and makes a wonderful summer lunch. The marinade is a delicious blend of Southeast Asian flavors.

INGREDIENTS
2 duck breasts
1 tablespoon sunflower oil
5 ounces sugar snap peas
2 carrots, cut into 3-inch sticks
8 ounces medium egg noodles
6 scallions, sliced
salt
2 tablespoons fresh cilantro leaves,
to garnish

FOR THE MARINADE
1 tablespoon sesame oil
1 teaspoon ground coriander
1 teaspoon Chinese five-
spice powder

FOR THE DRESSING
1 tablespoon vinegar
1 teaspoon soft light brown sugar
1 teaspoon soy sauce
1 garlic clove, crushed
1 tablespoon sesame seeds, toasted
3 tablespoons sunflower oil
3 tablespoons sesame oil
freshly ground black pepper

SERVES 4

1 Slice the duck breasts thinly across and place in a shallow dish. Mix together all the ingredients for the marinade, pour over the duck and turn well to coat thoroughly. Cover with plastic wrap and leave in a cool place for about 30 minutes.

2 Heat the oil in a frying pan, add the slices of duck and stir-fry for 3–4 minutes, until cooked. Remove from the pan and set aside.

3 Bring a pan of lightly salted water to the boil. Place the sugar snap peas and carrots in a steamer that will fit on top of the pan. When the water boils, add the noodles. Place the steamer on top and steam the vegetables while cooking the noodles.

4 Set the steamed vegetables aside. Drain the noodles, refresh under cold running water and drain again. Place them in a large serving bowl.

5 To make the dressing, mix the vinegar, sugar, soy sauce, garlic and sesame seeds in a bowl. Add a generous grinding of pepper, then whisk in the oils.

6 Pour the dressing over the egg noodles and toss well to mix. Add the sugar snap peas, carrots, scallions and duck slices and toss again to mix. Sprinkle the fresh cilantro leaves over the top and serve immediately.

BROILED SPICED QUAIL WITH MIXED LEAF AND MUSHROOM SALAD

• • •

This is a perfect supper dish for autumnal entertaining. Quail is at its best when the breast meat is removed from the carcass, so that it cooks quickly and can be served rare.

INGREDIENTS

8 quail breast portions
2 ounces/¼ cup butter
1 teaspoon paprika
salt and freshly ground
    black pepper

FOR THE SALAD
4 tablespoons walnut oil
2 tablespoons olive oil
3 tablespoons balsamic vinegar
1 ounce/2 tablespoons butter
3 ounces/generous 1 cup chanterelle
    mushrooms, sliced if large
1 ounce/3 tablespoons walnut
    halves, toasted
4 ounces mixed salad leaves

SERVES 4

1 Preheat the broiler. Arrange the quail portions on the broiler rack, skin-sides up. Dot with half the butter and sprinkle with half the paprika and a little salt.

2 Broil the quail portions for 3 minutes. Turn and dot with the remaining butter and sprinkle with the remaining paprika and a little salt. Broil for a further 3 minutes, or until cooked. Transfer to a warmed dish, cover and set aside.

3 To make the dressing, whisk the oils with the balsamic vinegar, then season to taste with salt and pepper.

Cook's Tip
Take care when toasting the walnuts, as they scorch quickly. The best way to toast them is to heat a non-stick frying pan until hot. Add the walnuts and cook for 3–5 minutes, or until golden, turning them frequently.

4 Melt the butter in a frying pan. Cook the chanterelles for about 3 minutes, or until just beginning to soften. Add the walnuts and heat through. Remove from the heat.

5 Thinly slice the cooked quail portions and arrange them on four individual serving plates with the chanterelles, walnuts and mixed salad leaves. Drizzle the oil and vinegar dressing over the salad and serve warm.

PROSCIUTTO SALAD WITH AN AVOCADO FAN

• • •

Avocados are amazingly versatile, but they are at their most elegant when sliced thinly and fanned on a plate.

INGREDIENTS

3 avocados
5 ounces prosciutto
3–4 ounces arugula leaves
24 marinated black
olives, drained

FOR THE DRESSING

1 tablespoon balsamic vinegar
1 teaspoon lemon juice
1 teaspoon prepared
English mustard
1 teaspoon sugar
5 tablespoons olive oil
salt and freshly ground
black pepper

SERVES 4

1 To make the dressing, combine the balsamic vinegar, lemon juice, mustard and sugar in a bowl. Gradually whisk in the olive oil, season to taste with salt and pepper and set aside.

2 Cut two of the avocados in half. Remove and discard the pits and skins, and cut the flesh into ½-inch thick slices. Gently toss with half the dressing. Place the prosciutto, avocado slices and arugula on four serving plates. Sprinkle the olives and the remaining dressing over the top.

3 Halve, pit and peel the remaining avocado. Slice each half lengthwise into eighths. Gently draw a sharp knife across the quarters at ½-inch intervals to create regular stripes.

4 Using a sharp knife, make four cuts lengthwise down each avocado eighth, leaving ½ inch intact at the end. Carefully fan out the slices and arrange one fan on the side of each plate.

MELON AND PROSCIUTTO SALAD

· · ·

Sections of cool, fragrant melon covered with thin slices of air-dried ham – a classic appetizer.

INGREDIENTS

1 large melon (cantaloupe or Charentais)
6 ounces prosciutto, thinly sliced

FOR THE SALSA
8 ounces strawberries
1 teaspoon superfine sugar
2 tablespoons sunflower oil
1 tablespoon orange juice
1/2 teaspoon finely grated orange rind
1/2 teaspoon grated fresh root ginger
salt and freshly ground black pepper

SERVES 4

1 Halve the melon and take the seeds out with a spoon. Cut the rind away with a paring knife, then slice the melon flesh thickly. Cover with plastic wrap and chill until ready to serve.

2 To make the salsa, hull the strawberries and cut them into large dice. Place in a small mixing bowl with the sugar and crush lightly to release the juices. Add the sunflower oil, orange juice and rind and ginger. Season with salt and a generous twist of pepper.

3 Arrange the melon slices on a serving plate and lay the prosciutto over the top. Serve the salsa separately in a small bowl.

WILD MUSHROOM SALAD WITH PROSCIUTTO

. . .

Autumn provides a wealth of ingredients for the salad maker. Most treasured of all are wild mushrooms, found mainly in deciduous woodland. If you are not familiar with edible species, larger supermarkets and specialist delicatessens often sell a wide range.

INGREDIENTS

6 ounces prosciutto, thickly sliced
½ oak leaf lettuce
½ frisée lettuce
1 tablespoon walnut oil
1½ ounces/3 tablespoons butter
1 pound wild or cultivated mushrooms such as chanterelles, field blewits, oyster mushrooms, champignons de Paris, sliced
60ml/4 tbsp brandy
salt and freshly ground black pepper

FOR THE HERB PANCAKE
3 tablespoons all-purpose flour
5 tablespoons milk
1 egg, plus 1 egg yolk
4 tablespoons grated Parmesan cheese
3 tablespoons chopped fresh mixed herbs such as parsley, thyme, tarragon, marjoram, chives

SERVES 4

1 To make the pancakes, combine the flour with the milk in a pitcher. Beat in the egg and egg yolk with the Parmesan and herbs. Season with salt and pepper. Place a non-stick frying pan over a steady heat. Pour in enough batter to coat the base of the pan.

2 When the batter has set, turn the pancake over and cook briefly on the other side. Remove the pancake and leave to cool. Continue until you have used all the batter.

3 Roll the pancakes together and cut into ½-inch ribbons. Cut the prosciutto into ribbons and toss with the pancake ribbons.

4 Moisten the salad leaves with the walnut oil and divide among four plates. Place the pancake and prosciutto ribbons in the center.

5 Melt the butter in a heavy frying pan. Add the mushrooms and cook for 6–8 minutes. Add the brandy and ignite with a match or taper. When the flames have subsided, spoon the mushrooms onto the salad, season to taste with salt and pepper and serve immediately while still warm.

WARM SALAD OF BAYONNE HAM AND NEW POTATOES

∘ ∘ ∘

INGREDIENTS

8 ounces new potatoes, halved
if large
2 ounces green beans
4 ounces young spinach leaves
2 scallions, sliced
4 eggs, hard-boiled, shelled
and quartered
2 ounces Bayonne ham or other
cured ham, cut into strips
juice of 1/2 lemon
salt and freshly ground
black pepper

FOR THE DRESSING

4 tablespoons olive oil
1 teaspoon ground turmeric
1 teaspoon ground cumin
2 ounces/1/2 cup shelled hazelnuts

SERVES 4

1 Cook the potatoes in salted boiling water for 10–15 minutes, or until tender, then drain well. Cook the beans in salted boiling water for 2 minutes, then drain.

2 Toss the potatoes and green beans with the spinach and scallions in a bowl.

3 Arrange the egg quarters on the salad and sprinkle the strips of ham over the top. Sprinkle with the lemon juice and season with plenty of salt and pepper.

4 Heat the dressing ingredients in a large frying pan and cook, stirring frequently, until the nuts turn golden. Pour the hot, nutty dressing over the salad and serve before the leaves wilt.

Variation

Replace the potatoes with a 14-ounce can drained and rinsed mixed beans and peas.

PERUVIAN SALAD

. . .

This really is a spectacular-looking salad. It could be served as a side dish or would make a delicious light lunch. In Peru, white rice would be used, but brown rice adds an interesting texture and flavor.

INGREDIENTS

8 ounces/2 cups cooked long grain
  brown or white rice
1 tablespoon chopped fresh parsley
1 red bell pepper, halved
  and seeded
1 small onion, sliced into rings
olive oil, for sprinkling
4 ounces green beans, halved
2 ounces/½ cup baby corn cobs
4 quail eggs, hard-boiled
1–2 ounces Serrano ham
  or proscuitto, cut into
  thin slices (optional)
1 small avocado
lemon juice, for sprinkling
3 ounces mixed salad leaves
1 tablespoon capers
about 10 stuffed olives, halved

FOR THE DRESSING
1 garlic clove, crushed
4 tablespoons olive oil
3 tablespoons sunflower oil
2 tablespoons lemon juice
3 tablespoons plain yogurt
½ teaspoon mustard
½ teaspoon sugar
salt and freshly ground
  black pepper

SERVES 4

1 To make the dressing, whisk all the ingredients in a bowl with a fork until smooth.

2 Put the rice in a large salad bowl and spoon in half the dressing. Stir in the parsley and set aside.

3 Place the bell pepper, cut-side down, in a small roasting pan. Add the onion rings. Sprinkle the onion with a little olive oil and place the pan under a hot broiler for 5–6 minutes, until the pepper blackens and blisters and the onion turns golden. Stir the onion once or twice so that it cooks evenly.

4 Stir the sliced onion into the rice. Put the pepper in a plastic bag and knot the bag. When cool enough to handle, peel the pepper halves and cut the flesh into thin strips.

5 Cook the green beans in boiling water for 2 minutes, then add the corn and cook for 1–2 minutes more, until tender. Drain, refresh under cold water, then drain again. Place the vegetables in a mixing bowl and add the pepper strips, quail eggs and ham, if using.

6 Peel the avocado, remove the pit and cut the flesh into slices or chunks. Sprinkle with the lemon juice. Put the salad leaves in a separate mixing bowl, add the avocado and mix lightly. Arrange the mixture on top of the rice.

7 Stir about 3 tablespoons of the remaining dressing into the green bean and pepper mixture. Pile this on top of the avocado mixture.

8 Sprinkle the capers and stuffed olives on top and serve the salad with the remaining dressing.

BEEF AND HERBED PASTA SALAD

Marinated beef is broiled and served warm with pasta salad.

INGREDIENTS

*1 pound beef tenderloin
1 pound fresh tagliatelle with
sun-dried tomatoes and herbs
4 ounces cherry tomatoes
½ cucumber*

*FOR THE MARINADE
1 tablespoon soy sauce
1 tablespoon sherry
1 teaspoon grated fresh root ginger
1 garlic clove, crushed*

*FOR THE HERB DRESSING
2 tablespoons horseradish sauce
¼ pint/⅔ cup plain yogurt
1 garlic clove, crushed
2–3 tablespoon chopped fresh
mixed herbs such as chives,
parsley, thyme
salt and freshly ground
black pepper*

SERVES 6

1 To make the marinade, mix all the ingredients together in a shallow dish. Add the beef tenderloin and turn to coat well. Cover with plastic wrap and leave in a cool place for 30 minutes to allow the flavors to penetrate the meat.

2 Preheat the broiler. Lift the beef out of the marinade and pat it dry with paper towels. Place the beef on a broiler rack and broil for 8 minutes on each side, basting with the marinade.

3 Transfer the beef to a plate, cover with foil and leave to stand for 20 minutes.

4 To make the herb dressing, put all the ingredients into a bowl and mix thoroughly. Cook the pasta in a large pan of lightly salted boiling water according to the packet instructions until it is *al dente*. Drain thoroughly, rinse under cold water and leave to dry.

5 Halve the cherry tomatoes. Cut the cucumber in half lengthwise, scoop out the seeds with a teaspoon and slice the flesh thinly into crescents.

6 Put the tagliatelle, tomato halves, cucumber and dressing into a mixing bowl and toss to coat. Slice the beef and arrange on individual serving plates with the pasta salad. Serve warm.

ROCKBURGER SALAD WITH SESAME CROÛTONS

This salad plays on the ingredients that make up the classic all-American beefburger in a sesame-seed bun.

INGREDIENTS

2 pounds lean ground beef
1 egg
1 medium onion, finely chopped
2 teaspoons Dijon mustard
½ teaspoon celery salt
4 ounces Roquefort or other
blue cheese
1 large sesame-seed loaf
3 tablespoons olive oil
1 small iceberg lettuce
2 ounces arugula leaves
4 fluid ounces/½ cup
French Dressing
4 ripe tomatoes, quartered
4 scallions, sliced
freshly ground black pepper

SERVES 4

1 Place the ground beef, egg, onion, mustard, celery salt and pepper in a mixing bowl. Combine thoroughly. Divide the mixture into 16 equal portions.

2 Flatten the pieces between two sheets of waxed paper to form 5-inch rounds.

3 Place ½ ounce of the blue cheese on eight of the burgers. Sandwich with the remaining burgers and press the edges firmly. Stack the burgers between sheets of waxed paper and chill until ready to cook.

4 To make the sesame croûtons, preheat the broiler to a moderate temperature. Remove the sesame-seed crust from the loaf, then cut the crust into short fingers. Moisten with olive oil and toast evenly for 10–15 minutes.

5 Broil the burgers at the same temperature for 10 minutes, turning once.

6 Toss the salad leaves with the French Dressing, then distribute among four large serving plates. Place two rockburgers in the center of each plate and arrange the tomatoes, scallions and sesame croûtons around the edge.

Cook's Tip

If you can't find a sesame-seed loaf, use French bread. Cut the stick into slices of about ½ inch, brush with olive oil and place on a baking sheet. Bake in the oven on a low heat for about 15 minutes until the bread rounds are crisp and golden.

THAI BEEF SALAD

○ ○ ○

A hearty salad of beef and crunchy vegetables, laced with a tangy chile and lime dressing.
Cooking the meat on the barbecue would give a truly delicious flavor to the salad.

INGREDIENTS

2 sirloin steaks, about
8 ounces each
1 red onion, thinly sliced
½ cucumber, thinly sliced
into matchsticks
1 lemon grass stalk,
finely chopped
2 tablespoons chopped scallions
juice of 2 limes
1–2 tablespoons Thai fish sauce
2–4 red chiles, thinly sliced, fresh
cilantro, bok choy and mint,
to garnish

SERVES 4

1 Pan-fry the steaks or cook on the barbecue until medium-rare. Leave the steaks to rest for 10–15 minutes.

2 When the steaks have cooled slightly, slice them thinly, using a heavy knife, and put the slices into a large bowl.

3 Add the sliced onion, cucumber matchsticks and chopped lemon grass

4 Add the scallions. Toss and season with lime juice and Thai fish sauce. Serve at room temperature or chilled, garnished with the chiles, cilantro, bok choy and mint.

NEW ORLEANS STEAK SALAD

° ° °

*The New Orleans "Poor Boy" started life in the Italian Creole community, as a sandwich filled
with leftover scraps. This salad, made with tender beef steak, is a variation on the sandwich.*

INGREDIENTS

*4 sirloin or round steaks,
about 6 ounces each
1 head of escarole
1 bunch watercress
4 tomatoes, quartered
4 large gherkins, sliced
4 scallions, sliced
4 canned artichoke hearts, halved
6 ounces white mushrooms, sliced
12 green olives
4 fluid ounces French Dressing
salt and freshly ground
black pepper*

SERVES 4

1 Season the steaks with plenty
of black pepper and cook under a
preheated hot broiler or on a hot
barbecue, for 4–6 minutes, turning
once, until they are medium-rare.
Transfer them to a plate, cover with
foil and leave the steaks to rest in a
warm place.

2 Combine the salad leaves with all the
ingredients except the steak, and toss
with the French Dressing.

3 Divide the salad among four plates.
Slice each steak diagonally and arrange
the slices over the salad. Season with
salt and fresh black pepper and serve.

The perfect end to a summer lunch, *al fresco* supper, a barbecue or picnic, fruit salad is a favorite with young and old alike. The recipes in this chapter make full use of the massive range of fruits available, from familiar to exotic and from fresh to dried.

FRUIT SALADS

FRESH FRUIT SALAD

· · ·

This basic fruit salad is always welcome, especially after a rich main course. It is endlessly adaptable – when peaches and strawberries are out of season, use bananas and grapes, or any other fruit.

INGREDIENTS

2 eating apples
2 oranges
2 peaches
16–20 strawberries
2 tablespoons lemon juice
1–2 tablespoons orange flower water
confectioners' sugar
a few fresh mint leaves, to decorate

SERVES 6

1 Peel and core the apples and cut into thin slices. Peel the oranges with a sharp knife, removing all the pith, and segment them, catching the juice in a bowl.

2 Plunge the peaches for 1 minute into boiling water, peel off the skin and cut the flesh into thick slices, discarding the pit.

3 Hull the strawberries and halve or quarter if larger. Place all the fruit in a large serving bowl.

4 Blend together the lemon juice, orange flower water and orange juice. Taste and add a little confectioners' sugar to sweeten. Pour the fruit juice mixture over the salad and serve decorated with mint leaves.

DRIED FRUIT SALAD

· · ·

This wonderful combination of fresh and dried fruit makes an excellent dessert throughout the year. You can use frozen raspberries and blackberries during the winter months.

INGREDIENTS

4 ounces/¹/₂ cup dried apricots
4 ounces/¹/₂ cup dried peaches
1 pear
1 apple
1 orange
4 ounces/²/₃ cup mixed raspberries and blackberries
1 cinnamon stick
2 ounces/¹/₄ cup superfine sugar
1 tablespoon clear honey
1 tablespoon lemon juice

SERVES 4

1 Soak the dried apricots and peaches in water for 1–2 hours, until plump, then drain and halve or quarter. Peel and core the pear and apple and cut into cubes.

2 Peel the orange with a sharp knife, removing all the pith, and cut into wedges. Place all the fruit in a large pan with the raspberries and blackberries.

3 Add 2¹/₂ cups water, the cinnamon stick, sugar and honey and bring to the boil. Cover and simmer very gently for 10–12 minutes, then remove the pan from the heat.

4 Stir in the lemon juice. Leave to cool, then transfer to a bowl and chill in the refrigerator for about 1–2 hours before serving.

COOL GREEN FRUIT SALAD

• • •

A sophisticated, simple fruit salad for any time of the year.

INGREDIENTS

3 honeydew melons
4 ounces seedless green grapes
2 kiwi fruit
1 carambola
1 green apple
1 lime
6 fluid ounces/¾ cup sparkling grape juice

SERVES 6

1 Halve the melons and remove the seeds. Keeping the shells intact, scoop out the flesh with a melon baller or use a spoon, then cut into cubes. Reserve the melon shells.

2 Remove any stems from the grapes and, if they are large, cut them in half. Peel and chop the kiwi fruit. Thinly slice the carambola. Core and thinly slice the apple and place in a mixing bowl with the melon, grapes, kiwi fruit and carambola.

3 Thinly pare the rind from the lime and cut it in fine strips. Blanch the lime strips in boiling water for 30 seconds, drain and rinse in cold water. Squeeze the juice from the lime and toss the juice into the bowl of fruit.

4 Spoon the prepared fruit into the reserved melon shells and chill the shells in the refrigerator until required. Just before serving, spoon the sparkling grape juice over the fruit and sprinkle with the strips of lime rind.

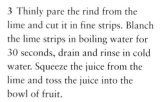

Cook's Tip

On a hot summer's day, serve the filled melon shells nestling on a platter of crushed ice to keep them beautifully cool.

WINTER FRUIT SALAD

INGREDIENTS

*8-ounce can pineapple cubes in
fruit juice
7 fluid ounces/scant 1 cup freshly
squeezed orange juice
7 fluid ounces/scant 1 cup
unsweetened apple juice
2 tablespoons orange or
apple liqueur
2 tablespoons clear
honey (optional)
2 oranges, peeled
2 green apples, chopped
2 pears, chopped
4 plums, pitted
and chopped
12 fresh dates, pitted
and chopped
115g/4oz/¹/₂ cup ready-to-eat
dried apricots
fresh mint sprigs,
to decorate*

SERVES 6

1 Drain the pineapple, reserving
the juice. Put the pineapple juice,
orange juice, apple juice, liqueur
and honey, if using, in a large
serving bowl and stir.

2 Using a small sharp knife,
segment the oranges, catching any
juice in the bowl. Put the orange
segments and pineapple in the fruit
juice mixture.

3 Add the chopped apples and
pears to the bowl.

4 Stir in the plums, dates and dried
apricots, cover with plastic wrap
and chill in the refrigerator for
several hours. Decorate with fresh
mint sprigs before serving.

Cook's Tip

Use other unsweetened fruit
juices, such as pink grapefruit
and pineapple juice, in place of
the orange and apple juice.

ITALIAN FRUIT SALAD AND ICE CREAM

In the summer in Italy, little pavement fruit stores sell small dishes of macerated soft fruits. Delectable on their own, they also make wonderful ice cream.

INGREDIENTS

2 pounds mixed summer fruits such as strawberries, raspberries, blueberries, peaches, apricots, plums, melons
juice of 3–4 oranges
juice of 1 lemon
1 tablespoon liquid pear and apple concentrate
3 tablespoons whipping cream
2 tablespoons orange liqueur (optional)
fresh mint sprigs, to decorate

SERVES 6

1 Prepare all the fruit according to type and then cut it into fairly small pieces.

2 Put the fruit into a serving bowl and pour over enough orange juice to cover. Add the lemon juice and chill for 2 hours.

3 Set half the macerated fruit aside to serve as it is. Process the rest in a blender or food processor to a smooth purée.

4 Gently warm the pear and apple concentrate and stir into the fruit purée. Whip the cream and fold it in, then add the liqueur, if using.

5 Churn the mixture in an ice-cream maker, following the manufacturer's instructions, or place it in a freezerproof container. Freeze until ice crystals form around the edge, then beat the mixture until smooth.

6 Repeat the process once or twice, then freeze until firm.

7 Transfer the ice cream to the refrigerator to soften slightly before serving in scoops, with the fruit, decorated with sprigs of mint.

Cook's Tip
The macerated fruit also makes a delicious drink. Purée in a blender or food processor, then press through a strainer.

WATERMELON, GINGER AND GRAPEFRUIT SALAD

∘ ∘ ∘

*This pretty, pink combination is
very light and refreshing for any
summer meal.*

INGREDIENTS

*1 pound/2 cups watermelon flesh
2 ruby or pink grapefruit
2 pieces stem ginger and
2 tablespoons of the syrup*

SERVES 4

1 Remove any seeds from the
watermelon and cut the flesh into
bitesize chunks.

2 Using a small, sharp knife, cut
away all the peel and white pith
from the grapefruit. Carefully cut
between the membranes and lift
out the segments, catching any
juice in a bowl.

Cook's Tip

Toss the fruits gently –
grapefruit segments will break
up easily, and the appearance
of the dish will be spoiled.

3 Finely chop the stem ginger and
place in a serving bowl with the
melon cubes and grapefruit
segments, adding the reserved juice.

4 Spoon over the ginger syrup
and toss the fruits lightly to mix.
Cover with plastic wrap and chill
before serving.

FRESH FRUIT WITH MANGO COULIS

· · ·

This bright, flavorful sauce is easy to prepare and ideal for making a simple fruit salad seem special.

INGREDIENTS

1 large ripe mango, peeled, pitted and chopped
rind of 1 unwaxed orange
juice of 3 oranges
superfine sugar, to taste
2 peaches
2 nectarines
1 small mango, peeled
2 plums
1 pear or ½ small melon
juice of 1 lemon
1–2 ounces/heaping tablespoon wild strawberries (optional)
1–2 ounces/heaping tablespoon raspberries
1–2 ounces/heaping tablespoon blueberries
small fresh mint sprigs, to decorate

SERVES 6

1 In a food processor fitted with a metal blade, process the large mango until smooth. Add the orange rind and juice and sugar to taste and process again until very smooth. Press through a strainer into a bowl and chill.

2 Slice and pit the peaches, nectarines, small mango and plums. Quarter the pear and remove the core or, if using, slice the melon thinly and remove the skin.

3 Place the sliced fruits on a large plate, sprinkle with the lemon juice, cover with plastic wrap and chill in the refrigerator for up to 3 hours before serving. (Some fruits discolor if cut too far ahead of time.)

4 To serve, arrange the sliced fruits attractively on serving plates, spoon the berries on top, drizzle with a little mango coulis and decorate with mint sprigs. Serve the remaining coulis separately.

FRUITS-OF-THE-TROPICS SALAD

INGREDIENTS

1 medium pineapple
14-ounce can guava halves
in syrup
2 medium bananas, sliced
1 large mango, peeled,
pitted and diced
4 ounces stem ginger and
2 tablespoons of the syrup
4 tablespoons coconut milk
2 teaspoons sugar
1/2 teaspoon grated nutmeg
1/2 teaspoon ground cinnamon
strips of coconut,
to decorate

SERVES 4–6

1 Peel, core and cube the pineapple, and place in a serving bowl. Drain the guavas, reserving the syrup, and chop. Add the guavas to the bowl with one of the bananas and the mango.

2 Chop the stem ginger and add to the pineapple mixture.

3 Pour the 2 tablespoons of the ginger syrup and the reserved guava syrup into a blender or food processor and add the remaining banana, the coconut milk and the sugar. Process to make a smooth, creamy purée.

4 Pour the banana and coconut purée over the fruit and add a little grated nutmeg and a sprinkling of cinnamon on top. Cover with plastic wrap and chill before serving, decorated with strips of coconut.

481

EXOTIC FRUIT SALAD

A variety of fruits, depending on what is available, can be used for this salad. Look for mandarin oranges, carambolas, papaya, physalis and passion fruit.

INGREDIENTS

3 ounces/scant ½ cup sugar
2 tablespoons preserved stem
    ginger syrup
2 pieces star anise
1 inch cinnamon stick
1 clove
juice of ½ lemon
2 fresh mint sprigs
1 mango
2 bananas
8 lychees, fresh or canned
8 ounces/2 cups strawberries
2 pieces stem ginger, cut into sticks
1 medium pineapple

SERVES 4

3 With a long, sharp knife, cut the pineapple in half lengthwise down the center. Loosen the flesh with a small, serrated knife and remove to form two boat shapes. Cut the pineapple flesh into large chunks and place in the cooled syrup.

4 Spoon the fruit salad carefully into the pineapple halves and bring to the table on a large serving platter or board. There will be enough fruit salad left over to refill both the pineapple halves for a second serving.

1 Place the sugar in a pan and add 1¼ cups water, the ginger syrup, spices, lemon juice and mint. Bring to the boil and simmer for 3 minutes. Strain into a large bowl.

2 Remove both the top and bottom from the mango and remove the outer skin. Stand the mango on one end and remove the flesh in two pieces either side of the flat pit. Slice evenly and add to the syrup. Add the bananas, lychees, strawberries and ginger. Chill until ready to serve.

MELON AND STRAWBERRY SALAD

A beautiful and colorful fruit salad, this is equally suitable to serve as a refreshing appetizer or to round off a meal.

INGREDIENTS

1½ honeydew melons
1 watermelon
8 ounces/2 cups strawberries
1 tablespoon lemon juice
1 tablespoon clear honey
1 tablespoon chopped fresh mint
1 fresh mint sprig (optional)

SERVES 4

1 Prepare the melons by cutting them in half and discarding the seeds. Use a melon baller to scoop out the flesh into balls or use a knife to cut it into cubes. Place these in a fruit bowl.

2 Rinse and hull the strawberries, cut in half and add to the melon balls or cubes.

Cook's Tip

Use whichever melons are available: replace honeydew with cantaloupe or watermelon with Charentais, for example. Try to choose melons with a variation in color for an attractive effect.

3 Mix together the lemon juice and honey and add 1 tablespoon water to make it easier to spoon over the fruit. Mix into the fruit gently.

4 Sprinkle the chopped mint over the top of the fruit. Serve the fruit salad decorated with the mint sprig, if you like.

BLUEBERRY, ORANGE AND LAVENDER SALAD

• • •

Delicate blueberries feature in a simple salad of sharp oranges and sweet little meringues.

INGREDIENTS

6 oranges
12 ounces/3 cups blueberries
8 fresh lavender sprigs, to decorate

FOR THE MERINGUE

2 egg whites
4 ounces/generous ½ cup
superfine sugar
1 teaspoon fresh lavender flowers

SERVES 4

1 Preheat the oven to 275°F. Line a baking sheet with six layers of newspaper and cover with parchment paper. To make the meringue, whisk the egg whites in a large mixing bowl until they hold their weight on the whisk. Add the sugar, a little at a time, whisking thoroughly before each addition. Gently fold in the lavender flowers.

2 Spoon the lavender meringue into a pastry bag fitted with a ¼-inch plain nozzle. Pipe as many small buttons of meringue onto the prepared baking sheet as you can fit in. Dry the meringues near the bottom of the oven for 1½–2 hours.

3 To segment the oranges, remove the peel from the top, bottom and sides with a small, sharp, serrated knife. Loosen the segments by cutting with a paring knife between the flesh and the membranes, holding the fruit over a bowl to catch the juice.

4 Arrange the orange segments decoratively on four plates.

5 Combine the blueberries with the lavender meringues and pile in the center of each serving plate. Decorate with sprigs of lavender and serve immediately.

FRESH FIG, APPLE AND DATE SALAD

* * *

Sweet figs and dates combine well with crisp apples. A hint of almond unites the flavors.

INGREDIENTS

6 large eating apples
juice of ½ lemon
6 ounces/generous 1 cup fresh dates
1 ounce white marzipan
1 teaspoon orange flower water
4 tablespoons plain yogurt
4 ripe green or purple figs
4 almonds, toasted

SERVES 4

1 Core the apples. Slice thinly, then cut into fine matchsticks. Moisten with lemon juice to prevent them from turning brown.

2 Remove the pits from the dates and cut the flesh into fine strips, then combine them with the apple slices.

3 Soften the marzipan with the orange flower water and combine with the yogurt. Mix well.

4 Pile the apples and dates in the center of four serving plates. Remove the stem from each of the figs and divide the fruit into quarters without cutting right through the base. Squeeze the base with the thumb and forefinger of both hands to open up the fig.

5 Place a fig in the center of each fruit salad, spoon in the yogurt filling. Decorate with a toasted almond and serve.

BLACKBERRY SALAD WITH ROSE GRANITA

∘ ∘ ∘

INGREDIENTS

5 ounces/²/₃ cup superfine sugar
1 fresh red rose, petals
removed and
finely chopped
1 teaspoon rose water
2 teaspoons lemon juice
1 pound/2²/₃ cups blackberries
confectioners' sugar,
for dusting
fresh rose petals,
to decorate

FOR THE MERINGUE
2 egg whites
4 ounces/generous ¹/₂ cup
superfine sugar

SERVES 4

1 To make the granita, bring ²/₃ cup water to the boil in a stainless-steel or enamel pan. Add the sugar and rose petals, then simmer for 5 minutes.

2 Strain the syrup into a deep metal tray, add a further scant 2 cups water, the rose water and lemon juice and leave to cool. Freeze the mixture for about 3 hours, or until solid.

3 Meanwhile preheat the oven to 275°F. Line a large baking sheet with six layers of newspaper and then cover with parchment paper.

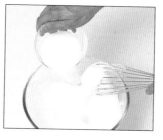

4 To make the meringue, whisk the egg whites until they hold their weight on the whisk. Add the superfine sugar, a little at a time, and whisk until firm.

Cook's Tips
Blackberries are widely cultivated from late spring to autumn and are usually large, plump and sweet. The finest wild blackberries have a bitter edge and a strong depth of flavor – best appreciated with a sprinkling of sugar.

Make sure that the rose petals are free of pollution, pesticides and any other chemicals.

5 Spoon the meringue into a pastry bag fitted with a ¹/₂-inch plain nozzle. Pipe the meringue in lengths across the parchment-lined baking sheet. Dry the meringue near the bottom of the oven for 1¹/₂–2 hours.

6 Break the meringue into 2-inch lengths and place three or four pieces on each of four large serving plates. Pile the blackberries next to the meringue.

7 With a tablespoon, scrape the granita finely. Shape into ovals and place over the meringue. Dust with confectioners' sugar, decorate with rose petals, and serve immediately.

RASPBERRIES WITH MANGO CUSTARD

· · ·

Sharp, fresh raspberries unite with a fragrant mango custard.

INGREDIENTS

1 large mango
3 egg yolks
2 tablespoons superfine sugar
2 teaspoons cornstarch
7 fluid ounces/scant 1 cup milk
8 fresh mint sprigs,
to decorate

FOR THE RASPBERRY SAUCE
1 pound/2⅔ cups raspberries
3 tablespoons superfine sugar

SERVES 4

1 To prepare the mango, remove the top and bottom with a serrated knife. Cut away the outer skin, then remove the flesh by cutting either side of the flat central pit. Reserve half of the mango flesh for decoration and coarsely chop the remainder.

2 For the custard, combine the egg yolks, sugar, cornstarch and 2 tablespoons of the milk to a smooth paste in a small bowl.

5 Pour the custard into a food processor, add the chopped mango and blend until smooth. Leave the custard to cool.

3 Rinse out a small pan with cold water to prevent the milk from catching. Pour the rest of the milk into the pan, bring to the boil and pour it over the ingredients in the bowl, stirring evenly.

6 To make the raspberry sauce, place 2 cups of the raspberries in a stain-resistant pan. Add the sugar, soften over a gentle heat and simmer for 5 minutes. Rub the fruit through a fine nylon strainer to remove the seeds. Set aside to cool.

7 Spoon the raspberry sauce and mango custard into two pools on four serving plates. Slice the reserved mango and fan out or arrange in a pattern over the raspberry sauce. Sprinkle the remaining raspberries over the mango custard. Decorate each plate with two sprigs of mint and serve immediately.

4 Put the mixture through a strainer back into the pan, stir to simmering point and cook until the mixture has thickened.

Cook's Tip

Mangoes are ripe when they yield to gentle pressure. Some varieties show a red-gold or yellow flush when they are ready to eat.

Variation

Substitute loganberries for the raspberries.

PINEAPPLE CRUSH WITH STRAWBERRIES AND LYCHEES

· · ·

*The sweet, tropical flavors of
pineapple and lychees combine
well with aromatic strawberries.*

INGREDIENTS

2 small pineapples
1 pound/4 cups strawberries
14-ounce can lychees
3 tablespoons kirsch or
white rum
2 tablespoons confectioners' sugar

SERVES 4

1 Remove the crowns from both
pineapples by twisting sharply.
Reserve the leaves for decoration.

2 Cut both pineapples in half
diagonally using a long-bladed,
serrated knife.

3 Cut around the flesh inside the
skin of all the pineapple halves
with a small, sharp, serrated knife,
keeping the skin intact. Remove the
core from the pineapple and
discard. Chop the flesh. Reserve
the skins.

4 Hull the strawberries and gently
combine with the pineapple and
lychees, taking care not to damage
the fruit.

5 Mix the kirsch or rum with the
confectioners' sugar, pour over the
fruit and freeze for 45 minutes.

6 Turn out the fruit into the
pineapple skins, decorate
with the reserved pineapple leaves
and serve immediately.

Cook's Tip

A ripe pineapple will resist
pressure when squeezed and
will have a sweet, fragrant
smell. In winter, freezing
conditions can cause the flesh
to blacken.

MUSCAT GRAPE FRAPPÉ

. . .

The flavor and perfume of the Muscat grape is rarely more enticing than when captured in this sophisticated, icy-cool salad. Because of its alcohol content this dish is not suitable for young children.

INGREDIENTS

*½ bottle Muscat wine, Beaumes de Venise, Frontignan or Rivesaltes
1 pound Muscat grapes*

SERVES 4

1 Pour the wine into a stainless-steel or enamel tray, add ⅔ cup water, mix well and freeze for for about 3 hours, or until the wine is completely solid.

2 Remove the seeds from the grapes with a pair of tweezers. If you have time, you can also peel the grapes. Scrape across the frozen wine with a tablespoon to make a fine ice. Combine the grapes with the ice, spoon into four shallow glasses and serve immediately.

GRAPEFRUIT SALAD WITH CAMPARI AND ORANGE

The bitter-sweet flavor of Campari combines especially well with citrus fruit, such as grapefruit and oranges. Because of its alcohol content, this dish is not suitable for young children.

INGREDIENTS

3 tablespoons superfine sugar
4 tablespoons Campari
2 tablespoons lemon juice
4 grapefruit
5 oranges
4 fresh mint sprigs, to decorate

SERVES 4

1 Bring ⅔ cup water to the boil in a small pan, add the sugar and simmer until dissolved. Transfer to a bowl; leave to cool.

2 Add the Campari and lemon juice to the syrup and stir well to mix. Cut the peel from the top, bottom and sides of the grapefruit and oranges with a serrated knife. Segment the fruit into a bowl by slipping a small paring knife between the flesh and the membranes. Combine the fruit with the Campari syrup, cover it with plastic wrap and chill until ready to serve.

3 Spoon the salad into four dishes, decorate with a sprig of fresh mint and serve.

Cook's Tip
When buying citrus fruit, choose brightly colored varieties that feel heavy for their size.

493

DRESSED STRAWBERRIES

∘ ∘ ∘

Fragrant strawberries release their finest flavour when moistened with this sauce.

INGREDIENTS

*12 ounces/2 cups raspberries, fresh or frozen
3 tablespoons superfine sugar
1 passion fruit
1½ pounds/6 cups small fresh strawberries
8 plain finger cookies, to serve*

SERVES 4

4 Pass the blended fruit sauce through a fine nylon strainer to remove the seeds, pressing it through with the back of a spoon.

5 Fold the strawberries into the sauce, then spoon into four stemmed glasses. Serve with plain finger cookies.

1 Place the raspberries and sugar in a stain-resistant pan and soften over a gentle heat to release the juices. Simmer for 5 minutes. Leave to cool.

2 Halve the passion fruit and scoop out the seeds and juice.

3 Transfer the raspberries into a food processor or blender, add the passion fruit and process until a smooth purée forms.

494

MIXED MELON SALAD WITH WILD STRAWBERRIES

° ° °

Ice-cold melon is a delicious way to end a meal. Here three varieties are combined with strongly flavored wild or woodland strawberries.

INGREDIENTS

1 Charentais melon
1 cantaloupe melon
2 pounds watermelon
6 ounces/1½ cups wild
    strawberries
4 fresh mint sprigs, to decorate

SERVES 4

1 Cut all the melons in half using a large knife.

2 Remove the seeds from the Charentais and cantaloupe melons with a spoon.

3 With a melon baller, take out as many balls as you can from all three melons. Combine in a large bowl, cover with plastic wrap and chill in the refrigerator until ready to serve.

4 Add the wild strawberries to the melon balls and transfer to four stemmed glass dishes.

5 Decorate with sprigs of fresh mint and serve while still very cold and refreshing.

FRUIT KEBABS WITH MANGO AND YOGURT SAUCE

This colorful dessert is ideal for a party.

1/2 pineapple, peeled, cored
and cubed
2 kiwi fruit, peeled and cubed
5 ounces/scant 1 cup strawberries,
hulled and cut in half lengthwise
1/2 mango, peeled, pitted
and cubed

FOR THE SAUCE
4 fluid ounces/1/2 cup fresh
mango purée
4 fluid ounces/1/2 cup thick
plain yogurt
1 teaspoon sugar
few drops of vanilla extract
1 tablespoon finely shredded
fresh mint leaves
1 fresh mint sprig, to decorate

SERVES 4

1 To make the sauce, beat together the mango purée, yogurt, sugar and vanilla with an electric hand mixer.

2 Stir in the shredded mint. Cover the sauce and chill until required.

Cook's Tip
Use 1–1½ peeled and pitted mangoes for the purée.

3 Thread the fruit onto twelve 6-inch wooden skewers, alternating the pineapple, kiwi fruit, strawberries and mango.

4 Transfer the mango and yogurt sauce to an attractive bowl, decorate with a mint sprig and place in the center of a large serving platter. Surround with the kebabs and serve.

TROPICAL FRUITS IN CINNAMON SYRUP

These glistening fruits are best prepared a day in advance to allow the flavors to develop and mingle.

INGREDIENTS
1 pound/2¼ cups superfine sugar
1 cinnamon stick
1 large or 2 medium papayas
(about 1½ pounds), peeled,
seeded and cut lengthwise
into thin pieces
1 large or 2 medium mangoes
(about 1½ pounds) peeled,
pitted and cut lengthwise
into thin pieces
1 large or 2 small carambolas
(about 8 ounces) thinly sliced

SERVES 6

1 Sprinkle about one-third of the sugar over the base of a large, heavy pan. Add the cinnamon stick and half of the papaya, mango and carambola pieces.

2 Sprinkle half of the remaining sugar over the fruit pieces in the pan. Add the remaining papaya, mango and carambola and sprinkle with the remaining sugar.

3 Cover the pan and cook the fruit over medium heat for about 35–45 minutes, until the sugar dissolves completely. Gently shake the pan occasionally, but do not stir or the fruit will collapse and become soggy.

4 Uncover the pan and simmer for about 10 minutes, until the fruit becomes translucent. Remove the pan from the heat and leave to cool. Discard the cinnamon stick.

5 Transfer the fruit and syrup to a bowl, cover and chill overnight before serving.

BANANA AND MASCARPONE

. . .

If you are a fan of cold banana custard, you'll love this recipe. It is an adult version of an old favorite. No one will guess that the secret is ready-made custard sauce.

INGREDIENTS

9 ounces/generous 1 cup mascarpone cheese
½ pint/1¼ cups fresh ready-made custard sauce
¼ pint/⅔ cup strained plain yogurt
4 bananas
juice of 1 lime
2 ounces/½ cup pecan nuts, coarsely chopped
4 fluid ounces/½ cup maple syrup

SERVES 4–6

1 Combine the mascarpone, custard sauce and yogurt in a large bowl and beat together with a wooden spoon until smooth. Make this mixture up to several hours ahead, if you like. Cover and chill, then stir before using.

2 Slice the bananas diagonally and place in a separate bowl. Pour over the lime juice and toss together until the bananas are coated.

3 Divide half the custard mixture among four to six dessert glasses and top each portion with a spoonful of the banana mixture.

4 Spoon the remaining custard mixture into the glasses and top with the rest of the bananas. Sprinkle the nuts over the top. Drizzle maple syrup over each dessert and chill for 30 minutes before serving.

BANANAS WITH LIME AND CARDAMOM

. . .

Cardamom and bananas go together perfectly, and this luxurious dessert makes an original treat.

INGREDIENTS

6 small bananas
2 ounces/¼ cup butter
seeds from 4 cardamom pods, crushed
2 ounces/½ cup sliced almonds
thinly pared rind and juice of 2 limes
2 ounces/⅓ cup light brown sugar
2 tablespoons dark rum
vanilla ice cream, to serve

SERVES 4

1 Peel and halve the bananas lengthwise. Heat half the butter in a frying pan. Add half the bananas and cook until the undersides are golden. Turn carefully, using a metal spatula. Cook until golden all over.

2 Once cooked, transfer the bananas to a heatproof serving dish. Cook the remaining bananas in the same way.

3 Melt the remaining butter, then add the cardamom seeds and almonds. Cook, stirring until the almonds are golden.

4 Stir in the lime rind and juice, then the sugar. Cook, stirring, until the mixture is smooth, bubbling and slightly reduced. Stir in the rum. Pour the sauce over the bananas and serve immediately, with vanilla ice cream.

MELON TRIO WITH GINGER COOKIES

The eye-catching color of the three different types of melons really make this dessert.

INGREDIENTS

¼ *watermelon*
½ *honeydew melon*
½ *Charentais melon*
4 *tablespoons stem ginger syrup*

FOR THE COOKIES
1 *ounce/2 tablespoons sweet butter*
1 *ounce/2 tablespoons superfine sugar*
1 *teaspoon clear honey*
1 *ounce/¼ cup all-purpose flour*
1 *ounce/¼ cup luxury candied mixed fruit, finely chopped*
1 *piece of stem ginger in syrup, drained and finely chopped*
2 *tablespoons sliced almonds*

SERVES 4

1 Using a spoon, remove the seeds from the melons and discard. Cut them into wedges, then slice off the rind. Cut all the flesh into chunks and mix in a bowl. Stir in the ginger syrup, cover with plastic wrap and chill until ready to serve.

2 Meanwhile, make the biscuits. Preheat the oven to 350°F. Heat the butter, sugar and honey in a pan until melted. Remove from the heat and stir in the remaining ingredients.

3 Line a baking sheet with parchment paper. Space four spoonfuls of the cookie mixture on the parchment at regular intervals, leaving plenty of room for spreading. Flatten the mixture slightly into round shapes and bake for 15 minutes or until the tops are golden brown.

4 Let the cookies cool on the baking sheet for 1 minute, then lift each one in turn, using a metal spatula, and drape over a rolling pin to cool and harden. Repeat with the remaining ginger mixture to make eight cookies.

5 Serve the chilled melon chunks with some of the syrup and the ginger cookies.

Cook's Tip

For an even prettier effect, scoop the melon flesh into balls with the large end of a melon baller.

JAMAICAN FRUIT TRIFLE

. . .

INGREDIENTS

*1 large sweet pineapple,
peeled and cored,
about 12 ounces*
½ pint/1¼ cups heavy cream
*7 fluid ounces/scant 1 cup
crème fraîche*
*3 tablespoons confectioners'
sugar, sifted*
*2 teaspoons pure
vanilla extract*
*2 tablespoons white or
coconut rum*
*3 papayas, peeled, seeded
and chopped*
*3 mangoes, peeled, pitted
and chopped*
*thinly pared rind and juice
of 1 lime*
*1 ounce/⅓ cup coarsely shredded
or flaked coconut, toasted*

SERVES 8

1 Cut the pineapple into large chunks, place in a food processor or blender and process briefly until chopped. Tip into a strainer placed over a bowl and leave for about 5 minutes so that most of the juice drains from the fruit.

2 Whip the heavy cream to very soft peaks, then lightly, but thoroughly fold in the crème fraîche, sifted confectioners' sugar, vanilla extract and rum.

3 Fold the drained, chopped pineapple into the cream mixture. Place the chopped papayas and mangoes in a large bowl and pour over the lime juice. Gently stir the fruit mixture to combine. Cut the pared lime rind into thin shreds and add it to the bowl.

4 Divide the fruit mixture and the pineapple cream among eight dessert plates. Decorate with the lime shreds, toasted coconut and a few small pineapple leaves, if you like, and serve immediately.

Cook's Tip

It is important to let the pineapple purée drain thoroughly, otherwise the pineapple cream will be watery. Don't throw away the drained pineapple juice – mix it with sparkling mineral water for a refreshing drink.

TROPICAL FRUIT GRATIN

. . .

This out-of-the-ordinary gratin is strictly for adults. A colorful combination of fruit is topped with a simple sabayon before being flashed under the grill.

INGREDIENTS

2 tamarillos
¹/₂ sweet pineapple
1 ripe mango
6 ounces/1¹/₂ cups blackberries
4 fluid ounces/¹/₂ cup sparkling white wine
4 ounces/¹/₂ cup superfine sugar
6 egg yolks

SERVES 4

1 Cut each tamarillo in half lengthwise and then into thick slices. Cut the rind and core from the pineapple and take spiral slices off the outside to remove the eyes. Cut the flesh into chunks. Peel the mango, cut it in half and cut the flesh away from the central pit in slices.

2 Divide all the fruit, including the blackberries, among four 5¹/₂-inch gratin dishes set on a baking sheet and set aside. Heat the wine and sugar in a pan until the sugar has dissolved. Bring to the boil and cook for 5 minutes.

3 Put the egg yolks in a heatproof bowl. Set the bowl over a pan of simmering water and whisk until pale. Gradually pour in the hot sugar syrup, whisking constantly, until the mixture has thickened. Preheat the broiler.

4 Spoon the mixture over the fruit. Place the baking sheet on a low shelf under the hot broiler until the topping is golden. Serve hot.

BROILED PINEAPPLE WITH PAPAYA SAUCE

. . .

Pineapple cooked this way takes on a superb flavor and is sensational when served with the papaya sauce.

INGREDIENTS

1 sweet pineapple
melted butter, for greasing and brushing
2 pieces drained stem ginger in syrup, cut into fine matchsticks, plus 2 tablespoons of the syrup from the jar
2 tablespoons raw sugar
pinch of ground cinnamon
fresh mint sprigs, to decorate

FOR THE SAUCE
1 ripe papaya, peeled and seeded
6 fluid ounces/³/₄ cup apple juice

SERVES 6

1 Peel the pineapple and take spiral slices off the outside to remove the eyes. Cut it crosswise into six slices, each 1-inch thick. Line a baking sheet with a sheet of foil, rolling up the sides to make a rim. Grease the foil with melted butter. Preheat the broiler.

2 Arrange the pineapple slices on the lined baking sheet. Brush with butter, then top with the ginger matchsticks, sugar and cinnamon. Drizzle over the stem ginger syrup. Broil for 5–7 minutes or until the slices are golden and lightly charred on top.

3 Meanwhile, make the sauce. Cut a few slices from the papaya and set aside, then purée the remainder with the apple juice in a blender or food processor.

4 Press the purée through a strainer placed over a bowl, then stir in any juices from cooking the pineapple.

5 Serve the pineapple slices with a little sauce drizzled around each plate. Decorate with the reserved papaya slices and the mint sprigs.

CITRUS FRUIT FLAMBÉ

. . .

A flambé is a dramatic finale for a dinner party. The crunchy praline makes it extra special.

INGREDIENTS

4 oranges
2 ruby grapefruit
2 limes
2 ounces/¼ cup butter
2 ounces/⅓ cup light
brown sugar
3 tablespoons Cointreau
fresh mint sprigs, to decorate

FOR THE PRALINE
oil, for greasing
4 ounces/½ cup superfine sugar
2 ounces/½ cup shelled
pistachio nuts

SERVES 4

1 First, make the pistachio praline. Brush a baking sheet lightly with oil. Place the superfine sugar and nuts in a small heavy pan and cook over a low heat, gently swirling the pan occasionally until the sugar has completely melted.

2 Continue to cook over a fairly low heat until the nuts start to pop and the sugar has turned a dark golden color. Pour onto the oiled baking sheet and set aside to cool. Using a sharp knife, chop the praline into coarse chunks.

3 Cut all the rind and pith from the citrus fruits. Holding each fruit in turn over a large bowl, cut between the membranes with a paring knife so that the segments fall into the bowl, with any juice.

4 Heat the butter and brown sugar together in a heavy frying pan until the sugar has melted and the mixture is golden. Strain the orange, grapefruit and lime juices into the pan and continue to cook, stirring occasionally, until the juice has reduced and is syrupy.

5 Add the fruit segments and warm through without stirring. Pour over the Cointreau and set it alight. As soon as the flames die down, spoon the fruit flambé into serving dishes. Sprinkle some praline over each portion and decorate with mint.

> *Cook's Tip*
> Cointreau is the best-known brand name of an orange-flavored liqueur, generically known as triple sec.

EXOTIC TROPICAL FRUIT SALAD

Passion fruit makes a superb dressing for any other kind of fruit, but it really brings out the flavor of exotic varieties, such as papaya and kiwi fruit.

INGREDIENTS

1 mango
1 papaya
2 kiwi fruits
coconut or vanilla ice cream,
to serve

FOR THE DRESSING
3 passion fruit
thinly pared rind and juice of 1 lime
1 teaspoon hazelnut or walnut oil
1 tablespoon clear honey

SERVES 6

1 Peel the mango, cut it into three slices, then cut the flesh into chunks and place it in a large bowl. Peel the papaya and cut it in half. Scoop out and discard the seeds, then chop the flesh.

Cook's Tip

A clear golden honey scented with orange blossom or acacia blossom would be perfect for the dressing.

---

2 Cut both ends off each kiwi fruit, then stand them on a board. Using a small sharp knife, cut off the skin from top to bottom. Cut each kiwi fruit in half lengthwise, then cut into thick slices. Combine all the fruit in a large bowl.

3 Make the dressing. Cut each passion fruit in half and scoop the seeds out into a strainer set over a small bowl. Press the seeds well to extract all their juices. Lightly whisk the remaining dressing ingredients into the passion fruit juice, then pour the dressing over the fruit. Mix gently to combine. Cover and chill for 1 hour before serving with scoops of coconut or vanilla ice cream.

INDEX

A

Aioli 258

apple 240
  Apple and Celeriac Salad 276
  Apple Coleslaw 282
  Baked Apples in Honey and Lemon 205
  Chargrilled Apples on Cinnamon Toasts 192
  Fresh Fig, Apple and Date Salad 485
  preparing 250
  Radish, Mango and Apple Salad 290

apricots 240
  Apricot Duck with Beansprout Salad 456
  Carrot, Raisin and Apricot Coleslaw 283
  Chicken and Apricot Phyllo Pie 224
  preparing 251

artichoke, *see* Jerusalem artichoke

artichokes: Artichoke and Eggs Salad 331
  Shrimp and Artichoke Salad 374
  Stuffed Artichoke Bottoms 159
  Sweet-and-sour Artichoke Salad 305

arugula: 243
  Arugula and Cilantro Salad 262
  Arugula and Grilled Goat Cheese Salad 310
  Arugula, Pear and Parmesan Salad 300
  Fennel, Orange and Arugula Salad 280
  Roasted Cherry Tomato and Arugula
    Salad 339

asparagus: Asparagus and Langoustine Salad 433
  Asparagus and Orange Salad 328
  Grilled Asparagus with Salt-cured Ham 30
  Pasta, Asparagus and Potato salad 419
  Warm Pasta Salad with Asparagus 411

avocado 238
  Avocado and Smoked Fish Salad 325
  Avocado, Crab and Cilantro Salad 382
  Avocado, Tomato and Mozzarella Salad 416
  Egg, Bacon and Avocado Salad 334
  Fresh Spinach and Avocado Salad 289
  Guacamole 179
  Guacamole Salsa in Red Leaves 295
  Pasta, Olive and Avocado Salad 422
  Prosciutto Salad with an Avocado Fan 460
  Shrimp, Avocado and Citrus Salad 430

B

Baby Chickens with Lime and Chili 82

baby corn 238

Baby Eggplant with Raisins and Pine Nuts 317

bacon: Bacon Kofta Kebabs and Salad 52
  Chicken Liver, Bacon and Tomato Salad 404
  Egg, Bacon and Avocado Salad 334
  Frisée Salad with Bacon 328
  Mixed Grill Skewers with Horseradish
    Sauce 48
  Oyster and Bacon Brochettes 218
  Sausages with Prunes and Bacon 50
  Smoked Bacon and Green Bean Pasta
    Salad 410
  Trout with Bacon 118

Baked Apples in Honey and Lemon 205

Baked Bananas with Spicy Vanilla Filling 195

Baked Squash with Parmesan 146

Baked Stuffed Zucchini 150

bananas 240
  Baked Bananas with Spicy Vanilla Filling 195
  Banana and Mascarpone 498
  Bananas with Lime and Cardamom 498
  Plantain and Green Banana Salad 343

Barbecue Sauce 178

Barbecue-cooked Lamb with Potato Slices 64

Barbecue-cooked corn Salsa 175

barbecues: choosing 12
  cooking times 16
  fuel 14
  safety 15

Basic Barbecue Marinade 17

Basil and Lemon Mayonnaise 254

beans: Brown Bean Salad 356
  Fava Bean, Mushroom and Chorizo Salad 337
  Green Bean and Sweet Red Pepper Salad 320
  Green Bean Salad 344
  green beans 238
  Lamb Casserole with Garlic and Beans 229
  Peppery Bean Salad 352
  Red Bean and Mushroom Burgers 138
  Smoked Bacon and Green Bean Pasta
    Salad 410
  Smoked Ham and Bean Salad 353
  Tomato, Savory and Green Bean Salad 306
  Tuscan Tuna and Bean Salad 299
  Warm Fava Bean and Feta Salad 308
  White Bean and Celery Salad 354

beansprouts: Apricot Duck with Beansprout
  Salad 456
  Beansprout and Daikon Salad

beef: Beef and Herbed Pasta Salad 466
  Beef Rib with Onion Sauce 56
  New Orleans Steak Salad 471
  Pepper Steak 226
  Peppered Steaks in Beer and Garlic 54
  Polpettes with Mozzarella and Tomato 23
  Rockburger Salad with Sesame Croûtons 468
  Sirloin Steaks with Bloody Mary Sauce 55
  Spiced Beef Satay 58

  Spicy Meatballs 35
  Stilton Burgers 57
  Vegetable-stuffed Beef Rolls 59

beet: Sweet Potato, Egg, Pork and Beet Salad 406

Belgian endive: Belgian Endive Salad with
  Roquefort 430
  Belgian Endive, Fruit and Nut Salad 278

bell peppers: Chargrilled Tuna with Fiery Pepper
  Purée 116
  Couscous Stuffed Peppers 156
  Duck Breasts with Red Pepper Jelly Glaze 94
  Green Bean and Sweet Red Pepper Salad 320
  Grilled Bell Pepper Salad 326
  Leek and Grilled Red Bell Pepper Salad with
    Goat Cheese 338
  Mackerel Kebabs with Sweet Pepper Salad 102
  Pepper and Cucumber Salad 294
  Peppers with Tomatoes and Anchovies 314
  Roast Bell Pepper and Mushroom Pasta
    Salad 423
  Roasted Bell Pepper and Tomato Salad 318
  Roasted Bell Pepper Antipasto 21
  Stuffed Tomatoes and Peppers 154

Black and Orange Salad 262

blackberries 240
  Blackberry Salad with Rose Granita 486
  Blackened Cajun Chicken and Corn 80

Blue Cheese and Chive Dressing 253

blueberries 240
  Blueberry, Orange and Lavender Salad 484
  Smoked Mackerel with Blueberries 114

Brie Parcels with Almonds 28

Broiled Chicken Salad with Lavender 448

Broiled Pineapple with Papaya Sauce 502

Broiled Salmon and Spring Vegetable Salad 368

Broiled Spiced Quail with Mixed Leaf and
  Mushroom Salad 459

Brown Bean Salad 356

Buckwheat Noodles with Smoked Salmon 370

burgers: Lamb Burgers with Red Currant
  Chutney 62
  Red Bean and Mushroom Burgers 138
  Stilton Burgers 57